Holy Bible Re-examined

The Comprehensive Criticism

'A bold and thought-provoking examination of the Bible, this book challenges long-held beliefs with scholarly insight and historical depth. A must-read for anyone seeking a deeper, critical understanding of biblical texts.'
Shabir Yusuf, Author and Commentator on Religion.

'This book provides a comprehensive and rigorous critique of the Bible, addressing its contradictions, historical context, and textual complexities. It invites readers from all backgrounds to engage thoughtfully with the foundational texts of the faith. A compelling guide for those looking to question and explore the Bible beyond traditional views.'
Dr Feras Husseini, Researcher on Religious Texts

Holy Bible Re-examined

The Comprehensive Criticism

Mohamad Younes

Papyra

Holy Bible Re-examined: *The Comprehensive Criticism*

Copyright © 2025 Mohamad Younes. All rights reserved. No portion of this book may be reproduced in any form without written permission from the publisher or author, except as permitted by applicable copyright law.

Papyra Pty Ltd
Sydney, Australia
www.papyra.com.au

Paperback ISBN: 978-1-923486-00-3
eBook ISBN: 978-1-923486-01-0

Scripture quotations marked NIV are taken from the Holy Bible, New International Version®, NIV®. Copyright © 1973, 1978, 1984, 2011 by Biblica, Inc.® Used by permission of Zondervan. All rights reserved worldwide. www.zondervan.com. The "NIV" and "New International Version" are trademarks registered in the United States Patent and Trademark Office by Biblica, Inc.®

Scripture quotations marked ESV are taken from the ESV® Bible (The Holy Bible, English Standard Version®). Copyright © 2001 by Crossway, a publishing ministry of Good News Publishers. Used by permission. All rights reserved.

Scripture quotations marked KJV are taken from the King James Version. Public domain.

Scripture quotations marked NRSV are taken from the New Revised Standard Version Bible. Copyright © 1989 National Council of the Churches of Christ in the United States of America. Used by permission. All rights reserved worldwide.

Regarding quotations taken from New World Translation. Copyright © Watch Tower Bible and Tract Society of Pennsylvania. Used with respectful acknowledgement for educational and critical purposes.

Quranic translations quoted from The Qur'an with a Phrase-by-Phrase English Translation by Ali Quli Qarai. Copyright © Ali Quli Qarai. Used with respectful acknowledgement for educational and critical purposes.

بِسْمِ اللَّهِ الرَّحْمَٰنِ الرَّحِيمِ

In the Name of Allah, the Most Merciful, the Most Gracious

בשם אללה , הרחום , הכי אדיב

I dedicate this book to my family, my friends, and my brothers and sisters in the Muslim community across the world. I hope that this book will better equip you to seek the truth and challenge popular belief using your reasoning.

Contents

Introduction 1
0.1 Conversation with Christian friend 6

Evolution and Developments 9
1.1 The Bible 10
1.2 The Gospels 17
1.3 Marcan priority 26
1.4 Synoptic Influences 50
1.5 The Q Source, Thomas, and James 55

Discrepancies and Inconsistencies 62
2.1 Contradictions 63
2.2 Forgeries 87
2.3 Textual Criticism 95
2.4 Alterations of the Text 112

Gratuitous Sexual & Other Obscenity 127
3.1 Inspiring Bible passages 128
3.2 Are these from God? 132
3.3 Unnecessarily Pornographic and Violent Verses 134
3.4 Comparing Narratives in the Qur'an and Bible 145
3.5 Women in the Bible 157
3.6 Uncomfortable verses from the New Testament 163

Jesus' (Pbuh) Divinity in the Bible? 168
4.1 Is the Trinity in the Bible? 169
4.2 Indirect Proofs used by the Church 188
4.3 Church Fathers on the Trinity 224

Paul, an Apostle? 248
  5.1 Who is Paul? 249
  5.2 Paulianity or Christianity? 251
  5.3 Peter, John, James, and the Thirteenth Apostle 255
  5.4 Lost Paulitics 264
  5.5 Paul's Contradictions and Misquotations 267

Crucifixion and Resurrection 277
  6.1 Original Sin? 278
  6.2 Human Sacrifice for the Redemption of Sin? 281
  6.3 Atonement Dilemma 286
  6.4 Contradictions of Events 291

Canon 306
  7.1 Gnostic and Apocryphal Writings 307
  7.2 Differing Views in Early Christianity 313
  7.3 Canon in a Nutshell 319
  7.4 Church Fathers on the Canon 325
  7.5 Scholarly Treatment of Canon 329

Pagan Influences 335
  8.1 Incarnation 336
  8.2 Pagan Roots of Christian Holidays 341
  8.3 Conclusion 344

INTRODUCTION

What is the Bible? Is the Bible a holy book? Is the Bible, as Christians claim, the complete Word of God? These are the questions this book aims to answer.

What is a holy book? Answering this question is made easier by adopting a systematic criterion. This criterion should be based on evidence and reason. However, to strengthen any arguments against the Bible, we will only use criteria which the Bible encourages us to use. We should try to put aside our biases and begin with a neutral position.

Interestingly, the Bible instructs us not to blindly follow but produce evidence to support our position.

> "By wisdom a house is built, and by understanding it is established; by knowledge its rooms are filled with all precious and pleasant riches." (Proverbs 24: 3-4, ESV)

> "Prove all things; hold fast to that which is good." (1 Thessalonians 5:21, KJV)

Allow us to reason and prove all things. This book will begin by introducing a set of five essential criteria. Then, we will follow these criteria to determine whether the Bible is the only Word of God. When I say 'Word of God', this can be quite vague, as something may contain parts that are the words of God, but not in totality from God. The real question ought to be, is the Bible 100 percent the Word of God?

The following criteria for a book being 100 percent the Word of God is as follows:

1. **The book should be of divine origin.**

   "For the prophecy came not in old time by the will of man: but holy men of God spake as they were moved by the Holy Ghost." (2 Peter 1:21, KJV).

How do we know whether the Bible is inspired and who its authors were? What is the Holy Spirit, and were the authors really inspired by God?

2. **The book should contain beneficial teachings.**

   "All Scripture is God-breathed and is useful for teaching, rebuking, correcting, and training in righteousness." (2 Timothy 3:16, NIV)

If the Bible is "God-breathed", is it useful for teaching, rebuking, correcting, and training? Is it righteous, teaching righteousness? Does it properly rebuke, correct, and train?

3. **The book should not contain any failed prophecy.**

   "If what a prophet proclaims in the name of the LORD does not take place or come true, that is a message the LORD has not spoken." (Deuteronomy 18:22, NIV)

Does the Bible make prophecies? How specific are these prophecies? Does the Bible contain anything considered a failed prophecy?

Introduction

4. **The book should not call to the worship of other than God.**

   "They exchanged the truth about God for a lie, and worshiped and served created things rather than the Creator." (Romans 1:25, NIV)

What does the Bible say about Jesus? Does the Bible ask us to worship Jesus? Does Jesus claim to be God? Does the Bible contain in it a series of developments about Jesus (Pbuh)? Is Jesus a God-man?

5. **Finally, the book should be infallible in the truth and not contain any contradiction or confusing teachings.**

   "For God is not the author of confusion." (1 Corinthians 14:33, KJV, KJV)

   "Every Word of God is flawless." (Proverbs 30:5, NIV)

   "As for God, his way is perfect: The LORD's word is flawless..." (Psalm 18:30, NIV)

Do we find any contradictory statements or discrepancies within the Bible? Since God is perfect and his words are "flawless", do we find any errors that go against what God says?

In the process of addressing these five essential criteria for determining if the Bible is 100 percent the Word of God, this book will explore: early historical Christianity, questions over the canonization of the Bible, crucifixion, Paul, early disciples of Jesus, the deity of Jesus (Pbuh), and where necessary, a comparative study of Biblical and Qur'anic depictions of prophets, people, and women.

It is vital to approach this question with an open mind. Whether you are Christian, Muslim, or otherwise, scholarship—along with logic and evidence—should be presented as opposed to emotion and subjectivity.

"Come now, and let us reason together," sayeth the LORD." (Isaiah 1:18, KJV)

"Don't have anything to do with foolish and stupid arguments, because you know they produce quarrels. And the Lord's servant must not be quarrelsome but must be kind to everyone, able to teach, not resentful." (2 Timothy 2:23–24, NIV)

In order to evaluate how this text influences your thinking, start by asking yourself the following question.

Is the Bible the only complete and inerrant Word of God?
    (a) Yes, it is 100 percent the Word of God.
    (b) Not completely; however, it does contain the Word of God.
    (c) Maybe. I am not sure.
    (d) The Bible is not the Word of God.

Regardless of your answer, this book may be of use to you, in order to either challenge your perspective or strengthen your point of view. It is worth inspecting and seeking the evidence for yourself.

Regardless of whether you are Muslim, Christian, Atheist or of a different position, your time spent discovering, questioning, and engaging with an unclosed perspective will only benefit you and allow you to learn more.

Introduction

The Blind Men and the Elephant

The Buddha once gave a parable about a king in the town of Savathi. The king had gathered all of the blind men in the town. They were then divided into groups and taken to an elephant in the town. Each group of blind men was introduced to a different part of the elephant's body.

One group was introduced to the head, another to its legs, another to its body, and so forth. The king eventually asked each of the groups to describe what they thought an elephant was like. Those who made contact with the legs said it was like a post; those who made contact with the head said it was like a water pot; and so forth. The groups obviously had a difference of opinion and began arguing with each other, demanding that their experience was the true elephant and everyone else was wrong (Keown, D., 2013. Buddhism: A very short introduction (Vol. 3). Oxford University Press).

Understanding religion resembles the parable of the elephant. We must not make sweeping generalizations and assumptions about any particular position. Christianity, Islam, Buddhism, and other religions are large and complex subjects. We should be cautious about generalizations. In everything, it is important that we search for context and evidence. We need to assess, qualify, and substantiate the claims using evidence, reason, and rationality.

Using the Bible

Wherever possible, I have tried to use Biblical texts when illustrating a point or message in order to focus the reader on the conversation about the Bible and Christianity. At times, the Qur'an has been used for comparison, to show a potential alternative to the Bible's approach.

I have mostly used the New International Version, King James Version, and English Standard version of the Bible, but various other versions have been used where their text better illustrates the point being made. All Qur'an translations are from Ali Qali Qurai. The system of referencing followed is chapter then verse(s) (e.g., Qur'an 1:1 or Genesis 1:1).

Note for academics: At times arguments have been made along the lines that previous scholars/academics have argued. Their works are cited only in the bibliography, except when they are used as evidence for an otherwise unproven claim.

0.1 Conversation with a Christian friend

James: "Hello my friend, would you like to hear the good news?"

Mohamad: "Hi there. Sure, what's the good news?"

James: "The good news is that Jesus Christ died for your sins on the cross so that you can be set free!"

Mohamad: "Who do you say is Jesus Christ?"

James: "Jesus Christ is God of the world, who came down in the flesh to deliver his message to you, to me, to all of us!"

Introduction

Mohamad: "Jesus Christ is God? Why did he die for me, and how do you know this?"

James: "Yes, absolutely Jesus is God. He died because He was the perfect sinless being, the begotten son of God who took on all sin for humanity so that whoever believes in him shall have eternal life. This is written in God's book."

Mohamad: "Ok, this is starting to get a little confusing for me. First you said Jesus Christ died on the cross for me. Then you mentioned Christ being God, and now he is also the son of God?"

James: "Yes, exactly! It seems that you understand, all you need to do now is repent in the name of Jesus Christ and the Holy Spirit."

Mohamad: "Wait, wait, hold on. I don't for a moment accept what you have said. If Jesus is God, why would he need to die? That would mean God died, wouldn't it?"

James: "Hmmm, well, it doesn't mean he necessarily ceased to exist!"

Mohamad: "Ok, fair enough. Well what you mean by God? What do you mean by "Son of God" and "died"? And what evidence do you have for all these claims?"

James: "Great questions. I'm sorry I never introduced myself. My name is James. You are…?"

Mohamad: "My name is Mohamad. Nice to meet you, James."

James: "Nice to meet you, Mohamad. Oh, Mohamad! Are you a Muslim?"

Mohamad: "Yes I am, James."

James: "Great! So, Mohamad, being a Muslim, how do you know you're saved in Islam? Do you have any salvation? What assurance do you have in Islam? You do know the Qur'an came some 600 years after Jesus, why do you…"

Mohamad: "James, James, I'm sorry to interject here. Do you mind if we continue with our initial discussion? With an open mind, let us dialogue and have a fruitful and respectful discussion."

James: "Amen. Sounds great. Have you ever read the Bible by any chance? What is your response to it?"

Mohamad: "Absolutely, James. Let us begin with the Bible."

١

"How can you say, "We are wise, for we have the law of the LORD," when actually the lying pen of the scribes has handled It falsely?" (Jeremiah 8:8, NIV)

Evolution and Developments

"O People of the Book! Do not exceed the bounds in your religion, and do not attribute anything to Allah except the truth."

(Qur'an 4:171)

1.1 The Bible

The Bible is one of the most highly purchased and read books in the history of the West (Ehrman 2006). A majority of those who read the Bible approach it from a devotional perspective of belief and faith.

This book, however, is more interested in the Bible from an academic and historical perspective, which brings forth greater difficulties discovered by scholars. The Bible can have numerous and varying implications and meanings for different readers. The Bible can be widely interpreted, allowing for diverse views on ethical issues, understanding of inspiration, hermeneutics (interpretation), and exegesis (Brown 1993).

The result of this is the numerous denominations in Christianity, such as Nestorian, Monophysite, Orthodox, Catholic, Protestant, Anglican, Restorationist, and many other subdivisions. This also explains the varying beliefs of the early Christian Church.

Furthermore, to many people, the Bible is simply a nice and wonderful guide to faith and practice, treated with the utmost reverence. To such people, the Bible is the inerrant Word of God, and they are very much attached to the scripture. They consider the Bible must be 100 percent accurate and without any error—the eternal Word of the Almighty Lord.

> "As for God, his way is perfect: The LORD's word is flawless; he shields all who take refuge in him." (Psalms 18:30, NIV)

But what if we take a more objective approach rather than a subjective one? What if we analyze the Bible critically through our historical lenses without bias? Suppose we read through the Bible (Old and New

Testament) horizontally rather than vertically, studying and investigating each episode together. Can the below verse maintain its validity?

> "Every word of God is flawless; He is a shield to those who take refuge in Him." (Proverbs 30:5, NIV)

Could it be possible that some of the authors of the Bible were not who people claimed them to be? Do we even know when these writers lived? What were their cultural and theological assumptions? Could it be that these writings differed from each other and had conflicting perspectives?

What if we dig even further than that? Could we discover that the books of the Bible contain numerous unescapable discrepancies? Most importantly, what if we don't even have the original words and sayings of the Bible that our Christian friends read every day? Could we discover that scribes unintentionally or intentionally altered the texts in order to suit their theological beliefs? These are some of the questions one seeks to have answered through a more historical/academic perspective of the Bible.

Background Information

The Bible has two major sections. The first section is the Old Testament (thirty-nine books for Protestants, forty-six for Catholics). The Old Testament is divided very broadly into historical books, the wisdom books, and the prophets (Brown 1994). For Jews, however, the first five books of Moses (Genesis, Exodus, Leviticus, Numbers, and Deuteronomy) are known as the Torah (Pentateuch). After the

Pentateuch, the Old Testament contains a collection of religious writings of ancient Israelites including poetry, history, and wisdom.

The second section of the Bible is the New Testament, containing twenty-seven documents (thirty-five for Ethiopian Orthodox) of ranging lengths and types, such as the Gospels (Matthew, Mark, Luke, and John), historical texts (Acts of the Apostles), and Pauline and non-Pauline Epistles (Dunn 2013). The Gospels largely discuss the teachings and personhood of Jesus (Or for Muslims, Prophet Isa Pbuh) as well as events in first century Christianity.

The first four Gospels predominantly deals with the life and ministry of Jesus (Pbuh). These Gospels were originally written mostly in Greek, the common language of the Roman dominated Mediterranean at the time.

When discussing these texts, we ought to look at the evidence and establish a conclusion based on it. The Bible clearly affirms such reasoning (1 Thessalonians 5:21). When we look at the background information of Jesus (Pbuh), what we find are abundant memories, but unfortunately, no contemporary accounts written of him as far as we know.

We have memories of his life, his mission, and what he was all about. However, these memories were all written long after the fact and not by people who were there to observe him (Ehrman 2015). These memories are from late authors who heard about Jesus (Pbuh) from others who heard it from others who yet heard it from others and so on. They are, unfortunately, memories of memories of other memories.

Even though Jesus (Pbuh) lived up until 30AD, our earliest surviving account of him is around thirty or forty years later (Gospel

Evolution and Developments

of Mark). Even after gospels of Jesus were in circulation, there were also oral traditions circulated. It is obvious people were intrigued by Jesus (Pbuh). However, one must understand that truth about him was also being circulated with tales (Ehrman 2015).

> "But you must not mention 'a message from the Lord' again, because each one's word becomes their own message. So you distort the words of the living God, the Lord Almighty, our God." (Jeremiah 23:36, NIV)

According to the above verse in Jeremiah, Newman & Stine (2003), there is a clear perversion of people distorting the message of God during this time:

> "And you pervert the words of the living God. The verb rendered pervert has as its basic meaning "turn" or "overturn." New Jerusalem Bible has "twist" and New English Bible "make nonsense of"; An American Translation and New International Version prefer "distort." If the interpretation of burden given above is accepted, and you pervert the words of the living God would be "for otherwise you distort the words of the living God."

Moving forward to the New Testament we read in 2 Peter 3:16:

> "...His letters contain some things that are hard to understand, which ignorant and unstable people distort, as they do the other Scriptures, to their own destruction." (NIV)

According to John Gill's *Bible Exposition* (2009), the above verse refers to people "either adding unto or detracting from the scriptures."

Many people around the world see Jesus (Pbuh) in different ways, especially when it comes to the Abrahamic religions (Jews, Christians, and Muslims). Many people, including his disciples, saw him and remembered him in different ways. Indeed, many of the details presented are accurate based on the historical substantive evidence we have, but some may well be distorted as well.

It is very important to understand the concept of Jesus (Pbuh) and the eyewitnesses. Conservative scholars such as Richard Bauckham (Bruce and Kautzer 1978) attempt to emphasize that the Gospel authors are trusted to be reliable and historically accurate. However, New Testament scholars such as Ehrman (2015) point out that this particular view does not really hold outside of conservative evangelical Christian thinking.

I will submit that the gospel writings are indeed reliable, but only to a certain extent.

However, Reliability is very different from validity.

In this context, reliability is the *consistency* of writing, while validity is the *accuracy* of the writings. The manuscripts themselves may be reliable in terms of accurately transmitting the text as it was known at the time they were produced. However, the content of the text itself may not necessarily be true or accurate.

Reliability is if the Bibles are the same today as when they were written, while validity, is if they are true.

Evolution and Developments

Without going into too much detail just yet, below is a list of points suggesting the gospel writings are not as valid as we would like them to be (Ehrman 2015):

- Nearly all the people associated with Jesus (Pbuh) were lower-class, Aramaic-speaking Jews in the rural parts of Palestine.
- These followers were most likely illiterate, uneducated, poor, and had no time to travel.
- Jesus (Pbuh), according to history, does not seem to leave Palestine, remaining most of his life in Galilee before ending his journey in Jerusalem.
- The Gospel writers lived in different parts of the world than Jesus and his followers.
- The Gospel writers spoke Greek, not Aramaic and never directly claimed to be eyewitnesses.
- These writers learned the stories about Jesus (Pbuh), which were in circulation for years, in Greek.
- These writers at times modified and adjusted the accounts to fit their own liking.
- The four Gospels (Matthew, Mark, Luke, and John) are all anonymous, never indicating directly whom they are (Matthew and Mark are spoken about in the third person).
- Matthew was named after the tax collector in Matthew 9:9; Mark was named after a famous person related to Peter; and Luke was a companion of Paul and John, while John was simply named after John the disciple (son of Zebedee).

Dennis Smith and Joseph Tyson in *The Acts seminar report* (2013) have concluded that Acts was written around the second century and probably not written by Luke himself.

Despite these potential problems the Bible faces, we can be certain of these gospel writers having some form of information about Jesus with them. That is for sure. Some of these sources may have been written stories or, otherwise, stories passed on through oral traditions. Many of the stories in fact came from the oral gospel tradition (Dunn 2013).

All the stories about Jesus (Pbuh) in the Gospels represent the ways in which people remembered him. Even if these stories trace back to eyewitnesses of Jesus (Pbuh), this does not necessarily make them valid or accurate.

According to Apple (2016) in his book, *New Testament People*, "The historical Jesus may be beyond recovery…He was not a Christian but a Jew, who might not have endorsed later developments in Christianity." Evolution and corruption may have taken place, distorting the true message of Jesus (Pbuh). This development and distorting does not necessarily refer to a linear form of corruption.

1.2 THE GOSPELS

The Gospels of Matthew, Mark, and Luke are known as the *Synoptic Gospels*. They are called synoptic due to their common view and similarities. When these three Gospels are compared, it is undeniable that the accounts are strikingly similar to one another in content and expression. The Synoptic Gospels tell of Jesus travelling and preaching in parables mainly about the kingdom of God.

The overwhelming bulk of New Testament scholars agree on the dates and priorities of the Gospels (Collins 2001, Ehrman 2016, Brown 1997). Despite the order in our Bibles today, it is the scholarly consensus that Mark was the first written Gospel and became the source for Matthew and Luke. This hypothesis is known as the Marcan priority (Smith 2011).

According to most New Testament scholars, the dates of the Gospel of Mark range between 63–75AD; the Gospels of Matthew and Luke around the years 80–85AD; and the Gospel of John (or the spiritual Gospel, due to its more meditative portrayal of Jesus) is roughly dated between 90–100AD (Ehrman 2000).

Notice the dates vary from a minimum of thirty-three to seventy years after the life of Jesus (Pbuh). Therefore, just like the space between the train and the platform, we as readers must mind the gaps between Jesus and the Gospel writings (Stanton 2002). The following is an approximate order of the gospels.

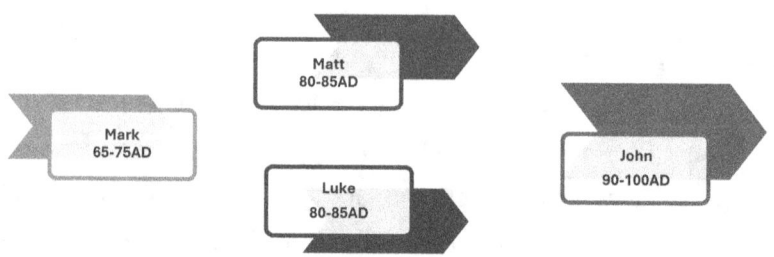

Below is a figure explaining the relationship known as the Two-source hypothesis:

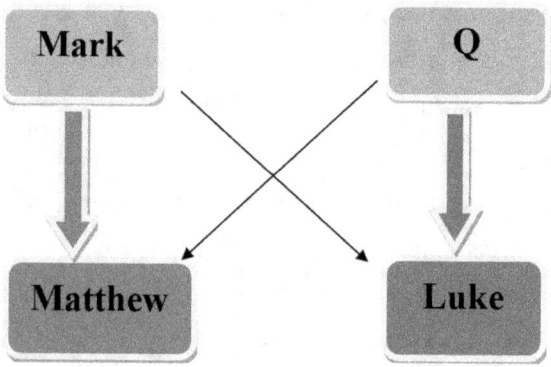

Never mind the letter Q for now; we will discuss that subsequently once we introduce the literary relationships of the Gospels.

Synoptic Problem

The synoptic problem refers to Matthew, Mark, and Luke being so similar, not only in regards to the material but also in the precise wording of the text.

It is insufficient to explain these similarities on the basis of common oral tradition alone (Kloppenborg 2008). Rather, some type of literary dependence must logically be assumed; that is to say, someone copied from another source or somebody's previously written text. Several of the evangelists must have used one or more of the earlier Gospels as sources for their own compositions. This is the basic idea of the synoptic problem.

However, the situation gets complicated, as some of the material is common to all three Synoptic Gospels. There is also content that's only found in two of them, i.e. Matthew and Luke. There is also content that is found exclusively in individual Gospels. The common material is not always presented in the same order in the various gospels. So, the question remains, who wrote first, and if so, who copied from who?

Considering the many other theories of the relationship between the Gospels (triple, double, and single traditions), the Two-source hypothesis is most likely to be the case. Keep in mind when we speak of "Mark, Matthew, Luke, and John," the scholarly consensus is that the authors are actually unknown.

Just as the Gospels were circulated anonymously, they were also composed anonymously. Anonymous in the sense that they do not contain explicit statements identifying their authors.

Irenaeus (bishop of Lyon in France) later attributed the names (Matthew, Mark, Luke, and John) in 185AD (Ehrman 2009). Irenaeus was a second-century Christian bishop and theologian, who played a significant role in the early church's recognition of these Gospels

Despite this, many New Testament scholars have accepted some of Irenaeus' claims. Mark is viewed as a student of Peter, named John Mark, who would have supposedly received the story from Peter, the disciple of Jesus. Matthew is believed to have been written by the disciple Matthew listed in the Gospels as a disciple of Christ. Luke is the third Gospel writer and would have been a companion of Paul.

There is little reason to believe the gospel writers themselves were eyewitnesses. The eyewitnesses would have been Aramaic speaking people almost entirely from rural Galilee. Mark, for example, was an educated, Greek-speaking Christian living outside of Palestine, while Luke, Matthew and John wrote decades after Jesus' death.

Luke states that eyewitnesses started passing along the oral traditions he had heard (Luke 1:1-4), not witnessed himself. In fact, as he was a gentile writer then that is strong evidence that he was not an eyewitness. The gospels of Luke are connected with Paul, but Paul himself was not an eyewitness of Jesus' life, even by his own claims.

Included in the canon of the Bible were two books that were written by claimed disciples of Jesus, "Matthew & John", and another two that are connected to the most "important" apostles "Paul & Peter".

Matthew is heavily based on Mark and another source (the Q source) which indicates it relied on these sources rather than an eyewitness account. Besides, the dating of both Matthew and Luke would be around 80-85AD with many eyewitnesses likely having passed away by this time.

Meanwhile, not only is John dated later, around 90-100AD, but it also differs significantly from the synoptic gospels in terms of content, style, and theology, shaped by a later perspective. By the time these Gospels were written, the oral traditions circulating in rural Galilee or Jerusalem would have likely been altered over time.

Having said all that, I will speak of Mark, Matthew, Luke, and John for the sake of convenience. The author of Mark would have written his gospel first and put that into circulation at the time and place in which he lived. As Mark wrote his Gospel first, Matthew and

Evolution and Developments

Luke used it later as the source for their Gospels. It seems very logical, since that source was already circulating, that they would use it to build on their own.

> "Many have undertaken to draw up an account of the things that have been fulfilled...I too decided to write an orderly account for you, most excellent Theophilus..." (Luke 1:1, 3, NIV)

Evaluating and identifying Gospel sources can be quite controversial in the case of Christianity. Interestingly, along the way, Matthew and Luke would start adding and making "improvements" to the stories of Mark while developing their Christology's.

Almost 90 percent of the Gospel of Mark is found in Matthew; over 70 percent in Luke. Around 45 percent of Matthew and 41 percent of Luke are based on the Gospel of Mark (Kloppenborg 2008).

It is clear that some form of literary relationship exists between the Gospels, hence the term synoptic. There is a definitely high degree of verbatim (word for word) agreement. This is clear when we examine the Gospels horizontally rather than vertically in order to find these striking similarities.

Since we do not have the autographs of any of the Gospels – our earliest manuscripts are all much later – we cannot be sure that the Greek texts of the Gospels that we use are identical with what the Synoptic evangelists wrote. We cannot even be sure that Matthew, Mark or Luke did not write multiple drafts of each of the Gospels. (Kloppenborg 2008)

Horizontal reading is a method of textual analysis used to compare multiple accounts of a similar event i.e. different Gospel episodes. Vertical reading is the way you would normally read any book, from top to bottom.

Shown here is a figure detailing the relationships in percentages.

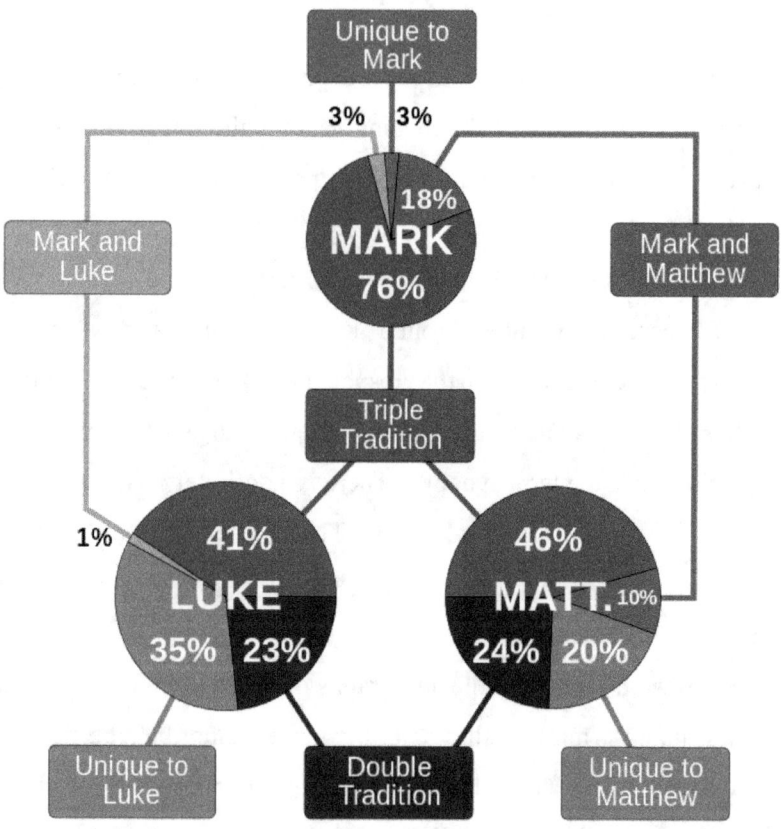

Evolution and Developments

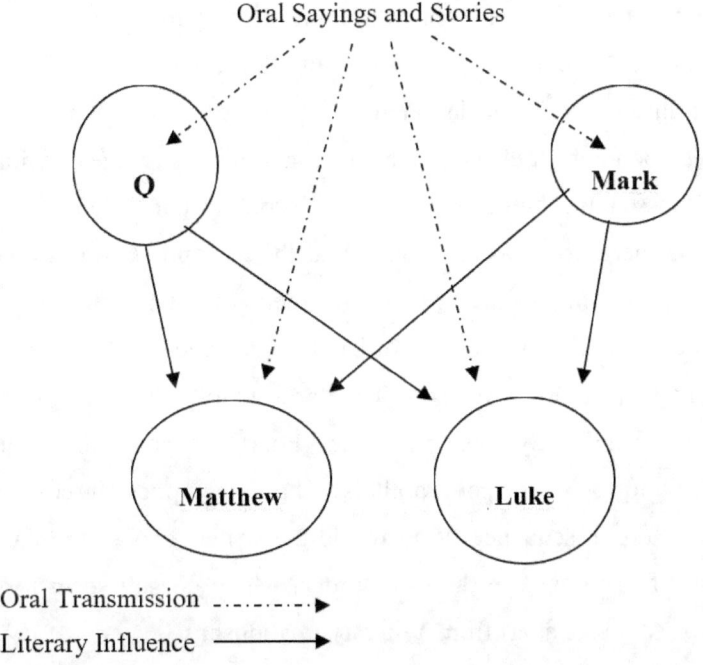

Let us compare Mark 1:16–20 and Matthew 4:18–20, for example, to help us further understand the correlation:

Mark 1:16–20	Matthew 4:18–20
"As Jesus walked beside the Sea of Galilee, he saw Simon and his brother Andrew casting a net into the lake, for they were fishermen. "Come, follow me," Jesus said, "and I will send you out to fish for people." At once they left their nets and followed him." (NIV)	"As Jesus was walking beside the Sea of Galilee, he saw two brothers, Simon, called Peter, and his brother Andrew. They were casting a net into the lake, for they were fishermen. "Come, follow me," Jesus said, "and I will send you out to fish for people." At once they left their nets and followed him." (NIV)

The passage from Mark contains eighty-two words, and the passage from Matthew contains eighty-nine. In Matthew, 62 percent is agreed upon in the Greek translation and 70 percent in Mark. Both of them agree upon almost every small detail; and this is just one example of countless similarities throughout the Gospels (Dunn 2013).

Another good reason to think that the Synoptic Gospels contain literary copying is the strong agreement in relating to the same incidents in the same relative order. This is evident through not only John Kloppenborg's work on "The Earliest Gospel" but also through Kurt Aland's Synopsis of the Four Gospels and Burton Throckmorton's Gospel Parallels. These synoptics agree almost completely in sequence. Why would the writers choose to relate all stories and sayings in the same order? There doesn't seem to be a reason to do so, apart from a literary relationship.

Take for example, the story of Jesus' argument with the Pharisees about washing hands (Matthew 15:1-20 & Mark 7:1-23). They both appear just before the story of the Syro-Phoenician women's daughter (Matthew 15:21-28 & Mark 7 24-30). Although Matthew changes the ethnicity of the women from Syro-Phoenician to Canaanite, it is in the exact same order.

Similarly, the issue of payment of taxes (Matthew 22:15-22 & Mark 12:13-17) comes just before the controversy about the resurrection (Matthew 22:23-33 & Mark 12:18-27). Luke and Mark agree even more strongly than Matthew and Mark, providing more evidence that copying has occurred. While it isn't entirely clear who is copying who, it is clear that the wording and sequence of the three Gospels have some copying involved.

Evolution and Developments

Below is an example of Matthew and Mark agreeing in their wording (in **bold**), and Mark and Luke agreeing (*in italic*). (Translations from Kloppenborg 2008)

Matthew 8:14-15	**And** coming **to the house** of Peter, Jesus saw his **mother-in-law** ill and burning with a fever. **And** he touched **her hand and the fever left her, and** being raised **she served** him.
Mark 1:29-31	**And** immediately, leaving *the synagogue* they came **to** *the house* of Simon and Andrew, with James and John. *Now the* **mother-in-law** of Simon was lying down, burning *with a fever*, and immediately they are telling him about her. **And** approaching he raised **her hand. And the fever left** *her* and *she served* them.
Luke 4:38-39	Now arising from *the synagogue*, he entered *the house of Simon. Now the mother-in-law of Simon* was afflicted with a serious fever, and they asked him *about her. And* standing over her, he rebuked the fever and it *left her*. Getting up at once *she served them*.

It is also clear that both Matthew and Luke improved Mark's syntax by eliminating redundant words and sayings. Both Matthew and Luke replace Mark's excessive use of "and" with more compact sentences. Matthew and Luke would use the verb "to approach" (*proserchomai*) instead of "to come" (*erchomai*). Another addition is the word "fringe" which can be seen below.

Matthew 9:20	…<u>approaching</u> (*proselthousa*) from behind, she touched <u>the fringe</u> of his garment, for she was saying to herself, "If I only touch his garment I will be saved,"
Mark 5:27	… coming up (*elthuousa*) from behind in the crowd she touched his garment for she was saying, "If I touch even his garment I will be saved."
Luke 8:44	<u>approaching</u> (*proselthousa*) from behind, she touched <u>the fringe</u> of his garment; and immediately her flow of blood ceased.

1.3 Marcan priority

Traditionally, Christians have long held that the order of the Gospels in the New Testament is Matthew, Mark, Luke, and John. This view was widely supported by early Church Fathers such as Origen, who in his Commentary on the Gospel of Matthew (Book 1), affirmed Matthew's prominence as the first Gospel.

However, this traditional ordering of the Gospels has been disputed by modern biblical scholarship, particularly through the theory of Markan priority.

The Marcan priority (Kloppenborg 2008) is only one proposed theory about the synoptic problem. The rationale is, as we touched upon earlier, that the Gospel of Mark was written first and was later used as a major source for the Gospels of Matthew and Luke.

Evolution and Developments

There are numerous reasons why New Testament scholars have come to this conclusion, in short, their arguments are based on the content, style, and length of each Gospel.

The story in Mark has a much simpler beginning and ending—no nativity story, genealogy, resurrection appearances (the women fled for they were afraid), or extended speeches. The Greek style used in Matthew and Luke are much more elegant and literary than Mark's simple Greek.

Generally speaking, when a story is used as a source, it becomes longer in length, but Mark is the shortest of the Gospels (Smith 2011). If the author of Mark copied Matthew or Luke, why would he shorten the story and remove some important mentions of Jesus' ministry? Even though we can explain the literary relationships within the Gospels, how can we explain the added or improved verses from the writers? This moves into our snowball Christology evolution and development discussion.

Snowball Christology

As mentioned previously, Matthew and Luke likely used Mark as a source to write their own gospels. Along the way, many improvements were made. By the time the Gospel John was written, there were evolutionary developments of Jesus (Pbuh). Interestingly for Muslims, this concept is not new.

> "So woe to them who write the Book with their hands and then say, "This is from Allah," that they may sell it for a paltry gain. So woe to them for what their hands have written, and woe to them for what they earn!" (Qur'an 2:79)

The late eminent Catholic scholar, Raymond Brown, wrote:

> "…neither evangelist liked Marks's redundancies, awkward Greek expressions, uncomplimentary presentation of the disciples and Mary, and embarrassing statements about Jesus. When using Mark, both expanded the Markan accounts in the light of post-resurrectional faith." (Brown 1997)

We see a transition from a messenger sent to preach the message of the coming kingdom of God, to him becoming God himself, as many Christians believe today. However, the Bible itself seems replete of statements denying Jesus' (Pbuh) divinity and the Trinity. So, do we then have a contradiction here between the Bible and Christian claims?

> "For I am God, and not a man— the Holy One among you." (Hosea 11:9, NIV)

> "Fellow Israelites, listen to this: Jesus of Nazareth was a man accredited by God to you by miracles, wonders and signs, which God did among you through him, as you yourselves know." (Acts 2:22, NIV)

Let us now dive into some examples of the improvements and changes over time by comparing the same incidents within the Gospels themselves, horizontally.

Evolution and Developments

Keep in mind as you read these contradictions, the following:

1. Mark, written around 65-70 CE, is generally considered the earliest Gospel and serves as the primary source for both Matthew and Luke. These Gospels closely follow Mark's structure, adapting his account, making notable theological and narrative changes.

2. Matthew, written 10-20 years after Mark, adjusts the narrative to address specific theological concerns, particularly presenting Jesus as the fulfillment of Jewish prophecy. He adds and alters details, such as the virgin birth, to emphasize Jesus' divine status and legitimacy as the Messiah.

3. Luke, the only known Gentile Gospel writer, was a Roman citizen and companion of Paul. Writing around 80-90 CE, he adapted Mark's account to appeal to a Roman audience, emphasizing themes of social justice and universal salvation.

4. John, written around 90-100 CE, known as the spiritual gospel diverges significantly from the Synoptic Gospels. It is the main if not only gospel that Christians use to focus on the divinity of Jesus, his pre-existence and role as the divine Logos.

All of the below are from the New International Version translation.

Mark 9:5	Matthew 17:4
Peter said to Jesus, "Rabbi, it is good for us to be here. Let us put up three shelters—one for you, one for Moses, and one for Elijah."	Peter said to Jesus, "Lord, it is good for us to be here. If you wish, I will put up three shelters—one for you, one for Moses, and one for Elijah."
Notice above, the earlier Gospel Mark calls Jesus **"Rabbi."**	In the later Gospel of Matthew, Jesus' title changes to **"Lord"**.

Mark 13:35	Matthew 24:42
"Therefore keep watch because you do not know when the owner of the house will come back."	"Therefore keep watch, because you do not know on what day your Lord will come."
Here in Mark, Jesus is referred to as **"the owner of the house."**	The Gospel of Matthew upgraded Jesus' title to **"Lord."**

Mark 3:35	Matthew 12:50
"Whoever does God's will is my brother and sister and mother."	"For whoever does the will of my Father in heaven is my brother and sister and mother."
Here in Mark, Jesus refers only to 'God'.	Here in Matthew, Jesus refers to God as 'my Father', a change in the language.

Evolution and Developments

Mark 8:29-30	Luke 2:11
"But what about you?" he asked. "Who do you say I am?" Peter answered, "You are the Messiah." Jesus warned them not to tell anyone about him.	Today in the town of David a Savior has been born to you; he is the Messiah, **the Lord**.
The title of "Messiah" (Christos in Greek) is revealed gradually and somewhat ambiguously in Mark. Jesus instructs Peter and the disciples to keep this revelation private (Mark 8:30).	In contrast Luke presents Jesus' as a saviour very early, both openly and direct. Luke also adds the Lord after the title of Messiah.

Mark 8:29	Matthew 16:16	Luke 9:20
"Peter answered, "You are the Messiah."	"Simon Peter answered, "You are the Messiah, **the Son of the living God**."	"But what about you?" he asked. "Who do you say I am?" Peter answered, "God's Messiah."
Jesus is known as the Messiah, according to Peter.	In the later Gospel of Matthew, Peter knows Jesus as the Messiah, son of the living God. This is another addition.	In Luke, Peter knows Jesus as "God's Messiah" Another addition.

Mark 4:38	Matthew 8:25
"Jesus was in the stern, sleeping on a cushion. The disciples woke him and said to him, "**Teacher**, don't you care if we drown?"	"The disciples went and woke him, saying, "**Lord**, save us! We're going to drown!"
Here in Mark, Jesus is 'Teacher'.	The wording is changed here to refer to Jesus as 'Lord'.

Mark 1:9	Matthew 3:13–14
"At that time Jesus came from Nazareth of Galilee and was baptized by John in the Jordan."	"Then Jesus came from Galilee to the Jordan to be baptized by John. But John tried to deter him, saying, "**I need to be baptized by you, and do you come to me?**"
Jesus is baptized by John the Baptist with no further questions asked. Expressed as a simple fact. Which also raises some questions; Did Jesus sin? Why was he baptized?	Interestingly in the Gospel of Matthew's account, John says, "I need to be baptized by Jesus," emphasizing the status of Jesus (Pbuh).

Evolution and Developments

Mark 15:34	Luke 23:46
And at three in the afternoon Jesus cried out in a loud voice, "Eloi, Eloi, lema sabachthani?" (which means "My God, my God, **why have you forsaken me?**").	Jesus called out with a loud voice, "**Father, into your hands I commit my spirit.**" When he had said this, he breathed his last.
The Jesus depicted by Mark is seen as a prophet of God in despair on the cross. He seems deeply disturbed, in shock and also in doubt.	In Luke, Jesus does not express despair or defeat on the cross nor quote the Psalm 22 lament. Instead, he directs those mourning him to consider his journey towards death calmly and confidently. This is an intentional rewording of the event by Luke, likely to appeal to a Roman audience.

Mark 6:5	Matthew 13:58
"**He could not do any miracles** there, except lay his hands on a few sick people and heal them."	"And **he did not do many miracles** there because of their lack of faith."
Here there is a difference of wording; Jesus simply *could not* perform any miracles.	In Matthew, Jesus *did not* perform any miracles. Again, a removal of limitations.

Mark 12:29	**Luke 10:27**
"The most important one," answered Jesus, "is this: 'Hear, O Israel: The Lord our God, the Lord is one."	He answered, "'Love the Lord your God with all your heart and with all your soul and with all your strength and with all your mind'; and, 'Love your neighbor as yourself.
This verse is an important one to understand. A Jew asked Jesus of all the commandments, which is the most important one? In Mark, Jesus clearly states The Shema Yisrael, which Jews recite every day, declaring that there is no God but Yahweh, or Jehovah.	Fast forward to the later Gospel of Luke, Jesus is asked the very same question; however, the Shema is removed. Jesus speaks about loving the Lord your God with all your heart and soul. Matthew has removed the emphasis on God.

Mark 14:71, 72	**Luke 22:60-61**
He began to call down curses, and he swore to them, "I don't know this man you're talking about." … Then Peter remembered the word **Jesus** had spoken to him	Peter replied, "Man, I don't know what you're talking about!" Just as he was speaking, the rooster crowed. The **Lord** turned and looked straight at Peter.

Evolution and Developments

Jesus is simply referred to by his name "Jesus" and nothing more.	In Luke, Jesus has now been referred to as "Lord" – in which he does another 12 times in his Gospel.

Mark 10:17–18	Matthew 19:16–17
"As Jesus started on his way, a man ran up to him and fell on his knees before him. "Good teacher," he asked, "what must I do to inherit eternal life?" "Why do you call me good?" Jesus answered. "No one is good—except God alone."	"Just then a man came up to Jesus and asked, "Teacher, what good thing must I do to get eternal life?" "Why do you ask me about what is good?" Jesus replied. "There is only One who is good."
Here the man calls Jesus 'Good Teacher'. Jesus replies by distinguishing himself *from* God.	The question is changed in order to get the answer he wants. By asking, "Teacher"—not *Good Teacher* but *Teacher*— "what Good Things must I do?" Jesus is asked about what is Good, rather than being called Good, like in Mark.

Mark 5:27–30	Matthew 9:20–22
"When she heard about Jesus, she came up behind him in the crowd and touched his cloak, because she thought, "If I just touch his clothes, I will be healed." Immediately her bleeding stopped and she felt in her body that she was freed from her suffering. At once Jesus realized that power had gone out from him. He turned around in the crowd and asked, **"Who touched my clothes?"**	"Just then a woman who had been subject to bleeding for twelve years came up behind him and touched the edge of his cloak. She said to herself, "If I only touch his cloak, I will be healed." **Jesus turned and saw her.** "Take heart, daughter," he said, "your faith has healed you."
Here in Mark, Jesus has to ask "Who touched my clothes?" This should a slight ignorance, especially since he was 100 percent God and 100 percent man. The divine nature should have known better.	Interestingly, when we get to Matthew's version of the story, the part where Jesus asks the question, "Who touched my clothes?" is missing. This change removes the limitation of Jesus and strengthens his image.

Evolution and Developments

Mark 11:12–13	Matthew 21:18–19
"The next day as they were leaving Bethany, Jesus was hungry. Seeing in the distance a fig tree in leaf, he went to find out if it had any fruit. When he reached it, he found nothing but leaves, **because it was not the season for figs.**"	"Early in the morning, as Jesus was on his way back to the city, he was hungry. Seeing a fig tree by the road, he went up to it but found nothing on it except leaves."
Here Mark makes it clear that the reason there were no figs was that it was not the season for figs, implying that Jesus was unsure about the tree and had made a mistake.	Matthew in this instance has removed the mention that it was not the season for figs, possibly to cover up the human limitations of Jesus.

Mark 14:33-35	Luke 22:40-41
and he began to be deeply **distressed** and **troubled.** "My soul is overwhelmed with **sorrow** to the point of death"…Going a little farther, he **fell** to the ground and prayed	On reaching the place, he said to them, "Pray that you will not fall into temptation." He withdrew about a stone's throw beyond them, knelt down and prayed

In Mark's account, Jesus is showing emotion and mentions that he fell on the ground.	Here in Luke, instead of falling to the ground in grief, Jesus is now in control and "kneels" down. Again, likely appealing to Roman ideas of strength and honour.

Mark 16:3–4	Matthew 28:1–3
And they asked each other, "Who will roll the stone away from the entrance of the tomb?" But when they looked up, they saw that the stone, which was very large, had been rolled away.	"…Mary Magdalene and the other Mary went to look at the tomb. There was a violent earthquake, for an angel of the Lord came down from heaven and, going to the tomb, rolled back the stone and sat on it."
Here, Mark states that the women were wondering who was going to roll away the stone, only to find that it already rolled. The obvious question that comes to mind is, 'Who rolled away the stone'? Mark does not answer this question.	Matthew has it that when the women arrived, an angel came down and rolled the stone. Matthew consciously reworded the event to have the women witness who rolled the stone, leaving no question as to who did, as in Mark. Again, this rewriting is covering up the problems contained therein.

Evolution and Developments

Mark 1:41	Luke 5:13
Jesus was **indignant**. He reached out his hand and touched the man.	Jesus reached out his hand and touched the man.
Mark 3:5	Luke 6:10
He looked around at them in **anger** and, **deeply distressed** at their stubborn hearts, said to the man, "Stretch out your hand."	He looked around at them all, and then said to the man, "Stretch out your hand."
Mark 6:34	Luke 9:11
When Jesus landed and saw a large crowd, he had **compassion** on them	…but the crowds learned about it and followed him.
Mark 10:21	Luke 18:22
Jesus looked at him and **loved** him. "One thing you lack," he said.	When Jesus heard this, he said to him, "You still lack one thing.

Mark 11:15–17	Luke 19:45–46
On reaching Jerusalem, Jesus entered the temple courts and began driving out those who were buying and selling there. **He overturned the tables of the money changers and the benches of those selling doves,** ¹⁶ and would not allow anyone to carry merchandise through the temple courts. And as he taught them, he said, "Is it not written: 'My house will be called a house of prayer for all nations'? But you have made it 'a den of robbers.'"	When Jesus entered the temple courts, he began to drive out those who were selling. "It is written," he said to them, "'My house will be a house of prayer'; but you have made it 'a den of robbers.'
Mark has very clearly depicted Jesus with human emotions, including pity, anger, sadness, wonder, compassion, indignation, and love.	The Gospel of Luke often omits or downplays these emotional displays of Jesus, slowly but surely elevating his status and minimizing portrayals that could suggest vulnerability.

Evolution and Developments

> **John 7:8, 10**
>
> """You go to the festival. I am not (yet) going to this festival, because my time has not yet fully come.""""
>
> "However, after his brothers had left for the festival, he went also, not publicly, but in secret."
>
> In this passage of John's gospel, Jesus does end up going to the feast, but in secret. This is because, according to the gospel of John, the Jews were seeking to kill him. So going publicly could have caused serious harm. The point here is not the question of whether he lied or changed his mind. Rather, the point I want to stress is that later writers saw this passage as a potential problem and, in attempt to reconcile the contradiction of verse 8 and 10, they added the word 'yet' in verse 8. This, according to Ellicott's commentary (1954) "is of doubtful authority." Furthermore, "it removes an apparent difficulty. Without it, the words do not involve a change of purpose." Keep in mind that, according to Trinitarian Christians, Jesus, being God, had technically lied for a greater purpose or simply changed his mind. This, according to Numbers 23:19, is contradictory.

Based on the above-mentioned verses, we can see some indication that the Gospels took on an evolutionary development. However, this is further established in the Gospel of John, the very last Gospel, where the situation was improved even further than the others. In Mark's Gospel, as well as Matthew and Luke, we still know Jesus to have limitations.

Even though those limitations are subdued and "improved", he still is submitting his will to God (Mark 14:32 and Matthew 26:39). In the Gospel according to John, Jesus would not have submitted his will to God such as the earlier Gospels:

> "Now my soul is troubled, and what shall I say? 'Father, save me from this hour'? No, it was for this very reason I came to this hour." (John 12:27, NIV)

Compare that with Matthew.

> "Going a little further, he fell with his face to the ground and prayed, "My Father, if it is possible, may this cup be taken from me. Yet not as I will, but as you will." (Matthew 26:39, NIV)

It is clearer now that, the later the gospel was written, the more evident the snowball effect. For example, why is it that most or all of the texts proving Jesus' divinity come from the Gospel of John? Have Christians tried proving Jesus' divinity through the Synoptics or through the Old Testament?

How many times does Jesus refer to the kingdom of God? In Mark, he refers to it 18 times, and in John, only five times. What about all of the I AM statements in the Gospels? There are nine in Mark and a striking 118 in John.

Even the expression of God as Father is much more frequent in John than in Mark. Mark only references it a few times, whereas in John, God is called *Father* seventy-three times and more specifically Jesus' own Father one hundred times.

Evolution and Developments

Furthermore, Mark Goodacre in his work on the synoptic Gospels observed that certain discrepancies in Luke and Matthew are because of what he calls "editor's fatigue" (Goodcare 1998). The basic idea is that when Matthew or Luke is writing their Gospel using Mark as a source, they initially make changes and additions as needed.

However, as the process goes on, fatigue sets in, causing them to overlook the adjustments. Consequently, words and phrases that they intended to modify are inadvertently copied from Mark, resulting in inconsistencies within the final version of Matthew (or Luke) that we know.

Mark 6 (NIV)	Matthew 14 (NIV)
14 King Herod heard about this… 26 The king was greatly distressed, but because of his oaths and his dinner guests, he did not want to refuse her.	1 At that time Herod the tetrarch heard reports about Jesus 9 The king was distressed, but because of his oaths and his dinner guests, he ordered that her request be granted

Matthew sets out to identify Herod Antipas more precisely as a tetrarch — since the Romans did not give him the title "king." However, after adapting a number of verses, Matthew became mentally fatigued and inadvertently repeated Mark's less exact title from the beginning. This is more evidence proving the Gospels were copied and tampered with by their authors.

Here is another example of this type of fatigue in the Gospel of Luke.

"And whatever house you enter, stay there, and from there depart. And wherever they do not receive you, when you leave that town shake off the dust from your feet as a testimony against them." (Luke 9:4-5, ESV).	"And whatever town or village you enter, find out who is worthy in it and stay there until you depart... And if anyone will not receive you or listen to your words, shake off the dust from your feet when you leave that house or town." (Matthew 10:11, 14, ESV)
In Luke's version, the second statement includes the phrase "their town," while the first statement and the preceding text in the passage do not mention any specific town. According to Goodacre's theory, this inconsistency in Luke's text is attributed to editorial fatigue. Luke used Matthew's account as a source and initially removed the reference to a town in the first statement. However, due to fatigue or oversight, he accidentally included the reference to a town in the second statement.	

The fact that Matthew and Luke freely altered and "corrected" Mark strongly suggests that they did not consider it to be inspired scripture. If they had treated Mark or any other early manuscript as inspired, logically, one would not feel the need to add or remove any letter from it unless they felt it was semi inspired and needed perfecting.

Another classic example of this fatigue can be seen through the parable of the Sower.

Evolution and Developments

The telling of the parable (Mark 4:4–8, ESV)	The interpretation (Mark 4:15–20, ESV)
A. And as he sowed, some seed fell on the path, and the birds came and devoured it.	A. When they hear, Satan immediately comes and takes away the word that is sown in them.
B-1. Other seed fell on rocky ground, where it did not have much soil, and it sprang up quickly, since it had no depth of soil.	B-1. And these are the ones sown on rocky ground: when they hear the word, they immediately receive it with joy.
B-2. And when the sun rose, it was scorched; and since it had no root, it withered away.	B-2. And they have no root in themselves, but endure for a while; then, when tribulation or persecution arises on account of the word, immediately they fall away.
C. Other seed fell among thorns, and the thorns grew up and choked it, and it yielded no grain.	C. And others are the ones sown among thorns. They are those who hear the word, but the cares of the world and the deceitfulness of riches and the desires for other things enter in and choke the word, and it proves unfruitful.
D. And other seed fell into good soil and produced grain, growing up and increasing and yielding thirtyfold and sixtyfold and a hundredfold.	D. But those that were sown on the good soil are the ones who hear the word and accept it and bear fruit, thirtyfold and sixtyfold and a hundredfold.

Mark intentionally structured his parable with each element in the telling linked to a corresponding interpretation from Jesus afterward, ensuring nothing was left out. Luke's version makes alterations to the parable's telling, and in the interpretation that follows, he occasionally overlooks some of his modifications.

The telling of the parable (Luke 8: 5–8, ESV)	The interpretation (Luke 8:12–15, ESV)
A. And as he sowed, some fell along the path and was trampled underfoot, and the birds of the air devoured it.	A. The ones along the path are those who have heard; then the devil comes and takes away the word from their hearts, so that they may not believe and be saved.
B-1.	B-1. And the ones on the rock are those who, when they hear the word, receive it with joy.
B-2. And some fell on the rock, and as it grew up, it withered away, because it had no moisture.	B-2. But these have no root; they believe for a while, and in time of testing fall away.
C. And some fell among thorns, and the thorns grew up with it and choked it.	C. And as for what fell among the thorns, they are those who hear, but as they go on their way they are choked by the cares and riches and pleasures of life, and their fruit does not mature.

D. And some fell into good soil and grew and yielded a hundredfold.	D. As for that in the good soil, they are those who, hearing the word, hold it fast in an honest and good heart, and bear fruit with patience.

There are at least three problems resulting from fatigue which can be seen below (Goodacre 2004):

1. Luke omits the part of the parable where the seed sprang up quickly because it lacked depth of soil. However, he still provides an interpretation for that part of the parable
2. Where Mark's seed on the rock withered "because it had no root", Luke changes the reason to be that "it withered for lack of moisture". However, his interpretation addresses Mark's original version — that it withered because it had no root. His interpretation does not address the lack of moisture.
3. Luke removes Mark's reference to the sun scorching the seed on the rocky ground, yet he provides an interpretation for it: the "testing" that causes people to fall away.

Whether the relationships of the Gospels are explained through Lukan Posteriority (Luke using both Mark and Matthew as a source) or Matthean posteriority (Matthew using Mark and Luke as a source), and/or editorial fatigue, there is clearly tampering with the Gospels.

Christian cannot deny the presence of errors and mistakes within Mark, because that would oppose the beliefs of the authors of Matthew and Luke, who felt the need to correct and edit stories within Mark countlessly.

Randel Helms writes:

> "All things considered, then, Mark does not begin his story of Jesus very satisfactorily. Indeed, within two or three decades of Mark's completion, there were at least two, and perhaps three, different writers (or Christian groups) who felt the need to produce an expanded and corrected version. Viewed from their perspective, the Gospel of Mark has some major shortcomings : It contains no birth narrative ; it implies that Jesus, a repentant sinner, became the Son of God only at his baptism ; it recounts no resurrection narratives appearances ; and it ends with the very unsatisfactory notion that the women who found the Empty Tomb were too afraid to speak to anyone about it..." (Helms 2009)

Although Matthew and Luke used Mark as a source, they also deviate from him and use other traditions in their own Gospels.

This begs the question, what were the other traditions or Gospels which existed at that time? Why don't we have any existing manuscripts of so many alleged writings that would have supposedly been in circulation shortly after the time of Jesus?

Why do we encounter such a plethora of apocryphal and Gnostic gospels, including the Gospel of Thomas, Gospel of Mary, Gospel of Judas, Gospel of Peter, and Gospel of Philip, prompting questions about their exclusion from the canonical New Testament? Some of these Gospels such as Thomas and Peter have been dated quite early generally around late 1st century to 2nd century but remain outside the current Canon.

Evolution and Developments

These Gospels were preserved by various Christian communities and reflect diverse theological ideas, and narratives that were influential in the early development of Christianity.

Mark, although dated the earliest of the four Gospels, is by no means void from this "retelling of Jesus" problem. Mark is very likely to have suffered from the same challenges as Matthew and Luke. Mark would have drawn upon written and/or oral sources, traditions, miracle stories, and parables to compose his Gospel.

According to Maurice Casey in his book "The Aramaic Sources of Mark's Gospel" (Casey 1999), Mark's Gospel may have drawn from earlier written sources in Aramaic. These sources could potentially include written collections of sayings or teachings of Jesus, that were circulating within the early Christian communities where Aramaic was spoken.

Richard Bauckham, in "Jesus and the Eyewitnesses," (Bauckham 2008) contends that Mark's material largely derives from oral traditions. Dennis MacDonald, in "The Homeric Epics and the Gospel of Mark," (MacDonald 2000) and Robyn Faith Walsh, in "The Origins of Early Christian Literature (Walsh 2021)," argue that some of Mark's content stems from his own creativity and the influence of earlier literary conventions and tropes which would have included Jewish writings.

Overall, there is a progression from Jesus initially depicted more as a man to increasingly portrayed as divine with the latest Gospel John, having Matthew and Luke offering intermediary perspectives. The initial message of Christ was authentically conveyed by his disciples, but over time, it began to shift, particularly through the interpretations of figures like Paul, and even more significantly during the Councils of Nicaea and Constantinople, where foundational doctrines were established that diverged from the original teachings.

1.4 SYNOPTIC INFLUENCES

As discussed before, most Christians tend to focus less on the literary aspects of the Bible than the emotional. Obviously, this does not apply to all Christians; that would be a gross generalization.

However, when we study the Gospels, it is vital that we ask whether the writers' influences were people and circumstances or other scripture/writings that existed during their time. It is generally understood that the writers of the Gospels did not write them from scratch. That is, they most likely had in their possession a copy of the Old Testament and of Paul's epistles while constructing their Gospels (Smith 2011). Could it be that these documents influenced their writings?

The similarities between these works are not new. In fact, it is the overwhelming opinion of New Testament scholars (Ehrman 2006, Kloppenborg 2008, and Dunn 2013), many of whom often noted the similar ideas reflected in the Gospels were derived from the epistles.

There is well-established documentation in regards to Old Testament references within the Synoptic Gospels, which can be found in the Bible translation footnotes to Old Testament passages.

In fact, many of the Gospel passages also align with Paul's epistles and the book of Hebrews. It could be that Paul and the Gospel writers had knowledge of the oral traditions circulating in the first century (Dunn 2013), but that may not be the best explanation.

Evolution and Developments

Rather, the most probable explanation is that the writers of the Synoptic Gospels had Paul's letters at hand and used them to influence their writings to some degree.

It has often been said to me by my Christian friends that it would not make any sense for Paul's letters to have been written before the Gospels. Some even suggest that Mark influenced Paul; however, historical evidence makes that difficult to believe. If there were proof that Paul's letters were in fact earlier than the Gospels, then it is possible that they influenced the Gospel writers in constructing their scripture.

When we speak about influencing, though, we first need to define what we mean by *influence*. Did the author of Mark, for example, adapt to the ideas and theological beliefs floating around the Pauline churches? Or were his writings a direct interpretation of Pauline verses?

To simplify the idea, let us say Mark was the first of the four Gospels to be written. An idea some scholars appeal to is that Mark would have written his Gospel based on some of the Old Testament stories and been further influenced by a number of epistles (Helms 1988).

Then, let us say Matthew was the second Gospel to be written. Not only would he have used Mark as a source of information, explained previously as the Two-source hypothesis, but he would have also had a copy of the Old and New Testament epistles. The third Gospel, Luke would have had Mark, Matthew, and the Old and New Testament epistles (Smith 2011).

Some scholars disagree with this theory and instead refer to the hypothetical construction of *Q*. We will address this in the next portion. Strictly speaking, both theories can be true, as they are not, by nature, incompatible with each other.

However, over the centuries, this idea had been pushed away, but the theory of Pauline influence on the Gospels is more prominent throughout the history of scholarship (Weeden 1971).

Before we continue, let us first clarify some things. When we look at ancient literature, including the Gospel of Mark and the Old Testament, we find that it was written in a chiastic structure (Smith 2011). Chiastic structure is a literary technique of passages, which can be illustrated as a sandwich.

    A—Bread
      B—Mustard
        C—Lettuce
        C—Tomato
      B—Mustard
    A—Bread

A and *A* are both related, as both are bread. *B*'s are both condiments and *C*'s are both vegetables.

Michael Turton (2004), in his historical commentary on the Gospel of Mark, identifies chiasm within chiasm in Mark. Keep in mind that the chapters and verses in the Bible are not original to the Gospel itself.

Writers of that time did not put spaces between words, nor did they use punctuation. Mark's chiasms are characterized by simple exterior structures that bracket interior structures. This implies Mark's familiarity with the Pauline scriptures.

Evolution and Developments

The writer of Mark knew and used the writings of Paul through the use of his chiastic structure. Having noted a chiastic structure in Mark, we can move on to the parallels of Paul and Mark.

Consider Mark 12:10–11, which tells of the stone the builders rejected by referencing Psalm 118:22 'The stone that the builders rejected has become the cornerstone'. In Romans 8, Paul also references Psalms 118. This is not an isolated occurrence; both Paul and Mark would often cite Old Testament passages. So far this is a coincidence at best, so let us look at more examples..

Both Mark 12:12–17 and Roman 13:1–7 command us to pay our taxes and obey the law. In Mark 12:18–23, Jesus (Pbuh) is posed with a tricky question from the Sadducees regarding the denial of resurrection. Compare this with 1 Corinthians 15:12–1. Both passages present the question about the resurrection of the dead. It seems as though Mark, having been written later than Paul, has put Pauline theology into Jesus' mouth.

Benjamin Bacon often uses Mark 4:1–23 combined with the idea of Isaiah 6:9 (with respect to Romans 9–11) as a Pauline influence on Mark. Without getting too technical, it is potentially vital to understand who Paul was and what his historical circumstances were as well as to investigate his letters.

Another often-used comparison is Mark 7:19 and Romans 14:14, conveying similarities on food laws:

> "I am convinced, being fully persuaded in the Lord Jesus, that nothing is unclean in itself. But if anyone regards something as unclean, then for that person it is un-clean."
>
> (Romans 14:14, NIV)

"For it doesn't go into their heart but into their stomach, and then out of the body." (Mark 7:19, NIV)

"…The Lord Jesus, on the night he was betrayed, took bread, and when he had given thanks, he broke it and said, "This is my body, which is for you; do this in remembrance of me." (1 Corinthians 11:23–24, NIV).

"And he took bread, gave thanks and broke it, and gave it to them, saying, "This is my body given for you; do this in remembrance of me." (Luke 22:19, NIV)

The above verses are assuming that Paul was a source for Mark; however, some scholars argue the other way around—or at least that both could have used traditions of first-century Christianity (Dunn 2003). The point here is to convey the extent of influencing power Paul had if his letters were indeed earlier.

There seems to be evidence to suggest that later sayings were added to the Gospels by people reading Paul's letters first and being influenced by them. Even though Paul makes the claim that his words are from God (Romans 1:1–5), we do not have much reason to accept this. Going further, he says he received information about Jesus from no man.

Paul, unfortunately, only states around seven facts about the life of Jesus in his works. These facts also could have been gathered from existing writings. The Synoptic Gospel writers used Old Testament stories as a basis for many of the incidents in the life of Jesus.

Evolution and Developments

1.5 The Q source, Thomas, and James

We have all heard of the letter *Q* in the English alphabet of course, but from a Biblical perspective what is the Q source? Where does it come from, and what does it mean?

If you had noticed previously with the Two-source hypothesis figure, the letter *Q* was a part of the diagram (p. 29). The idea of Q is not a new one, but rather part of scholarship spanning centuries (Marxsen 1970). What is new, however, is the reconstructing aspects of Q and the original sayings.

As we have already explored, Mark was likely the first written Gospel, followed by Matthew and Luke using it as a source. This is tested through an examination of passages of Matthew and Luke with complete correlation stemming from Mark (Kloppenborg 2008).

However, there remain passages of complete verbatim correlation present in Matthew and Luke that are *not* included in Mark, which are referred to as the *Q source*. Where do they come from? Maybe they are from epistles. If not Mark or the epistles, then where? What is the explanation for this literary relationship?

Matthew and Luke share over 4,980 words that are not from Mark, including the Sermon on the Mount, the woes against Pharisees, and the many parables Jesus used in his teachings. When analyzing Matthew and Luke, we find that the word agreement in the double tradition ranges from 90 percent to less than 10 percent. The double tradition is common material in Matthew and Luke that isn't in Mark.

The suggestion that these similarities and correlations are coincidental, taken merely from oral traditions, is almost impossible. They must have used a common source (Kloppenborg 2008).

Q is indeed that common source. The letter Q is based on the German word *Quelle*, meaning a source. Matthew and Luke in many cases are clearly citing the same source, with the occasional exception of a few adjustments here and there. Nevertheless, the structure, even when the word-agreement is not great, is still the same. Take, for instance, Matthew 11:21–23 and Luke 10:13–15.

Matthew 11:21–23	Luke 10:13–15
"Woe to you, Chorazin! Woe to you, Bethsaida! For if the miracles that were performed in you had been performed in Tyre and Sidon, they would have repented long ago in sackcloth and ashes. But I tell you, it will be more bearable for Tyre and Sidon on the day of judgment than for you. And you, Capernaum, will you be lifted to the heavens? No, you will go down to Hades." (NIV)	"Woe to you, Chorazin! Woe to you, Bethsaida! For if the miracles that were performed in you had been performed in Tyre and Sidon, they would have repented long ago, sitting in sackcloth and ashes. But it will be more bearable for Tyre and Sidon at the judgment than for you. And you, Capernaum, will you be lifted to the heavens? No, you will go down to Hades. (NIV)

The words in the story itself are strikingly similar, almost an identical account. The parallels between the Q writings are not only based on vocabulary, but also sequence and structure.

Evolution and Developments

We have already established that portions of writing absent from Mark but present in Matthew and Luke are called *Q*. This is not constructed through imagination, but rather a logical obligation in reading the Gospels. Furthermore, there remain passages unique to Matthew and passages unique to Luke. This has led to the conclusion that these passages share a common source, Q. Let us look at another example—Matthew 3:7–10 and Luke 3:7–9:

Matthew 3:7–10	Luke 3:7–9
"But when he saw many of the Pharisees and Sadducees coming to where he was baptizing, he said to them: "You brood of vipers! Who warned you to flee from the coming wrath? Produce fruit in keeping with repentance. And do not think you can say to yourselves, 'We have Abraham as our father.' I tell you that out of these stones God can raise up children for Abraham. The axe is already at the root of the trees, and every tree that does not produce good fruit will be cut down and thrown into the fire." (NIV)	"John said to the crowds coming out to be baptized by him, "You brood of vipers! Who warned you to flee from the coming wrath? Produce fruit in keeping with repentance. And do not begin to say to yourselves, 'We have Abraham as our father.' For I tell you that out of these stones God can raise up children for Abraham. The ax is already at the root of the trees, and every tree that does not produce good fruit will be cut down and thrown into the fire." (NIV)

Again, we see great similarity, ranging from 60–80 percent correlation with each other. With this in mind, where is the Q source now? Scholars mostly believe it to be a lost manuscript, which would have likely been earlier than the Gospel of Mark. But what does this tell us? And what can we gain from it?

Of note is that nothing will be found in Q which mentions the divinity of Christ, redemption of sins requiring a blood sacrifice, the Trinity of dual hypostatic nature or Original sin. Jesus (Pbuh) never called himself God during his public ministry, nor did he ever imagine that he was God. He was simply God's servant.

This further enforces the idea that the passages alleging the divinity of Christ are later editions in the snowball of Christology.

"The God of Abraham, Isaac and Jacob, the God of our fathers, has glorified His servant Jesus." (Acts 3:13, NIV)

"Fellow Israelites, listen to this: Jesus of Nazareth was a man accredited by God to you by miracles, wonders and signs, which God did among you through him, as you yourselves know." (Acts 2:22, NIV)

Chapter 1 Evolution and Developments

References:
Apple, R. (2016). *New Testament People*. 1st ed. Bloomington, IN: Authorhouse.

Bauckham, R., 2008. Jesus and the eyewitnesses: the gospels as eyewitness testimony. Wm. B. Eerdmans Publishing.

Bowden, John. *Jesus: the unanswered questions*. SCM Press, 1988.

Brown, R.E., 1994. *Introduction to the New Testament Christology*. AandC Black.

Brown, Raymond E. An Introduction to the New Testament. New York: Doubleday, 1997.

Brown, S., 1993. *The origins of Christianity: a historical introduction to the New Testament*. Oxford University Press.

Bruce, F.F. and Kautzer, K., 1978. *Are the New Testament Documents Still Reliable?*. T. Nelson.

Casey, M., 1999. Aramaic sources of Mark's Gospel (Vol. 102). Cambridge University Press.

Collins, Adela Yarbro. "Mark." In The Oxford Bible Commentary, edited by John Barton and John Muddiman, 907-934. Oxford: Oxford University Press, 2001.

Dunn, J.D., 1985. *The Evidence for Jesus*. Westminster John Knox Press.

Dunn, J.D., 2013. *The oral Gospel tradition*. Wm. B. Eerdmans Publishing.

Ehrman, B.D., 2006. *Whose word is it?: the story behind who changed the New Testament and why.* AandC Black.

Ehrman, Bart D. The New Testament: A Historical Introduction to the Early Christian Writings. New York: Oxford University Press, 2016.

Ellicott, C.J. ed., 1954. *Ellicott's Commentary on the Whole Bible: A Verse by Verse Explanation.* Zondervan.

Goodacre, M., 1998. Fatigue in the Synoptics. New Testament Studies, 44(1).

Goodacre, M., 2004. The synoptic problem: A way through the maze (Vol. 80). A&C Black.

Helms, R., 1988. *Gospel fictions.* Prometheus books.

Helms, Randel. Gospel fictions. Prometheus Books, 2009.

Honoré, A.M. (1986). "A statistical study of the synoptic problem". *Novum Testamentum* **10** (2/3): 95–147. DOI:10.2307/1560364.

Keown, D., 2013. *Buddhism: A very short introduction* (Vol. 3). Oxford University Press.

Kloppenborg, J.S., 2008. *Q, the earliest Gospel: an introduction to the original stories and sayings of Jesus.* Westminster John Knox Press.

MacDonald, D.R., 2000. *The Homeric epics and the Gospel of Mark*. Yale University Press.

Marxsen, W., 1970. *Introduction to the New Testament: an approach to its problems*. Fortress Press.

Smith, D.O., 2011. *Matthew, Mark, Luke, and Paul: The Influence of the Epistles on the Synoptic Gospels*. Wipf and Stock Publishers.

Walsh RF. The Origins of Early Christian Literature. In: The Origins of Early Christian Literature: Contextualizing the New Testament within Greco-Roman Literary Culture. Cambridge University Press; 2021:i-ii.

Weeden, T.J., 1971. *Mark: Traditions in conflict*. Fortress Press.

Newman, B.M. and Stine, P.C., 2003. A handbook on Jeremiah. United Bible Societies.

2

"As for God, his way is perfect: The Lord's word is flawless; he shields all who take refuge in him." (2 Samuel 22:31, NIV)

Discrepancies and Inconsistencies

"Do they not contemplate the Quran? Had it been from [someone] other than Allah, they would have surely found much discrepancy in it." (Qur'an 4:82)

Discrepancies and Inconsistencies

2.1 CONTRADICTIONS

Having introduced the Gospel narrative relationships and development, let's now delve into some alleged contradictions found in the Bible. It is crucial to note that from a biblical perspective, the book should not contain errors or contradictions because it is considered a holy book inspired by God, and therefore, it must adhere to principles of divine protection.

If a book like the Bible were found to contain errors or contradictions, it would cast doubt on its claim to be the complete Word of God. If God is flawless and does not err, then His Holy Book should reflect that perfection.

Psalm 18:30 (NIV) states, "As for God, His way is perfect," and Proverbs 30:5-6 (NIV) affirms, "Every word of God is flawless. Do not add to his words…"

While there are countless minor and inconsequential errors in the Bible, such as numerical discrepancies, there are also significant and seemingly irreconcilable contradictions throughout the Gospels. It is important to acknowledge that similar contradictions can also be found in the Old Testament, which we will briefly touch upon as well. Contradictions or inconsistencies should not exist because they can confuse believers, bearing in mind that "God is not the author of confusion" (1 Corinthians 14:33, KJV).

Before we demonstrate any contradictions, it is important to note that differences do sometimes occur but are not exactly contradictory. Creative interpretation allows for justification in many cases. Sometimes the verses may seem odd and therefore appear to be contradictory but close examination confirms otherwise.

However, there are verses that are in clear contradiction and are irreconcilable. For example, let us compare the genealogies of that Matthew and Luke give us:

Matthew 1:6–16	Luke 3:21–31
David, Solomon, Roboam, Abia, Asa, Josaphat, Joram, Ozias, Joatham, Achaz, Ezekias, Manasses, Amon, Josias, Jechonias, Salathiel, Zorobabel, Abiud, Eliakim, Azor, Sadoc, Achim, Eliud, Eleazar, Matthan, Jacob, Joseph, *Jesus*	*David,* Nathan, Mattatha, Menan, Melea, Eliakim, Jonan, Joseph, Juda, Simeon, Levi, Matthat, Jorim, Eliezer, Jose, Er, Elmodam, Cosam, Addi, Melchi, Neri, Salathiel, Zorobabel, Rhesa, Joanna, Juda, Joseph, Semei, Mattathias, Maath, Nagge, Esli, Naum, Amos, Mattathias, Joseph, Janna, Melchi, Levi, Matthat, Heli, Joseph, *Jesus*

Both Matthew and Luke are giving the genealogies of Joseph. As you can see, the genealogies are not parallel. Does God want to give us differing genealogies of Jesus (Pbuh)? You may not consider this to be a solid contradiction. If a person is clever enough, they could make them match somehow, but would they be genuine in doing so?

Some of the classical contradictions encountered by readers of the Bible lie mainly in three categories: 1) differences in chronology of events, 2) variations in Jesus' wording in parallel passages, and 3) perhaps most challenging, differences in descriptions of events.

Discrepancies and Inconsistencies

Assess these as you read them, and come to your own conclusions based on the evidence. Do you think the Word of God would contain such mistakes?

The New Testament stands as a cornerstone of Christian faith, presenting supposed firsthand witness testimonies crucial to shaping beliefs, ethics, and life decisions centered around the life of Jesus Christ. These writings are foundational, influencing how Christians understand their worldview. Given the pivotal role of these texts, their reliability and internal coherence are of high importance.

In a hypothetical trial, where four witnesses are pivotal in a criminal trial seeking a severe judgment, consistency among their testimonies would be expected. Similarly, within the Gospels of Mark, Matthew, Luke, and John, we find variations in details and perspectives, redactions to the same scenarios, rewriting and reshaping of Jesus teachings.

If I were a juror in a court case, seeing the redactions and contradictions in the gospel narratives would make me wonder why later writers felt the need to modify earlier accounts.

If the Gospel of Mark, for instance, is considered divinely inspired, it raises questions about how and why these alterations were made. The discrepancies would definitely make me rethink how reliable these testimonies are and how they shape our understanding of faith and theology.

All of the following are from the King James Version unless otherwise cited.

1. Jairu's Daughter

Was Jairus' daughter alive when he approached Jesus? Matthew clearly states that the daughter is now dead, but Mark states that she is at the point of death. We ask, which one is true? This depends on the gospel we read. Either the daughter was at the point of death or not, it cannot be both.

> "While he spoke these things unto them, behold, there came a certain ruler, and worshipped him, saying, "My daughter is even now dead. But come and lay thy hand upon her, and she shall live." (Matthew 9:18)

> "And, behold, there cometh one of the rulers of the synagogue, Jairus by name; and when he saw him, he fell at his feet, and besought him greatly, saying, "My little daughter is at the point of death. I pray thee, come and lay thy hands on her, that she may be healed; and she shall live." (Mark 5:22–23)

2. Blind Man

Was the blind man healed after leaving Jericho or before entering Jericho? Matthew again says something different than Luke. Matthew states that it was as he was departing from Jericho, and Luke says it was as he was approaching Jericho.

> "And as they departed from Jericho, a great multitude followed him. And, behold, two blind men sitting by the way side, when

they heard that Jesus passed by, cried out, saying, "Have mercy on us, O Lord, thou son of David." (Matthew 20:29-30)

"And it came to pass, that as he was come nigh unto Jericho, a certain blind man sat by the way side begging." (Luke 18:35)

3. *What did Jesus ride on into Jerusalem?*

Matthew mentions that Jesus entered Jerusalem on an ass and colt:

"Tell ye the daughter of Sion, Behold, thy King cometh unto thee, meek, and sitting upon an ass, and a colt the foal of an ass. And the disciples went, and did as Jesus commanded them and brought the ass, and the colt, and put on them their clothes, and they set him thereon." (Matthew 21:5–7)

Mark mentions a colt:

"And they brought the colt to Jesus, and cast their garments on him; and he sat upon him." (Mark 11:7)

John mentions a young ass:

"And Jesus, when he had found a young ass, sat thereon." (John 12:14)

One could ask, 'What if Jesus rode on all three?' Why didn't all our witnesses mention Jesus riding all three?

4. *When was Jesus born?*

Matthew states Jesus was born during the days of Herod the king. This would be clearly before 4 BC, as that was the year of the king's death:

"Now when Jesus was born in Bethlehem of Judaea in the days of Herod the king." (Matthew 2:1)

Luke states Jesus was born after 6AD:
"And it came to pass in those days, that there went out a decree from Caesar Augustus that all the world should be taxed. (And this taxing was first made when Cyrenius was governor of Syria.)...Joseph also went up from Galilee, out of the city of Nazareth, in Judea...to be taxed with Mary his espoused wife, being great with child." (Luke 2:1–4)

Cyrenius had become governor of Syria in 6AD, nine years after King Herod's death.

In Luke (Luke 2:2), there's also a historical mistake about a census that took place during Jesus' birth. Luke says the census happened when Quirinius was governor of Syria. However, historical records, such as Josephus in his writing "The antiquities of the Jews", show that Quirinius only became governor around 6 CE. Jesus' birth is typically dated to 6-4 BCE, before Quirinius took office. This means the census described in Luke couldn't have occurred at the time of Jesus' birth, making it a historical error.

5. *Where were the women during the crucifixion?*

During the crucifixion, did the women stand near or far?

"And many women were there beholding afar off." (Matthew 27:55)

Discrepancies and Inconsistencies

"There were also women looking on afar off." (Mark 15:40)

"And the women that followed him from Galilee, stood afar off, beholding these things." (Luke 23:49)

All three synoptic gospels state the women were watching from afar. In John 19:25, they did not stand from afar, but rather stood near the cross:

> "Now there stood by the cross of Jesus his mother, and his mother's sister, Mary the wife of Cleophas, and Mary Magdalene."
> (John 19:25)

Afar or near? It cannot be both.

6. *When was Jesus crucified?*
Was Jesus crucified before or after the Passover?

> "Then led they Jesus from Caiaphas unto the hall of judgment: and it was early; and they themselves went not into the judgment hall, lest they should be defiled; but that they might eat the Passover." (John 18:28)

> "And it was the preparation of the Passover, and about the sixth hour: and he sayeth unto the Jews, "Behold your King!" But they cried out, "Away with him, away with him, crucify him." Pilate sayeth unto them, "Shall I crucify your King?" The chief priests answered, "We have no king but Caesar." (John 19:14–16)

"And the first day of unleavened bread, when they killed the Passover, his disciples said unto him, "Where wilt thou that we go and prepare that thou mayest eat the Passover?" (Mark 14:12)

"And it was the third hour, and they crucified him." (Mark 15:25)

In Mark, Jesus ate the Passover meal and was crucified the next morning. In John, Jesus did not eat the Passover meal and was crucified before the Passover meal was to be eaten.

7. *What time was Jesus crucified?*
Was Jesus crucified in the third or sixth hour?

"And it was the third hour, and they crucified him." (Mark 15:25) (Put on the cross at 9 a.m. and death at 3 p.m.)

"And it was the preparation of the Passover, and about the sixth hour." (John 19:14)

He couldn't have been crucified on the third and sixth hour at the same time, unless he was crucified on the third hour first, resurrected himself, and then was crucified a second time without anyone noticing it on the sixth hour.

8. *Was the body of Jesus wrapped in spices or not?*
The Gospel of John makes it very clear it was wrapped in spices:
"Then took they the body of Jesus, and wound it in linen clothes with the spices, as the manner of the Jews is to bury." (John 19:40)

However, this goes against Mark, because the women are seen buying spices on Saturday and Sunday morning to anoint the body of Jesus:
> "And when the sabbath was past, Mary Magdalene, and Mary the mother of James, and Salome, had bought sweet spices, that they might come and anoint him." (Mark 16:1)

9. Who carried Jesus' cross?

Did Jesus carry his own cross, as mentioned in John?
> "And he, bearing his cross, went forth into a place called the place of a skull" (John 19:17).

Or did Simon of Cyrene carry it, as mentioned in Matthew?
> "And as they came out, they found a man of Cyrene, Simon by name; him, they compelled to bear his cross" (Matthew 27:32).

Usually, the argument for this is that both could have held the cross. Why would our witnesses neglect to mention this?

10. When did the women arrive at the tomb, and who arrived?

Was it whilst still dark? And was it Mary Magdalene?
> "The first day of the week cometh Mary Magdalene early, when it was yet dark, unto the sepulcher, and seeeth the stone taken away from the sepulcher." (John 20:1)

Or was it at sunrise? And was it Mary Magdalene and the other Mary?
> "As it began to dawn toward the first day of the week, came Mary Magdalene and the other Mary to see the sepulcher." (Matthew 28:1)

Perhaps it was Mary, Mary Magdalene, mother of James and Salome, very early in the morning.

> "And when the Sabbath was past, Mary Magdalene, and Mary the mother of James, and Salome, had bought sweet spices, that they might come and anoint him. And very early in the morning the first day of the week, they came unto the sepulcher at the rising of the sun." (Mark 16:1–2)

11. Did the women immediately tell the disciples?

Mark 16:8 is where the Gospel actually ends, with the women telling nobody about it since "they were afraid."

Compare this with Matthew 28:8. They depart with fear, just like in Mark; however, in this passage, they had great joy along with their fear and, interestingly, ran to tell the disciples. Luke 24:8 has it also that they told the rest.

We can see a gradual evolution of how the story is told.

12. Why do only Matthew and Luke know of the virgin birth?

Of all the writers of the New Testament, only Matthew and Luke mention the virgin birth. Had something as miraculous as the virgin birth taken place, one would expect that Mark and John would have also mentioned it. Similarly, Paul also never mentions the virgin birth, nor numerous other important pieces of information, even though it would have strengthened his position of authority as an apostle.

Moreover, the angel's message and the date and location of the virgin birth are contradictory in Matthew and Luke. We discussed the contradiction in the date above.

Discrepancies and Inconsistencies

While both Matthew and Luke have it that Jesus was born in Bethlehem, there are differences in where each Gospel says they resided.

In Luke, Mary and Joseph travel from their home in Nazareth in Galilee to Bethlehem in Judea for the birth of Jesus (Luke 2:4). In Matthew, it was not until after the birth of Jesus that Mary and Joseph resided in Nazareth—and then only because they were afraid to return to Judea (Matthew 2:21–23).

13. The Ascension

According to Luke, Jesus' ascension took place in Bethany on the day of his resurrection:

> "And he led them out as far as to Bethany, and he lifted up his hands, and blessed them. And it came to pass, while he blessed them, he was parted from them, and carried up into heaven." (Luke 24:50-51)

However, according to Acts, Jesus' ascension took place at Mount Olivet, forty days after his resurrection:

> "And when he had spoken these things, while they beheld, he was taken up; and a cloud received him out of their sight.... "Ye men of Galilee, why stand ye gazing up into heaven? this same Jesus, which is taken up from you into heaven, shall so come in like manner as ye have seen him go into heaven." Then returned they unto Jerusalem from the mount called Olivet, which is from Jerusalem a sabbath day's journey." (Acts 1:9–12)

14. Where would Jesus meet the disciples?

In the forty days between the alleged resurrection and ascension of Jesus, the Apostles, as Luke has it, "never left Jerusalem."

> "…Stay in the city until you have been clothed with power from on high." (Luke 24:49, NIV)

How could they have broken such a clear order, especially when they received the order in person? In contrast from Luke, according to the Gospels of Mark and Matthew, the disciples did leave Jerusalem (for Galilee, per Jesus' other command).

> "But after I have risen, I will go ahead of you into Galilee." (Mark 14:28, NIV)

> Then Jesus said to them, "Do not be afraid. Go and tell my brothers to go to Galilee; there they will see me." (Matthew 28:10, NIV)

15. Did Jesus contradict himself or give a false prediction?

The Bible provides clear criteria to follow when determining whether a prediction is from God or not. Does Jesus (Pbuh) ever contradict this verse?

> "You may say to yourselves, "How can we know when a message has not been spoken by the Lord?" If what a prophet proclaims in the name of the Lord does not take place or come true, that is a message the Lord has not spoken. That prophet has spoken presumptuously, so do not be alarmed." (Deuteronomy 18:21–22, NIV)

Discrepancies and Inconsistencies

Jesus below is reported to have said clearly the sign in which he will demonstrate will be like the sign of Jonah.

> "For as Jonah was three days and three nights in the whale's belly; so shall the Son of man be three days and three nights in the heart of the earth." (Matthew 12:40, NIV)

When we look closely, though, we find that Jesus was not buried for three days and three nights as reported. It is generally accepted that Jesus was crucified Friday afternoon and arose sometime Saturday night or Sunday morning (McKinsey 1995).

In either instance, this does not equate to three days and three nights, but rather approximately a day and a half. Now, one may say that would be considered three days in Jewish times where the day begins at sunset rather than midnight. Unfortunately, even in this instance, even if we stretch the definition of day, it is still only three days and 2 nights.

The Bible seems to be at odds with its own Gospel stories. The examples we have covered so far are only some of the many differences that we can examine through a horizontal reading of the Bible. Simple differences, like that of Matthew (16:34) and Mark (14:30) telling of the number of times the cock will crow, may be considered meaningless. But big differences about important events are clearly significant.

16. Does Matthew mention a prophecy that cannot be identified?

Matthew 2:23 (NIV) ends by arguing that Jesus' life in Nazareth fulfilled a messianic prophecy, which he quotes:

> "and he went and lived in a town called Nazareth. So was fulfilled what **was said through the prophets, that he would be called a Nazarene**."

However, no such prophecy is found in the Old Testament, or any other known source. Where is Matthew getting this information?

Some scholars suggest that he is using extra canonical writings which we no longer have access to. Others suggest it is a mistranslation or misunderstanding.

Either way this has caused scholarly debate, as Matthew is very confidently stating that it was said through the prophets and absolutely nothing is found in the Old Testament. Even if this was an unintentional error, how could this be divinely inspired by misinformation?

17. Why did Jesus have to be born of a virgin?

Luke says that the reason Jesus had to be born of a virgin is through the Holy spirit.

> "The Holy Spirit will come on you, and the power of the Most High will overshadow you. So the holy one to be born will be called the Son of God." (Luke 1:35, NIV)

In Matthew, we see a different reason. Matthew claims that she had to be a virgin to fulfil the scriptures.

Discrepancies and Inconsistencies

"""All this happened so that what the Lord had spoken through the prophet came true: "The virgin will become pregnant and give birth to a son, and they will name him Immanuel," which means "God is with us."" (Matthew 1:23, NIV)

Here, Matthew is referring to Isaiah 7:14 where it states: "Therefore the Lord himself will give you a sign: The virgin will conceive and give birth to a son, and will call him Immanuel." The problem is that Matthew is quoting this verse from Isaiah in the Greek translation of the Old Testament, and when you read this very own verse in Hebrew, it does not say a **virgin will conceive and give birth to a son.**

The Hebrew word used in Isaiah 7:14 for a virgin is *Alma* which generally means a young woman. There is actually a Hebrew word specifically for a virgin and that word is *bethula*, which was never used in Isaiah. Matthew was reading a Greek Translation of the Old Testament known as the Septuagint, when writing his Gospel and mistranslated "almah" young woman in Hebrew as "parthenos" meaning virgin in Greek.

Furthermore, the passage itself is not specifically referring to a future messiah but is a prophecy given to King Ahaz during a time of political crisis, assuring him of God's protection.

18. Did Jesus, Mary, and Joseph go to Egypt or Nazareth?

In Matthew 2:14-15, all three are stated to have left for Egypt.

"So he got up, took the child and his mother during the night and left for Egypt, where he stayed until the death of Herod. And so was fulfilled what the Lord had said through the prophet: "Out of Egypt I called my son" (NIV)

However, in Luke 2:39, all three are stated to return to Nazareth.

"When Joseph and Mary had done everything required by the Law of the Lord, they returned to Galilee to their own town of Nazareth." (NIV)

19. Who was the high priest Jesus refers to?

In Mark 2:25-26 Jesus and his disciples were criticized by the Pharisees for picking grain on the Sabbath, to which Jesus responded by referencing how David and his companions ate bread when they were hungry.

"He answered, "Have you never read what David did when he and his companions were hungry and in need? In the days of Abiathar the high priest, he entered the house of God and ate the consecrated bread.." (NIV)

The problem with this verse is that it goes against the Old Testament which says in 1 Samuel 21:1-6 that it was *Ahimelech* who was the high priest and not *Abiathar* as mentioned in Mark. Someone made a mistake - Was it Jesus in recalling the story or Mark in recording Jesus' words?

20. What were the instructions of Jesus?

In Mark 6:8, Jesus instructs his disciples to take nothing for their journey except a staff, while in Matthew 10:10, he advises them not to take a staff. Which one was it?

"These were his instructions: "Take nothing for the journey **except a staff**—no bread, no bag, no money in your belts.""
(Mark 6:8, NIV)

> """Do not get any gold or silver or copper to take with you in your belts— **no** bag for the journey or extra shirt or sandals **or a staff**, for the worker is worth his keep." (Matthew 10:9-10, NIV)

Matthew 24

Keeping in mind the criteria for a false prophet is that they make false prophecies (Deuteronomy 18:21–22), we can see that Jesus makes false prophecies in Matthew 24. The first prediction is of the destruction of the temple, and the other is the apocalypse.

Assuming that Jesus (Pbuh) is a true Prophet, these predictions would not have been from his mouth. Somebody else would have attributed these predictions to him. The Gospel narratives all have small differences in regards to the predictions.

> "Jesus left the temple and was going away, when his disciples came to point out to him the buildings of the temple. But he answered them, "You see all these, do you not? Truly, I say to you, there will not be left here one stone upon another that will not be thrown down"…As he sat on the Mount of Olives, the disciples came to him privately, saying, "Tell us, when will these things be, and what will be the sign of your coming and of the end of the age?"…"For as the lightning comes from the east and shines as far as the west, so will be the coming of the Son of Man. Wherever the corpse is, there the vultures will gather. "Immediately after the tribulation of those days the sun will be darkened, and the moon will not give its light, and the stars will fall from heaven, and the powers of the heavens will be shaken"…"Truly, I say to you, this generation will not pass away until all these things take place." (Matthew 24:1-2, 3, 27-29, 34, ESV)

According to scholars such as Raymond Brown, these things did not happen, which caused some embarrassment for Christians attempting to reconcile them.

> "Far from being a clear prophecy, this saying seems to have been an embarrassment in the Synoptic Gospel tradition: Jesus had spoken about the destruction and rebuilding of the Temple, but he had died without the Temple being destroyed or his rebuilding it. Luke omits the saying…Mark Adds qualifications…Matthew reduces the prediction to a possibility…John is giving us still another reinterpretation designed to remove the difficulty." (Brown 1967).

Christians have attempted to reconcile such difficulties by suggesting the term 'generation' in verse 34 does not necessarily mean the generation during the time of Jesus (Pbuh). Others have also suggested that this prediction could still yet occur someday upon Jesus' return. Unfortunately, when we analyze the histories and intentions of the verses within their contexts, all of those suggestions become very unlikely and unreasonable to even entertain. In Ellicott's commentary on the whole Bible (1954), he states:

> "The natural meaning of the words is, beyond question, that which takes "generation" in the ordinary sense (as in Matthew 1:17, Acts 13:36, and elsewhere)…So it was on "this generation" that the accumulated judgments were to fall. The desire to bring the words into more apparent harmony with history has led some interpreters to take "generation" in the sense of "race" or "people" …But for this meaning, there is not the shadow of authority; nor does it remove the difficulty which it was invented to explain."

Discrepancies and Inconsistencies

If a prophecy, such as the above, regarding Jesus' return and the end times, failed to come true, it would indeed contradict the criteria set forth in Deuteronomy 18:22:

> "If what a prophet proclaims in the name of the Lord does not take place or come true, that is a message the Lord has not spoken. That prophet has spoken presumptuously, so do not be alarmed." (NIV)

According to this passage, a prophet's predictions must come to pass to be considered from God, any discrepancy between prophecy and outcome raises significant theological questions.

In several places in Paul's epistles, and most clearly in (1 Thessalonians 4:13-18), Paul states his belief that Jesus would return in his own lifetime, "we who are alive, who are left until the coming of the Lord" (1 Thessalonians 4:15, ESV).

Even after he died, Jesus did not return, and this was becoming an embarrassment for some Christians. Some scholars even go as far as to suggest that a forger ended up writing 2 Thessalonians in Paul's name to save his reputation and to eliminate this as a source of lies.

2 Thessalonians says not to be troubled by a previous letter written as if by Paul, which could be referring to 1 Thessalonians, saying that the day of Christ is at hand.

To refute the earlier epistle, this author has to discredit it by claiming it was a forgery written in Paul's name (2 Thessalonians 2:2-3, KJV) by "a man of sin" and "the son of perdition", who opposes and exalts himself above the word of God.

Although the letter states it was written by Paul, it was actually authored by someone else who intended for the reader to believe it was from Paul (Ehrman, 2012)

Old Testament discrepancies

The Old Testament is the Christian name for the Hebrew (Jewish) Bible, considered the first section of the Christian Bible before the New Testament. It was written in Hebrew and, in small parts, Aramaic (for example, Daniel, Ezra, and Jeremiah).

The Hebrew Bible (Masoretic text) was standardized by the tenth century (900AD). Jewish scholars known as Masoretes had established a standardized text of the Hebrew Bible. This became the authoritative version of the Hebrew Bible for Jewish communities. The translation of this Bible into Koine Greek is known as the Septuagint, long used in Greek-speaking churches and retained in some Orthodox churches today (Barr 1980). The canon of the Septuagint, however, included additional books, which are deemed apocryphal by Protestant Christians.

Overall, the Old Testament is a collection of 39 books (not including the seven Catholic-accepted books) about the history and way of the people of Israel. Unfortunately, the authors of these books are unknown, and each book has a unique style and tone.

The stories mentioned include laws and sayings proposed to serve as a model for ethics and religion. Sadly, this collection of books is infected with countless discrepancies within the stories, details, descriptions, and figures. Whether the contradictions are minor or major, the book as a whole can no longer remain flawless as stated in Psalm 18:30. These inconsistencies are not unique to the New Testament. Here are only some examples within the Old Testament.

I should clarify here that I do not intend to belittle Christians or the Bible itself, but to challenge what is portrayed in line with 1 Corinthians 14:33, KJV: "For God is not the author of confusion..."

Discrepancies and Inconsistencies

Whether these errors are numerical or copyist errors, they are errors nonetheless, which are confusing.

Would a university student submit an assessment to their professor and proudly admit to him/her that it had some errors? No, instead, it would be quite embarrassing; do you think God would have authored the following and previous errors mentioned?

1. How many fighting men were found in Israel?
2 Samuel 24:9: Eight hundred thousand.
1Chronicles 21:5: One million, one hundred thousand.

2. God sent his prophet to threaten David with how many years of famine?
2 Samuel 24:13: Seven.
1 Chronicles 21:12: Three.

3. How old was Ahaziah when he began to rule over Jerusalem?
2 Kings 8:26: Twenty-two.
2 Chronicles 22:2: Forty-two.

4. How long did he rule over Jerusalem?
2 Kings 24:8: Three months.
2 Chronicles 36:9: Three months and ten days.

5. Solomon built a facility containing how many baths?
1 Kings 7:26: Two thousand.

2 Chronicles 45: Over three thousand.

6. How many were the children of Adin?
Ezra 2:15: Four hundred and fifty-four.
Nehemiah 7:20: Six hundred and fifty-five.

7. Who was the father of Uzziah?
Matthew 1:8: Joram.
2 Chronicles 26:1: Amaziah.

8. Does God change his mind?
1 Samuel 15:10–11: Yes. "The word of the Lord came to Samuel: "I repent that I have made Saul King."" (ESV)
1 Samuel 15:29: No. "the Glory of Israel will not lie or have regret, for he is not a man, that he should have regret." (ESV)
Genesis 6:6: "And the Lord regretted that he had made man." (ESV)
Exodus 32:14: "And the Lord relented from the disaster that he had spoken of bringing on his people." (ESV)

9. How many were the children of Zattu?
Ezra 2:8: Nine hundred and forty five
Nehemiah 7:13: Eight hundred and forty five

10. How many horsemen did David capture?
2 Samuel 8:4: One thousand seven hundred
1 Chronicles 18:4: Seven thousand

Discrepancies and Inconsistencies

11. To whom did the Midianites sell Joseph?
Genesis 37:28: Ishmaelites.
Genesis 37:36: Officer of Pharoah.

12. Did Joshua capture Jerusalem?
Joshua 10:23, 40: Yes.
Joshua 15:63: No.

13. How many chief officers?
1 Kings 5:16: 3,300.
2 Chronicles 2:18: 3,600.

14. How many baths?
1 Kings 7:26: 2,000 baths.
2 Chronicles 4:5: 3,000 baths.

15. How many sons did Michal have?
2 Samuel 6:23: Michal had no sons,
2 Samuel 21:8: Five sons.

16. How many days?
2 Kings 25:8: The seventh day
Jer. 52:12: The tenth day

17. How did Saul die?
1 Samuel 31:4: He killed himself;
2 Samuel 21:12: He was killed by a Philistine.

2 Samuel 1: 10: He was killed by an Amalekite.

18. How many men drawing swords?
Samuel 24:9: 500,000 men.
I Chronicles 21:5 470,000 men.

19. Does God tempt us?
James 1:13: God tempts no man.
Genesis 22:1: God tempted Abraham.

20. Does God allow lying?
Proverbs 12:22: "Lying lips are abomination to the Lord" (ESV)
But 1 Kings 22:23 says: "The Lord has put a lying spirit in the mouth of all these your prophets." (ESV)

21. How many stalls?
1 Kings 4:26: 40,000.
2 Chronicles 9:25: 4,000.

22. How old was Jehoiachin when he reigned?
In 2 Kings 24:8: Eighteen years.
2 Chronicles 36:9: Eight years old.

These are only a few of the hundreds of errors in the Bible (Ally 2001). These above contradictions are limited to the writing of the Bible. We will cover the transmission and corruption of the Bible in later portions of this chapter.

Why would the Word of God contain so many discrepancies? Was this part of a divine plan, or was it corrupted/changed?

Discrepancies and Inconsistencies

As a further example, why are 2 Kings 19:1–13 and Isaiah 37:1–13 identical?

"As soon as King Hezekiah heard it, he tore his clothes and covered himself with sackcloth and went into the house of the Lord. And he sent Eliakim, who was over the household, and Shebna the secretary, and the senior priests, covered with sackcloth, to the prophet Isaiah the son of Amoz." (Isaiah 37:1-2, ESV)

"As soon as King Hezekiah heard it, he tore his clothes and covered himself with sackcloth and went into the house of the Lord. And he sent Eliakim, who was over the household, and Shebna the secretary, and the senior priests, covered with sackcloth, to the prophet Isaiah the son of Amoz." (2 Kings 19:1-2, ESV)

2.2 FORGERIES

Why do people, both modern and ancient, forge writings? Could the Word of God ever contain a forgery or forgeries? These are important questions readers of the Bible must ask themselves in investigating the veracity of the book.

How do we know the authors of the Bible were who they said they were? Is it possible that people wrote in the name of others for a particular reason?

Holy Bible Re-examined

To begin with, this is a list of the books of the Protestant Bible:

Old Testament		*New Testament*	
Genesis	Ecclesiastes	Matthew	1 Peter
Exodus	Song of Solomon	Mark	2 Peter
Leviticus		Luke	1 John
Numbers	Isaiah	John	2 John
Deuteronomy	Jeremiah	Acts (of the Apostles)	3 John
Joshua	Lamentations		Jude
Judges	Ezekiel	Romans	Revelation
Ruth	Daniel	1 Corinthians	
1 Samuel	Hosea	2 Corinthians	
2 Samuel	Joel	Galatians	
1 Kings	Amos	Ephesians	
2 Kings	Obadiah	Philippians	
1 Chronicles	Jonah	Colossians	
2 Chronicles	Micah	1 Thessalonians	
Ezra	Nahum	2 Thessalonians	
Nehemiah	Habakkuk	1 Timothy	
Esther	Zephaniah	2 Timothy	
Job	Haggai	Titus	
Psalms	Zechariah	Philemon	
Proverbs	Malachi	Hebrews	
		James	

We have will mainly been going over the New Testament in respect to forgery; however, let us take a look at some examples from the Old Testament.

Discrepancies and Inconsistencies

The first five books are believed to have been written by Moses (Pbuh), but after a little investigating, this does not seem likely. Coogan (2008) mentions one particular challenge for the Old Testament, presented in Deuteronomy 34:5: "And Moses the servant of the LORD died there in Moab, as the LORD had said."

The above verse clearly mentions the death of Moses. How could Moses have written his own obituary? Obviously, Moses did not write it. Would this be considered a forgery?

Some suggest that Joshua would have written the rest of the book for Moses, as he was second in command to Moses. But in Joshua 24:29, Joshua also ends up dying: "After these things Joshua the son of Nun, the servant of the LORD, died, being 110 years old." So the same problem occurs again.

Coogan (2008) indicates other reasons why Moses would not have written the first five books. For example, the text frequently refers to times after Moses: "These are the words Moses spoke to all Israel…" (Deuteronomy 1:1, ESV) Additionally, the texts often speak of Moses in the third person, which is quite suspect regarding authenticity.

Similarly, in the Gospel of Matthew, we have Matthew referring to himself in the third person:

> "As Jesus passed on from there, he saw a man called Matthew sitting at the tax booth, and he said to him, "Follow me." And he rose and followed him." (Matthew 9:9, ESV).

Another example from the Old Testament can be seen in the book of Jeremiah, which contains strong critiques of the religious leadership in Jerusalem. Jeremiah accuses the scribes of falsifying documents.

In one key verse (Jeremiah 8:8) condemns the scribes for creating lies through their writing. He denunciates false practices which align with some of the ideas found in Deuteronomy, which emerged later.

Jeremiah's central conflict was rooted in disagreements over what constituted the true covenant between God and Israel. He rejected the system of offerings and festivals as part of this covenant, emphasizing that true worship meant ethical living and devotion to God alone. Jeremiah criticized the idea that external rituals or sacrifices could atone for the people's failure to live out the ethical demands of the covenant. He believed that these practices were not part of the authentic covenant that he understood, which emphasized justice, righteousness, and the worship of God alone (Jeremiah 7:21-23; 9:23-24).

Jeremiah 8:8 suggests that there was some form of corruption or distortion of the biblical texts by the religious leaders and scribes of his time. The verse indicates that the scribes, who were responsible for writing and preserving religious documents, had altered or misrepresented the law of God, leading people to believe false interpretations or teachings.

While this specific passage does not directly indicate a complete forgery in the sense of creating entirely false documents, it does point to the manipulation or corruption of existing sacred writings.

According to Gill's Exposition of the entire Bible:

"…the pen of the scribes was in vain, when employed in **writing out false copies of the law,** or false glosses **and interpretations of it,** such as were made **by the Scribes**…" (Gill 2009)

Discrepancies and Inconsistencies

Generally speaking, a forgery is the process of making, adapting, or imitating things, especially documents, with the intent to deceive for some gain.

Ehrman (2011) provides a good example of a recently-discovered forgery known as *The Hitler Diaries*. On April 22, 1983, an alleged discovery of Adolf Hitler's personal diaries was released. It was a voluminous work covering the period between 1932–1945. This created a media frenzy around the world, with many people bidding on the diaries, from magazine and news organizations to journalists and historians.

The diaries ended up being a massive collection of forgeries. The forger himself, Konrad Kujau, used to sell fake Nazi memorabilia to wealthy, gullible collectors. Surprisingly, his forged copies of the diaries sold to people without much expert analysis verifying whether they were authentic. Eventually, evidence proved them fake through a comparative examination of the writings themselves. Small things began to reveal themselves, such as the difference in signatures. The case of the fake Hitler diaries is just one example of forgery.

In ancient times, forgery was common. Many people did it for different reasons, but mainly for monetary gain. In the past, there were fewer experts to identify forgeries, which made it quite easy to get away with. In fact, many early Christian forgers faked many documents for many different reasons (Ehrman 2005).

Today, we can find a multitude of forged documents that came from the early churches—Gospels and letters all claiming to be written by apostles or messengers. One example is the Gospel account written by Peter, detailing the resurrection event.

There are Gospels that were allegedly written by Jesus' brother Thomas, his disciple Philip, and even Mary Magdalene. There are also non-Gospel books describing the adventures of Jesus' 'apostles' like 'acts of Paul'. These have, however, been fabricated by church leaders in Turkey in second-century Christianity. We can see this through Tertullian's writings claiming the forger went on trial for what he had done.

As these forgeries all occurred between the second to fourth centuries, you may be wondering if there were forgeries during the time of the apostles. The answer is yes. Some of them come from Apostle Paul. Paul supposedly wrote 13 of the 27 books in the New Testament; however, most scholars would say that is not completely accurate. For example, as discussed earlier:

> "Concerning the coming of our Lord Jesus Christ and our being gathered to him, we ask you, brothers and sisters, not to become easily unsettled or alarmed by the teaching allegedly from us—whether by a prophecy or by word of mouth or by letter." (2 Thessalonians 2:1-2, NIV)

This passage mentions a letter that would have been in circulation during the time of Paul, and he suggests not to be led astray by it. The irony, as mentioned previously, is that most scholars do not believe that Paul wrote the book of 2 Thessalonians itself based on the discrepancies of 1 and 2 Thessalonians.

Ancient forgers employed strategies in order to make sure their own writings appeared real. One such strategy is warning against other fake writings. This old trick aims to makes the reader naturally

Discrepancies and Inconsistencies

assume the author (although a forger himself) is not a forger but genuine and looking out for the common good.

These types of forgeries were intentionally deceitful. Some may argue that some forgeries may have been done in an effort to correct rather than to deceive, but when forgeries are made by people who claimed to be followers of Jesus, we must question such deceitful actions.

There have also been forgeries in the name of Peter and Paul. Some scholars such as Bart Ehrman conclude that at least 11 of the 27 books in the New Testament were forged. 1 and 2 Peter, according the Hengel (2010), were probably not written by the disciple Peter. Scholars generally believe 2 Peter to be less authentic than 1 Peter.

Below is a list of books in the New Testament whose authenticity are disputed, according to general scholarly consensus (Wilson 2008).

Disputed	Possibly pseudonymous	Probably pseudonymous
Hebrew 2 Peter James 2 & 3 John Revelation	Ephesians Colossians 2 Thessalonians	1 Timothy 2 Timothy Titus

There is much more to be said on the topic of possible forgery within the Bible. For now, I will leave you to ponder some examples of Bible verses that are no longer included in modern translations due to omissions, textual variants, footnotes stating that these verses are not found in earlier manuscripts, and even clear forgeries.

Bible verses not included in some modern translations

The following is a list of many sections of the New Testament that are often not included (or come with a disclaimer) in modern translations as they are considered later editions.

1 John 5:7	Acts 8:37	Mark 16:18	Luke 22:44	Mark 16:17
John 7:53-8:11	Acts 15:34	Luke 22:20	John 3:16	James 1:8
Mark 16:9-20	Matthew 17:21	Matthew 6:13	Matthew 18:11	2 Corinthians 13:14
Mark 15:28	John 5:4	Luke 24:40	Mark 1:1	Acts 17:29
Luke 24:51-52	Rom 16:24	Mark 16:15	Luke 23:34	1 John 4:9

The presence of textual variances and missing verses in modern Bible translations raises significant questions about the authenticity and preservation of the biblical text.

These differences are often the result of discrepancies found in the earliest manuscripts and versions of the Bible. Some verses, such as John 7:53–8:11 (the story of the woman caught in adultery) and Mark 16:9–20 (which includes the resurrection appearances of Jesus), do not appear in the earliest and most reliable manuscripts.

This leads to uncertainty about whether these verses were originally part of the text or were later additions by scribes. Similarly, verses like 1 John 5:7, which refer to the Trinity, are absent from the majority of ancient Greek manuscripts, suggesting they were later interpolations.

Verses such as Mark 16:17–18, which speak of signs following believers, are missing in many of the earliest texts. Similarly, phrases like the one found in Matthew 6:13 ("For thine is the kingdom, and the power, and the glory, forever and ever") are absent from earlier manuscripts.

This inconsistency in the text not only raises questions about the reliability of the Bible but also points to the influence of later theological developments on the transmission of the text.

The existence of these textual variances challenges the notion that the Bible we have today is an exact, unchanged record of the original teachings and events.

Instead, it suggests that over centuries, the text has undergone alterations, whether intentional or accidental, as it was copied, translated, and edited by countless scribes. As a result, the question arises: how much of the current Bible truly reflects the original words and intentions of its authors? This we are yet to uncover as we delve further into the upcoming chapters.

2.3 Textual Criticism

It was not until the fifteenth century that the printing press was invented, so in ancient times, the only way to make record of anything, including the New Testament, was by copying it down sentence-by-sentence and letter-by-letter.

Some of the most-used ancient materials for writing were clay, tablets, stone, bone, wood papyrus, and parchments. The New Testament of the Bible was mainly written on papyrus and parchment (Metzger 1992). Papyrus is a flowering aquatic plant, which was used significantly in ancient times to make sandals and ropes and many other things. Papyrus was at its peak in Egypt, growing in the waters of the Nile.

Holy Bible Re-examined

Travelling back to the Greco–Roman world, they published their literary works on scrolls made of papyrus plants glued together, then wound up with a strip around a stick. This was called a volume, from the Latin word *volumen*, which means 'something rolled up.'

At this time, there were two main styles of writing manuscripts that were each used to write the New Testament—uncial letters and minuscule letters. Minuscule letters were smaller than uncial letters, so they took up less space and were more economically feasible.

According to Metzger (1993), the uncials were the earlier style of writing, while the minuscules came later and profoundly changed the textual tradition of the Greek Bible. Here are some examples:

Minuscule
(Codex Ebnerianus)

Uncial
(Codex Sinaiticus Luke 11)

Discrepancies and Inconsistencies

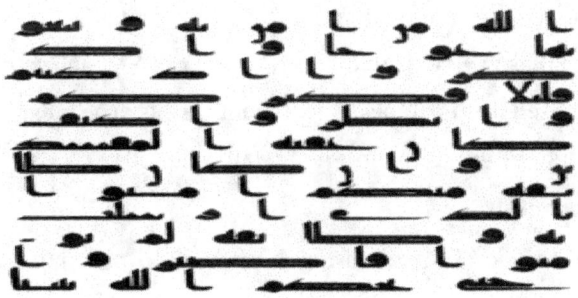

Kufic Script

Similarly, the Arabic script in the Qur'an contains numerous diacritical marks, such as I'jam (consonant pointing), Tashki'l (supplementary aids), and the Harakat (vowels), that were added later in order to help determine the correct pronunciation of words. The Bible also had different markings to help the reader (Metzger 1993), such as:

- Punctuation
- Pictures: Greeks of the Byzantine period used graphics to help readers understand the significance of the writings.
- Cola and commata: These helped readers with proper pauses.
- Chapter divisions: These are present to us in the Codex Vaticanus of the fourth century, with 170 sections in Matthew, 62 in Mark, 152 in Luke, and 50 in John.
- Titles: Codex Alexandrinus, one of the three earliest and most important manuscripts of the entire Bible in Greek.

It is important to note the many versions of the Bible we currently possess. Missionaries helping with the expansion of the Christian faith across a variety of different languages made the earliest versions. These languages included mainly Syriac, Latin, and Coptic. Many of the translations were limited and not well translated from Greek. Do not confuse these versions with the NIV, KJV, ESV, and so on, which are later revised forms of the ancient manuscripts. The most important of these versions are of the following (Ehrman 2011):

Syriac versions
- Old Syriac: Two manuscripts of four Gospels, now shown in the British Museum
- Syriac Vulgate: New Testament in fourth century – almost complete
- Philoxenian and Harclean
- Palestinian Syriac: Aramaic

Latin versions
- Old Latin: Third century; circulated in North Africa and Europe
- Codex Palatinus: Fifth century; four Gospels
- European Old Latin: Oldest European manuscript
- Latin Vulgate: Fourth century

There are other versions, as well, such as Coptic, Gothic, Armenian, Georgian, Ethiopic, and, interestingly, Arabic. Due to the rise of Islam, many books of the New Testament were translated into Arabic from Greek, Syriac, Coptic, and Latin. According to Sidney Griffith (2013),

Jews and Christians produced hundreds of manuscripts containing portions of the Bible in Arabic from the first centuries of Islam, well into the Middle Ages.

Discrepancies and Inconsistencies

In comparison, Qur'anic manuscripts have only one version in only one language, Arabic. It is often asserted that nothing exists from the first century of Hijra (migration), which is untrue. Many fragments of early Qur'anic manuscripts were shown by Orientalists, notably Nabia Abbott in her work *The Rise of the North Arabic script and its Kur'anic development, with a full description of the Qur'an manuscripts in the Oriental Institute* (1939, University of Chicago Press).

The Great Mosque of Sana'a in Yemen found a large collection of manuscripts dating from the first century. This particular mosque dates back to the sixth year of Hijra. When we look at the evidence for the Qur'anic manuscripts, both first- and second-century manuscripts can be found. This is evident in Masahif Sana (1985, Dar al-Athar al-Islamiyyah).

Amongst the abundant manuscripts of the Qur'an (Ma'ili, Yaquit, Kufi, Naskh, Mamluk, and others), we have the Kufic script codex attributed to Imam Ali (Pbuh), for example, containing 275 folios and is comprised of about 87 percent Qur'anic text.

The Uthmanic codex should not go without mentioning. The Uthmanic codex is a manuscript that was also written in Kufic script and contains 408 folios. The extant folios contain more than 99 percent Qur'anic text. There is also the codex Parisino-petropolitanus and other first century findings.

The University of Birmingham has a Qur'anic manuscript that is among the oldest in the world. Thanks to modern science, radiocarbon dating has established the parchment text, found to be from the years 568 and 645AD, with approximately 96 percent accuracy. A laboratory in the University of Oxford conducted the analysis. These results have placed the parchments close to the time of the Prophet Muhammad (Pbuh), generally believed to have lived between 570 and 632AD.

This research is part of the University's 'Mingana' collection of manuscripts in the Cadbury Research Library. Philanthropist Edward Cadbury funded the research at the University of Birmingham. For the sake of comparison, the reader should note that these manuscripts conform perfectly with the modern day Qur'an. Unlike the Bible, they prove there have been no lasting errors in the transmission of the Qur'an.

Errors in the transmission

So far, we have mentioned the sources used to write the different versions of the Bible and the adjustments that were made to it. But were any kinds of errors in the process of writing and transmitting the New Testament texts? Yes, but before we identify the errors, we should examine the reasons why these errors have occurred.

To begin with, most changes that we see are just pure mistakes. Slips of the pen, accidental omissions, additions, misspellings, and blunders. That is mainly what we will encounter upon analyzing them (Metzger 1993).

These are unintentional changes, involuntary changes within the Bible. Often times, scribes who were copying words of the ancient world found it difficult to distinguish between the Greek letters, which looked similar, especially when the copyist before them wrote carelessly. So similar-looking letters in the script were sometimes applied incorrectly. For the most part, this was not on purpose, but these minor errors took place quite frequently (Ehrman 2009).

Discrepancies and Inconsistencies

Parablepsis is another type of error that occurred when the scribes' eyes would wander from one line to another, mixing them together. This was sometimes accompanied by *homoeteleuton,* which is similar in its effect, having the sentences end with the same verbs (Ehrman 2009).

There are also those errors, unintentional of course, arising from faulty hearing. In ancient times, scribes would translate mostly by dictation, which could bring about confusion over some words with the same sounds as others but differences in spelling. Confusion was common with some Greek (Koine) vowels, and that confusion exists, in part, still to this day. In addition to similar-sounding vowels, there were also consonants that were interchangeable (Ehrman 2009).

Other errors such as the errors of the mind were quite common. In fact, copyists would often struggle to fix the orders of a sequence because of the transposition of letters and memory. Substitutions of synonyms, sequence changes, and letter transpositions were frequently a problem (Ehrman 2009).

Sometimes it is difficult to know if these were intentional or unintentional errors. Scribes more than likely meant well, but perhaps some were incompetent or just tired. We have some documented examples of these errors. Codex Sinaiticus, for example, is one of the oldest manuscripts, and in it, we see a number of omissions due to carelessness. The following omissions (Codex Sinaiticus) are widely understood to be mistakes by most if not all textual critics.

John 6:55

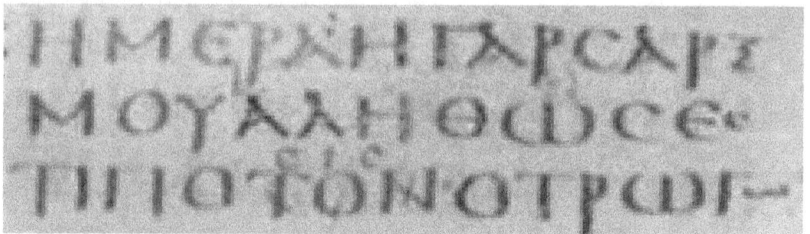

This passage should say, "*η γαρ σαρξ μου αληθως εστιν βρωσις και το αιμα μου αληθως εστιν ποσις* (For my flesh is meat indeed, and my blood is drink indeed)." However, Codex Sinaiticus only states, "For my flesh is drink indeed."

1 Corinthians 13:1–2

32 Greek words were omitted from this passage. When the scribe finished copying the first "αγαπην δε μη εχω," his eyes jumped to the second "αγαπην δε μη εχω" and resumed copying from there. Another scribe later inserted the omitted words in the top margin, as you can see.

Luke 17:35

Here, there appear to be words repeated. *αφεθησεται* appears twice.

Variations between Majority Text/Textus Receptus and Critical Text

The Majority Text (MT) is the Greek New Testament text based on the majority of Byzantine manuscripts. The Textus Receptus (TR) is a 16th-century compilation of Greek manuscripts used as the basis for the King James Version.

The Critical Text (CT) is a scholarly reconstructed text based on earlier and more diverse manuscripts, aiming for the most accurate representation of the original New Testament.

Modern translations like the NIV, ESV, and NASB are based on the Critical Text (CT), using the oldest manuscripts (e.g., Codex Sinaiticus, Codex Vaticanus).

The Majority Text (MT) is still used in some translations like the New Majority Text Bible.

Below are some examples of the variations which accumulated over time in the Majority Text (from KJV) and Textus Receptus (from KJV) compared to the Critical Text (from ESV):

Matthew 5:44

MT: But I say to you, love your enemies, bless those who curse you, do good to those who hate you, and pray for those who spitefully use you and persecute you.
CT: But I say to you, love your enemies, and pray for those who persecute you.

Matthew 6:13

MT: And lead us not into temptation, but deliver us from evil: For thine is the kingdom, and the power, and the glory, for ever. Amen.
CT: And lead us not into temptation, but deliver us from evil.

Matthew 17:21

MT: Howbeit this kind goeth not out but by prayer and fasting.
CT: Verse omitted.

Matthew 18:11

MT: For the Son of Man has come to save that which was lost.
CT: Verse omitted.

Discrepancies and Inconsistencies

Matthew 20:16

MT: So the last will be first, and the first last. For many are called, but few chosen.

CT: So the last will be first, and the first last.

Matthew 20:22-23

MT: But Jesus answered and said, Ye know not what ye ask. Are ye able to drink of the cup that I shall drink of, and to be baptized with the baptism that I am baptized with? They say unto him, We are able. And he saith unto them, Ye shall drink indeed of my cup, and be baptized with the baptism that I am baptized with: but to sit on my right hand, and on my left, is not mine to give, but it shall be given to them for whom it is prepared of my Father.

CT: Jesus answered, "You do not know what you are asking. Are you able to drink the cup that I am to drink?" They said to him, "We are able." He said to them, "You will drink my cup, but to sit at my right hand and at my left is not mine to grant, but it is for those for whom it has been prepared by my Father."

Matthew 23:14

MT: Woe unto you, scribes and Pharisees, hypocrites! for ye devour widows' houses, and for a pretence make long prayer: therefore ye shall receive the greater damnation.

CT: Verse omitted.

Matthew 24:36

MT: But of that day and hour knoweth no man, no, not the angels of heaven, but my Father only.

CT: But concerning that day and hour no one knows, not even the angels of heaven, nor the Son, but the Father only.

Mark 6:11

MT: And whosoever shall not receive you, nor hear you, when ye depart thence, shake off the dust under your feet for a testimony against them. Verily I say unto you, It shall be more tolerable for Sodom and Gomorrha in the day of judgment, than for that city.

CT: And if any place will not receive you and they will not listen to you, when you leave, shake off the dust that is on your feet as a testimony against them.

Mark 7:8

MT: For laying aside the commandment of God, ye hold the tradition of men, as the washing of pots and cups: and many other such like things ye do.

CT: You leave the commandment of God and hold to the tradition of men.

Mark 7:16

MT: If any man have ears to hear, let him hear.
CT: Verse omitted.

Discrepancies and Inconsistencies

Mark 9:43-46

MT: And if thy hand offend thee, cut it off: it is better for thee to enter into life maimed, than having two hands to go into hell, into the fire that never shall be quenched: Where their worm dieth not, and the fire is not quenched. And if thy foot offend thee, cut it off: it is better for thee to enter halt into life, than having two feet to be cast into hell, into the fire that never shall be quenched: Where their worm dieth not, and the fire is not quenched.

CT: And if your hand causes you to sin, cut it off. It is better for you to enter life crippled than with two hands to go to hell, to the unquenchable fire. And if your foot causes you to sin, cut it off. It is better for you to enter life lame than with two feet to be thrown into hell.

Mark 9:49

MT: For every one shall be salted with fire, and every sacrifice shall be salted with salt.

CT: For everyone will be salted with fire.

Mark 10:24

MT: And the disciples were astonished at his words. But Jesus answereth again, and saith unto them, Children, how hard is it for them that trust in riches to enter into the kingdom of God!

CT: And the disciples were amazed at his words. But Jesus said to them again, "Children, how difficult it is to enter the kingdom of God!"

Mark 11:26

MT: But if ye do not forgive, neither will your Father which is in heaven forgive your trespasses.

CT: Verse omitted.

Mark 14:19

MT: And they began to be sorrowful, and to say unto him one by one, Is it I? and another said, Is it I?

CT: They began to be sorrowful and to say to him one after another, "Is it I?"

Mark 15:28

MT: And the scripture was fulfilled, which saith, And he was numbered with the transgressors.

CT: Verse omitted.

Mark 16:9-20

MT: Long ending of Mark included.

CT: Long ending of Mark omitted.

Luke 1:28

MT: And the angel came in unto her, and said, Hail, thou that art highly favoured, the Lord is with thee: blessed art thou among women.

CT: And he came to her and said, "Greetings, O favored one, the Lord is with you!"

Discrepancies and Inconsistencies

Luke 9:55-56

MT: But he turned, and rebuked them, and said, Ye know not what manner of spirit ye are of. For the Son of man is not come to destroy men's lives, but to save them. And they went to another village.

CT: But He turned and rebuked them. And they went on to another village.

Luke 11:2-4

MT: And he said unto them, When ye pray, say, Our Father which art in heaven, Hallowed be thy name. Thy kingdom come. Thy will be done, as in heaven, so in earth. Give us day by day our daily bread. And forgive us our sins; for we also forgive every one that is indebted to us. And lead us not into temptation; but deliver us from evil.

CT: And he said to them, "When you pray, say: "Father, hallowed be your name. Your kingdom come. Give us each day our daily bread, and forgive us our sins, for we ourselves forgive everyone who is indebted to us. And lead us not into temptation.""

Luke 11:11

MT: If a son shall ask bread of any of you that is a father, will he give him a stone? or if he ask a fish, will he for a fish give him a serpent?

CT: What father among you, if his son asks for a fish, will instead of a fish give him a serpent;

Luke 22:43-44

MT: And there appeared an angel unto him from heaven, strengthening him. And being in an agony he prayed more earnestly: and his sweat was as it were great drops of blood falling down to the ground.

CT: Verses marked as a later addition.

Luke 23:17

MT: (For of necessity he must release one unto them at the feast.)

CT: Verse omitted.

Luke 23:34

MT: Then said Jesus, Father, forgive them; for they know not what they do. And they parted his raiment, and cast lots.

CT: First part of verse marked as a later addition, followed by "And they cast lots to divide his garments."

John 1:18

MT: No man hath seen God at any time, the only begotten Son, which is in the bosom of the Father, he hath declared him.

CT: No one has ever seen God; the only God, who is at the Father's side, he has made him known.

Discrepancies and Inconsistencies

John 5:3-4

MT: In these lay a great multitude of impotent folk, of blind, halt, withered, waiting for the moving of the water. For an angel went down at a certain season into the pool, and troubled the water: whosoever then first after the troubling of the water stepped in was made whole of whatsoever disease he had.

CT: In these lay a multitude of invalids—blind, lame, and paralyzed.

John 6:69

MT: And we believe and are sure that thou art that Christ, the Son of the living God.

CT: And we have believed, and have come to know, that you are the Holy One of God.

John 7:53-8:11

MT: The story of the woman caught in adultery is included.

CT: The story of the woman caught in adultery is omitted.

John 8:59

MT: Then took they up stones to cast at him: but Jesus hid himself, and went out of the temple, going through the midst of them, and so passed by.

CT: So they picked up stones to throw at him, but Jesus hid himself and went out of the temple.

Matthew 27:35

TR: And they crucified him, and parted his garments, casting lots: that it might be fulfilled which was spoken by the prophet, They parted my garments among them, and upon my vesture did they cast lots.
CT: And when they had crucified him, they divided his garments among them by casting lots.

Luke 17:36

TR: Two men shall be in the field; the one shall be taken, and the other left.
MT/CT: Verse omitted.

2.4 Alterations of the Text

Given that the Bible claims to be the complete Word of God, any tampering with it would refute this claim. Even a single added word takes the Bible from 100% the word of God, to less than 100%.

So far, we have only touched upon some unintentional changes, which are to be expected to a certain degree. But what about intentional changes? Did those occur? The answer is yes.

As odd as it may seem and as deceitful as it may be, this is likely the reality when it comes to textual criticism of the Bible. When we talk about intentional changes, it is important to note that they could have been or most probably were made with good intentions.

Many times, copyists would make what they thought to be corrections to errors. Without realizing it, they would have introduced other errors by attempting to clear up confusion. For example, if they

Discrepancies and Inconsistencies

came across something that seemed like a contradiction, misspelling, or geographical error, they would, 'correct' it.

Take a look at the following manuscript of the Codex Vaticanus from the fourth century. A scribe has written between the two columns, "You fool and knave, leave the old reading, don't change it! (Ehrman, 2011)"

The scribe's frustration here is completely understandable, but we must also understand that the only way we were able to copy manuscripts in the ancient world was by hand, so it is necessary to expect mistakes from these scribes.

The oldest New Testament manuscript fragment is P52, which dates to about 125AD. However, the earliest manuscripts that provide distinguishable readings date to about 200AD (Metzger 1993). These manuscripts come from Egypt and are of Alexandrian text-type. The reliability of these manuscripts doesn't seem to be high based on this example from the third century church father's Origen.

> "...The differences among the manuscripts [of the Gospels] have become great, either through the negligence of some copyists or through the perverse audacity of others; they either neglect to check over what they have transcribed, or, in the process of checking, they lengthen or shorten, as they please." (Bruce Metzger, *The Text of the New Testament: Its Transmission, Corruption, and Restoration*, 3rd ed. (1991), pp. 151-15)

Origen was not the only one who noticed these changes and errors in the Bible. The pagan philosopher Celsus also realized this much earlier (Ehrman 2011):

> "Some believers, as though from a drinking bout, go so far as to oppose themselves and alter the original text of the gospel three or four or several times over, and they change its character to enable them to deny difficulties in the face of criticism."

Victor Tununensis, a sixth-century Bishop, states in his Chronicle (AD 566) that he "censored and corrected" the Gentile Gospels written by persons considered illiterate by the Emperor Anastasius. In the time of sixth-century Christianity, these changes may have been made to conform to the views of the Emperor or people of the time (Yusseff 1993).

Discrepancies and Inconsistencies

St Augustine, the highly praised and respected theologian, admitted to 'Secret doctrines' in the Christian religions. "There were many things true in the Christian religion which it was not convenient for the vulgar to know, and that some things were false, but convenient for the vulgar to believe in them." (Christopher Reyes 2010)

People generally believe there is a one true and unchanged Bible. The truth is, all versions of the Bible in possession today (e.g., KJB, NRSV, NWT, etc.) are the result of extensive truncation and pasting from various manuscripts without definitively knowing the authentic source.

There are countless cases of the inclusion of questionable verses in the Bible without any disclaimer. Let us look at the imposed threats in order to better understand the situation. For example, the book of Revelation 22:18–19 says:

> "For I testify unto every man that heareth the words of the prophecy of this book, "If any man shall add unto these things, God shall add unto him the plagues that are written in this book; and if any man shall take away from the words of the book of this prophecy, God shall take away his part out of the book of life, and out of the holy city, and from the things which are written in this book."" (KJV)

The writer gives a clear warning and then threatens the copyists of the book. When a scribe changed a text, whether on purpose or by accidentally, those changes then became permanent unless someone corrected it. The next scribe who copied that manuscript would unknowingly copy those mistakes and possibly add mistakes of his own, and on and on in a continuous cycle.

Take, for instance, the woman who had committed adultery in John 7:53–8:12.

This is one of the most famous stories of Jesus. The story goes that Jesus was teaching in the temple until some Pharisees confronted him. They brought with them a woman who had been caught in the act of adultery, and they wanted to see what Jesus would say and do—whether he would violate the law of Moses or contradict his own teachings:

> "…And the scribes and Pharisees brought unto him a woman taken in adultery… They say unto him, Master, this woman was taken in adultery, in the very act. Now Moses in the law commanded us, that such should be stoned: but what sayest thou? This they said, tempting him that they might have to accuse him. But Jesus stooped down, and with his finger wrote on the ground, as though he heard them not.… He lifted up himself, and said unto them, "He that is without sin among you, let him first cast a stone at her." And they which heard it, being convicted by their own conscience, went out one by one, beginning at the eldest, even unto the last: and Jesus was left alone, and the woman standing in the midst. … He said unto her, "Woman, where are those thine accusers? Hath no man condemned thee?" She said, "No man, Lord." And Jesus said unto her, "Neither do I condemn thee: go, and sin no more.""
> (John 8:3-11, KJV)

Despite the wonderful story and wisdom behind it, there lies an even deeper problem behind the story. The verses above were not originally in the book of John; in fact, they were not originally part of any of the Gospels but were added later by scribes.

Discrepancies and Inconsistencies

The writing style is very different from the rest of John and speaks of a concept foreign to the framework of John. Scholars widely agree that some scribes even inserted this inauthentic story in other places, such as Luke (Ehrman 2011).

Another question we have to raise is about the accuracy of even the original books. We can take the example of Paul's letter to the Galatians. This letter, like others of his, was likely not handwritten by Paul himself, but rather dictated to a secretary scribe, a common technique for the time (Sanders 2001).

We know this because Paul added a postscript to the letter in his own handwriting, and there is a difference of style and size from those before. Did the scribe write down word-for-word what Paul said? Did he add his own words to it? If some parts are different from what Paul dictated, then do we even have Paul's words at all?

Let us ponder over the Gospel of Mark. The original Gospel ends at verse 9 of chapter 16. Ending with, "And they went out and fled from the tomb... and they said nothing to anyone, for they were afraid." (ESV) Then there are an extra 12 verses in Mark that continue the narrative of Jesus appearing after his crucifixion to Mary Magdalene, who then tells the disciples about him. At the end of Mark, the women flee and say nothing. This is extremely difficult to understand.

Many questions arise: Why didn't they tell the disciples? Didn't Jesus appear to the rest? How can it end like that? Scribes would have had the same questions while reading the Gospel, which explains why 12 verses were added in an attempt to resolve confusion. Unfortunately, the added verses (Mark 16:9-20) play a major role for Christians who take them literally.

"And these signs shall follow them that believe; in my name shall they cast out devils; they shall speak with new tongues; They shall take up serpents; and if they drink any deadly thing, it shall not hurt them; they shall lay hands on the sick, and they shall recover." (Mark 16:17-18, KJV)

Besides the difference in style in these later verses of Mark, these verses are not found in the earliest manuscript sources such as Codex Sinaiticus and Codex Vaticanus. These passages were not original to Mark, but a scribe later added them.

According to Metzger (1971) he writes:

"The last twelve verses of the commonly received text of Mark are absent from the two oldest Greek manuscripts (א and B), from the Old Latin codex Bobiensis (it k), the Sinaitic Syriac manuscript, about one hundred Armenian manuscripts, and the two oldest Georgian manuscripts (written 897 and 913AD). Clement of Alexandria and Origen show no knowledge of the existence of these verses; furthermore Eusebius and Jerome attest that the passage was absent from almost all Greek copies of Mark known to them."

Does this addition have any importance, though? Yes, in fact, Pentecostal Christians use this scripture a lot, such as groups of Appalachian snake handlers who actually handle poisonous snakes in order to prove their faith in the supposed words of Jesus (Pbuh). Some risk their lives, and some even die.

This highly dangerous practice is based on words that Jesus did not actually say. Another addition found nowhere in the ancient

Discrepancies and Inconsistencies

manuscripts is in 1 John. This one affects the Trinitarian Christians rather than Unitarians.

> "For there are three that bear record in heaven, the Father, the Word, and the Holy Ghost: and these three are one." (1 John 5:7, KJV)

It would seem that the concept of the Holy Trinity is supported here, but it is just an added verse that cannot be found in the earliest manuscripts. The Trinitarian formula (known as the *Comma Johanneum*) made its way into the third edition of Erasmus' Greek New Testament (1522). Al-Kadhi (1995) highlights a quote by Sir Higgins, demonstrating another trace of corruption:

> "In Cleland's *Life of Lanfranc, Archbishop of Canterbury,* is the following passage: "Lanfranc, a Benedictine Monk, Archbishop of Canterbury, having found the Scriptures much corrupted by copyists, applied himself to correct them, as also the writings of the fathers, agreeably to the orthodox faith.""

As mentioned previously, the best way to find differences within the Gospels is to read the texts horizontally. Each Gospel must be read and taken at face value as they are each different in their own way. If we take the crucifixion account in both Mark and Luke, we see an interesting difference.

In the Gospel of Mark, Jesus is quite silent throughout his crucifixion. Jewish leaders, passersby, and both robbers mock him as he is hanging on the crucifix. Finally, Jesus cries out saying, *"Eloi, Eloi, lama sabachthani?"* which means, "My God, My God, why have You forsaken Me?"

If we compare this with Luke, Jesus is not silent during his crucifixion; he speaks with weeping women (Luke 23:26). While being nailed to the cross, he says, "Father, forgive them, for they know not what they do." (KJV) He also has a discussion with the two robbers, different from that of Mark's account. As it was time for Jesus to go, he cried out "Father, into thy hands I commend my spirit" (KJV).

In the Gospel of Luke, Jesus is more active and aware of what is happening. The point here is not the differences between the Gospels, but rather that a verse in Luke is actually omitted by some scribes: "Jesus said, "Father, forgive them, for they know not what they do"" (Luke 23:34). This verse is actually absent from some of the earliest and most reliable Greek manuscripts of the Gospel of Luke, raising questions about its original inclusion. Some early manuscripts are missing this prayer of Jesus' likely due to alteration by scribes (Whitlark and Parsons, 2006).

Another example is in Mark 1:41. Here, there are two different versions of the Bible. The NIV and KJV both have different feelings attributed to Jesus (Pbuh).

"Jesus was indignant. He reached out his hand and touched the man. "I am willing," he said. "Be clean!"" (NIV)

"And Jesus, moved with compassion, put forth his hand, and touched him, and sayeth unto him, "I will; be thou clean."" (KJV)

These are not the only examples. These examples can be viewed by comparing Bible translations.

Discrepancies and Inconsistencies

In Matthew 6:13, the Lord's Prayer, the phrase "For thine is the kingdom, and the power, and the glory, for ever" (KJV) is included in some later manuscripts but is absent from the earliest Greek texts.

The presence of later additions indicates a possibility of human influence, challenging the notion of divine inspiration in the text.

In Romans 8:1, some manuscripts include the phrase "who walk not after the flesh, but after the Spirit," (KJV) while others do not. The absence of this clause in early manuscripts suggests that later editors may have sought to clarify or emphasize theological points, which raises concerns about the integrity of the biblical message.

1 John 5:7–8, the Comma Johanneum, which discusses the Trinity, "For there are three that bear record in heaven, the Father, the Word, and the Holy Ghost: and these three are one" (KJV) appears in some late Latin manuscripts but is missing from the majority of Greek texts. This passage's late emergence in the biblical canon points to the likelihood of theological motivations behind its inclusion.

Acts 8:37, which includes the Ethiopian eunuch's confession of faith, is found in some later manuscripts but is absent from earlier texts.

Verse 37 states "And Philip said, If thou believest with all thine heart, thou mayest. And he answered and said, I believe that Jesus Christ is the Son of God." (KJV)

The verses in Luke 22:43–44 that describe Jesus' sweating blood are omitted in many manuscripts, leading to significant textual debate. Specifically, verses 43 and 44 are not found in early manuscripts.

> "[[Then an angel from heaven appeared to him and gave him strength. In his anguish he prayed more earnestly, and his sweat became like great drops of blood falling down on the ground.]]"

You'll see that in the NRSV (New Revised Standard Version), verses 43 and 44 are surrounded by double brackets [[ ]]. This indicates that the translators believe these verses were not part of the original text. Similar double brackets can also be found in the account of the woman caught in adultery (John 7:53-8:11) and in the final twelve verses of Mark (16:9-20).

Speaking of the woman caught in adultery, some manuscripts describe Jesus drawing in the dust, but the specifics vary across texts. John 8:6 is phrased in different terms in different versions, for example:

NIV: They were using this question as a trap, in order to have a basis for accusing him. But Jesus bent down and started to write on the ground with his finger.

KJV: This they said, tempting him, that they might have to accuse him. But Jesus stooped down, and with his finger wrote on the ground, as though he heard them not.

NRSV: They said this to test him, so that they might have some charge to bring against him. Jesus bent down and wrote with his finger on the ground.

So, we find that the phrase "as though he heard them not" available in KJV is not included in NIV and NRSV. Was the deletion done with a purpose, for example, out of fear that Jesus' behavior of showing ignorance of the question loudly put to him, could perhaps send a wrong message to the critics of his divinity?

Discrepancies and Inconsistencies

Why was the phrase "...as though he heard them not." deleted from many versions of John 8:6? This has a significant implication for the honesty and integrity of these texts. If they are truly divinely inspired, why would certain passages be missing from the original manuscripts? Would God have difficulty including them?

We have spoken of unintentional changes, but we now find intentional ones as well. These are just a few out of many textual variants. Keep in mind that most variants are not of this magnitude, but they still exist and are worthy of investigating.

According to New Testament scholar Mike Licona in his book *The resurrection of Jesus: A new historiographical approach* (2011) the appearance of angels at Jesus' tomb after the resurrection is legendary. He states:

"It can forthrightly be admitted that the data surrounding what happened to Jesus is fragmentary and could possibly be mixed with legend, as Wedderburn notes. We may also be reading poetic language or legend at certain points, such as Matthew's report of the raising of some dead saints at Jesus' death (Matthew 27:51–54) and the angel(s) at the tomb..."

In another book by Licona and Habermas, *The case for the resurrection of Jesus* (2004, p. 185) it is stated that:

"Skeptics sometimes try to raise more questions than can be fairly answered in the allotted time available. Throw it back on them: "If you want to speculate with an opposing theory, the burden of proof is upon you to show that your theory is plausible. Why should I be stuck with the responsibility of thoroughly researching and refuting every possible unsubstantiated assertion that can be thrown at me? Do the work yourself; then give me something credible to consider and I will consider it..."""

One of the goals of this book is to give people like Licona and Habermas plenty of credible criticisms to consider objectively. Credible work is provided throughout this book for anyone to respond to, challenge, and question. However, the burden of proof is on the shoulders of the one who makes the positive claim. The one who claims the Bible is the inerrant word of God bears the burden of proving it.

This book is a response to claims already made about the Bible (in whichever form it is) being the complete and inerrant Word of God.

Chapter 2 Discrepancies and Inconsistencies

References:
Abbott, N., 1939. *The Rise of the North Arabic Script and Its Kuranic Development with a Full Description of the Kuran Manuscripts in the Oriental Institute.* University of Chicago Press.

Barr, J., 1980. Childs' Introduction to the Old Testament as Scripture. *Journal for the Study of the Old Testament,* 5(16).

Brown, R.E., 1967. How Much Did Jesus Know?—A Survey of the Biblical Evidence. *The Catholic Biblical Quarterly.*

Bruce Metzger, A Textual Commentary on the Greek New Testament (Stuttgart, 1971).

Discrepancies and Inconsistencies

Bruce Metzger, *The Text of the New Testament: Its Transmission, Corruption, and Restoration*, 3rd ed. (1991).

Coogan, M., 2008. *The Old Testament: a very short introduction*. Oxford University Press.

Codex Sinaiticus (n.d.) Codex Sinaiticus - Home. Available at: http://www.codexsinaiticus.org/en/ (Accessed: 10 January 2025).

Ehrman, B.D. and Culp, J., 2009. *Jesus, interrupted: Revealing the hidden contradictions in the Bible (And why we don't know about them)*. HarperOne.

Ehrman, B.D., 2005. *Misquoting Jesus: The story behind who changed the Bible and why*. New York: HarperSanFrancisco.

Ehrman, B.D., 2011. Forged. *Writing in the Name of God–Why the Bible's Authors Are Not Who We Think They Are*.

Ehrman, B.D., 2012. Forgery and counter forgery: the use of literary deceit in early Christian polemics. Oxford University Press.

Griffith, S.H., 2013. *The Bible in Arabic: The Scriptures of the People of the Book in the Language of Islam*. Princeton University Press.

Habermas, G.R. and Licona, M.R., 2004. *The case for the resurrection of Jesus*. Kregel Publications.

Hayes, J.H. and Holladay, C.R., 2007. *Biblical exegesis: a beginner's handbook.* Westminster John Knox Press.

History of Christianity in the light of Modern knowledge, Higgins p.318. (What did Jesus really say? Misha'al Abdullah Al-Kadhi)

Licona, M.R., 2011. *The resurrection of Jesus: A new historiographical approach.* Intervarsity Press.

Metzger, B.M., The Text Of The New Testament: Its Transmission, Corruption and Restoration, 1992.

Reyes, E.C., 2010. *In His Name.* AuthorHouse.

Tregelles S. P., An Introduction to the Textual Criticism of the New Testament, London 1856.

Whitlark, J.A. and Parsons, M.C., 2006. The 'Seven' Last Words: A Numerical Motivation for the Insertion of Luke 23.34 a. New Testament Studies, 52(2).

Wilson, B 2008, 'If We Only Had Paul, What Would We Know of Jesus?' Humanities and Religious Studies York University, Toronto.

Yusseff, M.A., 1993. *The Dead Sea Scrolls, the Gospel of Barnabas, and the New Testament.* American Trust Publications.

3

"Nor should there be obscenity, foolish talk or coarse joking, which are out of place, but rather thanksgiving."

(Ephesians 5:4, NIV)

Gratuitous Sexual & Other Obscenity

"And when they hear vain talk, they avoid it and say, 'Our deeds belong to us, and your deeds belong to you. Peace be to you. We do not court the ignorant.'" (Qur'an 28:55)

3.1 Inspiring Bible Passages

No doubt, many verses in the Bible are inspiring and enliven the hearts and souls of their readers. Reason dictates that these verses must have some degree of truth to them, and that they may even be divine in origin.

> "Hear, O Israel: The Lord our God, the Lord is one. Love the Lord your God with all your heart and with all your soul and with all your strength." (Deuteronomy 6:4–5, NIV)

The Shema noted above is one of the most important declarations and fundamental concepts in Judaism, Christianity, and Islam.

> "Say, 'If you love Allah, then follow me; Allah will love you and forgive you your sins, and Allah is all-forgiving, all-merciful.'" (Qur'an 3:31)

In the Qur'an, all of humankind is consistently reminded to not take up partners or other associations with God:

> "Say, 'O People of the Book! Come to a common word between us and you: that we will worship no one but Allah, that we will not ascribe any partner to Him, and that some of us will not take some others as lords besides Allah.'" (Qur'an 3:64)

We see this message found before in the Old Testament abundantly expressing strict monotheism, such as:

> "The salvation of the righteous comes from the Lord; he is their stronghold in time of trouble." (Psalm 37:39, NIV)

"You were shown these things so that you might know that the Lord is God; besides him there is no other." (Deuteronomy 4:35, NIV)

"You alone are the Lord. You made the heavens, even the highest heavens, and all their starry host, the earth and all that is on it, the seas and all that is in them. You give life to everything, and the multitudes of heaven worship you." (Nehemiah 9:6, NIV)

"For this is what the Lord says— he who created the heavens, he is God; he who fashioned and made the earth, he founded it; he did not create it to be empty, but formed it to be inhabited—he says: "I am the Lord, and there is no other."" (Isaiah 45:18, NIV)

From the Old Testament we learn monotheism, righteousness to God Almighty, patience, and wisdom from the prophets. We learn love and mercy from God to his chosen people, and the rewards for faithfulness. Similarly we find Jesus (Pbuh) in the earliest Gospel (Mark) making the exact same declaration of the Shema in the Old Testament (Deuteronomy 6:4).

We read in Mark 12:28–29:

"One of the teachers of the law came and heard them debating. Noticing that Jesus had given them a good answer, he asked him, "Of all the commandments, which is the most important?" "The most important one," answered Jesus, "is this: 'Hear, O Israel: The Lord our God, the Lord is one.'"" (NIV)

The Sermon on the Mount, the Beatitudes, and the Lord's Prayer are some of the most moving passages one may come across (Matthew 5–7). We revere the moral teachings of Jesus (Pbuh), as he inspired and challenged men and women. The sermon introduces the kingdom of God to his followers as well as living a life of acceptance of God's grace in order to enter into heaven.

The Prodigal Son (Luke 15:11–32) teaches us about forgiveness and restoration. The lost son of the father is welcomed back after moving away from home on his own to another place. The son, after blowing all his money and living in such an awful environment, realized that even the servants back home lived better than he did. So, he attempted to return home as a servant and not a son, but, surprisingly, the father welcomed him back with a ring and robe, for the son was lost and then found. This beautiful parable teaches us about God welcoming us back with rejoice when we stray from the right path.

In the parable of the house on rocks and sand (Matthew 7:24–27), we learn that by acting upon the teachings of Jesus (Pbuh) like a wise man, our foundation becomes strong and firm. One who does not learn from the teachings, like a fool, has a weak foundation for his life, which cannot stand up to destruction.

The parable of the Pharisee and the Publican (Luke 18:9–14) compares the prayers of two men. One, a proud and self-righteous Pharisee, and the other a publican or tax collector who accepted he had wronged God. Jesus tells us that even though the Pharisee who had prayed constantly and thought he was righteous, was still caught in sin because he refused to humble himself before God and ask forgiveness. Jesus declared the tax collector righteous, however,

Gratuitous Sexual & Other Obscenity

because he recognized he was not perfect and required forgiveness from God almighty.

The parable of the hidden treasure in Matthew 13:44 teaches us to view the Kingdom of God as a treasure found in a field. Just as someone finds treasure is willing to give away whatever he had in order to purchase the treasure field, we should be willing to do the same for the Kingdom of God.

The parable of the Good Samaritan (Luke 10:25–37) teaches us to be merciful and compassionate to all people. From this, we learn how to be the best type of neighbor to those around us, showing love and compassion regardless of where one is from.

This is only a small list of inspiring passages from the Bible. If one were to read the Bible holistically, an abundance of similar passages would be apparent. But the point here is that, although there are wonderful and moving passages in the Bible, we will also assess corrupted, negative, and sexually gratuitous passages from its pages.

Ultimately, this is not a case of picking and choosing what we would like from the Bible; this is simply assessing the evidence found in the Bible. Anything that goes against reason should be rejected, especially when we come across sexually gratuitous passages and descriptive verses not appropriate for children or adults. Unfortunately, the Bible does contain these types of passages.

We will assess whether such atrocious stories and verses could be from God. Rather, I will submit if such a book is found to contain such sexually gratuitous imagery, it is not reasonable to suggest it is the complete Word of God. At the very least, such portions cannot be from God.

For comparison, we will, where possible, show how the Qur'an tells similar stories, to show that the obscenity is unnecessary.

3.2 Are these from God?

The following section contains discussions of themes related to rape, incest, graphic violence, slavery, racism, misogyny, and other disturbing imagery. Reader discretion is strongly advised. If you prefer to skip this content, please proceed to page 169.

Could it be that the very Word of God would contain in it gratuitously graphic sexual passages, to such an extent that it becomes pornographic? What about passages of violent punishment and instructions explicit in their description? Unfortunately, the Bible often does this in many of the books we often skim over (McKinsey 1995). Some of these explicit sexual passages will be presented in order for us to question whether they are from the Almighty God.

For starters, what do I mean by something that is extremely sexual and graphic? Let us consider one example. The following passages are from Ezekiel 23.

> "Oholah engaged in prostitution while she was still mine; and she lusted after her lovers…She gave herself as a prostitute to all the elite of the Assyrians and defiled herself with all the idols of everyone she lusted after. She did not give up the prostitution she began in Egypt, when during her youth men slept with her, caressed her virgin bosom and poured out their lust on her.
>
> "Therefore I delivered her into the hands of her lovers, the Assyrians, for whom she lusted. They stripped her naked, took away her sons and daughters and killed her with the sword. She

became a byword among women, and punishment was inflicted on her."

"Yet she became more and more promiscuous as she recalled the days of her youth, when she was a prostitute in Egypt. There she lusted after her lovers, whose genitals were like those of donkeys and whose emission was like that of horses. So you longed for the lewdness of your youth, when in Egypt your bosom was caressed and your young breasts fondled." (NIV)

This passage is explicit, and I wonder why the writer of this book would go into such detail as describing the genitals and emissions (Deedat 1985). A better question to ask would be why God would want to include this in the Holy Bible?

Look, for example, at what God declares in Isaiah 13:15–16:

"Whoever is captured will be thrust through; all who are caught will fall by the sword. Their infants will be dashed to pieces before their eyes; their houses will be looted and their wives violated." (NIV)

Why would Jesus, the all-loving second person of the Trinity, declare something like this? If Jesus is 100 percent God and everlasting, was he not a part of this? Our Christian friends will say the Father permitted this. Surely, the Son (Jesus) would have been aware of it since they are co-equal?

"I will gather all the nations to Jerusalem to fight against it; the city will be captured, the houses ransacked, and the women raped." (Zechariah 14:2, NIV)

You might think that these X-rated verses are the exception, but unfortunately, for the Old Testament, they are the norm. Let us continue in our reading so that you can come to a conclusion based on the evidence, rather than taking my word for it (1 Thessalonians 5:21).

3.3 Unnecessarily Pornographic and Violent Verses

As you read through these examples asked yourself the following questions. Why do these verses need to be so explicit? Are the following passages appropriate for children? Are they even appropriate for adults? Let us assess.

It's essential to recognize that some of these difficult verses in the Old Testament are presented as divine commands from God. In Christian theology, the Trinity—Father, Son, and Spirit—represents a unified presence, meaning that Jesus is intimately connected to the laws and commands established in the Old Testament. Which technically means the "Son" was involved in these commandments, killings, rapes and horrible rulings.

GENESIS

> "Lot went outside to meet them and shut the door behind him and said, "No, my friends. Don't do this wicked thing. Look, I have two daughters who have never slept with a man. Let me bring them out to you, and you can do what you like with them. But don't do anything to these men, for they have come under the protection of my roof."" (Genesis 19:6–8, NIV)

> "Dinah, the daughter Leah had borne to Jacob, went out to visit the women of the land. When Shechem son of Hamor the Hivite, the

ruler of that area, saw her, he took her and raped her. His heart was drawn to Dinah daughter of Jacob; he loved the young woman and spoke tenderly to her. And Shechem said to his father Hamor, "Get me this girl as my wife."" (Genesis 34:1–4, NIV)

"While Israel was living in that region, Reuben went in and slept with his father's concubine Bilhah, and Israel heard of it." (Genesis 35:22, NIV)

"Then Judah said to Onan, "Sleep with your brother's wife and fulfill your duty to her as a brother-in-law to raise up offspring for your brother." But Onan knew that the child would not be his; so whenever he slept with his brother's wife, he spilled his semen on the ground to keep from providing offspring for his brother. What he did was wicked in the LORD's sight; so the LORD put him to death also." (Genesis 38:8–10)

"When Judah saw her, he thought she was a prostitute, for she had covered her face. Not realizing that she was his daughter-in-law, he went over to her by the roadside and said, "Come now, let me sleep with you."… [He] slept with her, and she became pregnant by him. 19 After she left, she took off her veil and put on her widow's clothes again." (Genesis 38:15-16, 18-19, NIV)

EXODUS

"Anyone who curses their father or mother is to be put to death." (Exodus 21:17, NIV)

JOSHUA

"They devoted the city to the Lord and destroyed with the sword every living thing in it—men and women, young and old, cattle, sheep and donkeys. Joshua said to the two men who had spied out the land, "Go into the prostitute's house and bring her out and all who belong to her, in accordance with your oath to her." So the young men who had done the spying went in and brought out Rahab, her father and mother, her brothers and sisters and all who belonged to her. They brought out her entire family and put them in a place outside the camp of Israel. Then they burned the whole city and everything in it, but they put the silver and gold and the articles of bronze and iron into the treasury of the Lord's house." (Joshua 6:21–24, NIV)

SONG OF SONGS

"If only you were to me like a brother, who was nursed at my mother's breasts! Then, if I found you outside, I would kiss you, and no one would despise me. I would lead you and bring you to my mother's house— she who has taught me. I would give you spiced wine to drink, the nectar of my pomegranates His left arm is under my head and his right arm embraces me." (Song of Songs 8:1–3, NIV)

"Let him kiss me with the kisses of his mouth— for your love is more delightful than wine Pleasing is the fragrance of your perfumes; your name is like perfume poured out. No wonder the young women love you! Take me away with you—let us hurry!" (Song of Songs 1:2–4, NIV)

Gratuitous Sexual & Other Obscenity

"How delightful is your love, my sister, my bride! How much more pleasing is your love than wine and the fragrance of your perfume more than any spice!" (Song of Songs 4:10, NIV)

"I am a wall, and my breasts are like towers. Thus I have become in his eyes like one bringing contentment." (Song of Songs 8:10, NIV)

DEUTERONOMY

"If a man happens to meet in a town a virgin pledged to be married and he sleeps with her, you shall take both of them to the gate of that town and stone them to death—the young woman because she was in a town and did not scream for help, and the man because he violated another man's wife. You must purge the evil from among you." (Deuteronomy 22:23–24, NIV)

"If two men are fighting and the wife of one of them comes to rescue her husband from his assailant, and she reaches out and seizes him by his private parts, you shall cut off her hand. Show her no pity." (Deuteronomy 25:11–12, NIV)

"If a man happens to meet a virgin who is not pledged to be married and rapes her and they are discovered, he shall pay her father fifty shekels of silver. He must marry the young woman, for he has violated her. He can never divorce her as long as he lives." (Deuteronomy 22:28–29, NIV)

"No one who has been emasculated by crushing or cutting may enter the assembly of the Lord. No one born of a forbidden marriage nor any of their descendants may enter the assembly of the Lord, not even in the tenth generation." (Deuteronomy 23:1-2, NIV)

"Because of the suffering your enemy will inflict on you during the siege, you will eat the fruit of the womb, the flesh of the sons and daughters the Lord your God has given you. Even the most gentle and sensitive man among you will have no compassion on his own brother or the wife he loves or his surviving children, and he will not give to one of them any of the flesh of his children that he is eating." (Deuteronomy 28:53–55, NIV)

"If your very own brother, or your son or daughter, or the wife you love, or your closest friend secretly entices you, saying, "Let us go and worship other gods" (gods that neither you nor your ancestors have known, gods of the peoples around you, whether near or far, from one end of the land to the other), do not yield to them or listen to them. Show them no pity. Do not spare them or shield them. You must certainly put them to death. Your hand must be the first in putting them to death, and then the hands of all the people. Stone them to death, because they tried to turn you away from the Lord your God, who brought you out of Egypt, out of the land of slavery." (Deuteronomy 13:6-10, NIV)

"You will be pledged to be married to a woman, but another will take her and rape her. You will build a house, but you will not live in it. You will plant a vineyard, but you will not even begin to enjoy its fruit. Your ox will be slaughtered before your eyes, but you will eat none of it. Your donkey will be forcibly taken from you and will not be returned. Your sheep will be given to your enemies, and no one will rescue them…The Lord will afflict your knees and legs with painful boils that cannot be cured, spreading from the soles of your feet to the top of your head." (Deuteronomy 28:30-31, 35, NIV)

"If someone has a stubborn and rebellious son who does not obey his father and mother and will not listen to them when they discipline him, his father and mother shall take hold of him and bring him to the elders at the gate of his town. They shall say to the elders, "This son of ours is stubborn and rebellious. He will not obey us. He is a glutton and a drunkard." Then all the men of his town are to stone him to death. You must purge the evil from among you. All Israel will hear of it and be afraid." (Deuteronomy 21:18-21, NIV)

PSALM

"Happy is the one who seizes your infants and dashes them against the rocks." (Psalm 137:9, NIV)

2 SAMUEL

"Before your very eyes I will take your wives and give them to one who is close to you, and he will sleep with your wives in broad daylight." (2 Samuel 12:11, NIV)

"Amnon became so obsessed with his sister Tamar that he made himself ill. She was a virgin, and it seemed impossible for him to do anything to her. Now Amnon had an adviser named Jonadab son of Shimeah, David's brother... He asked Amnon, "Why do you, the king's son, look so haggard morning after morning? Won't you tell me?" Amnon said to him, "I'm in love with Tamar, my brother Absalom's sister." "Go to bed and pretend to be ill," Jonadab said. "When your father comes to see you, say to him, 'I would like my sister Tamar to come and give me something to eat. Let her prepare the food in my sight so I may watch her and then eat it from her hand."

"Send everyone out of here," Amnon said. So everyone left him. Then Amnon said to Tamar, "Bring the food here into my bedroom so I may eat from your hand." And Tamar took the bread she had prepared and brought it to her brother Amnon in his bedroom. But when she took it to him to eat, he grabbed her and said, "Come to bed with me, my sister." "No, my brother!" she said to him. "Don't force me! Such a thing should not be done in Israel! Don't do this wicked thing. What about me? Where could I get rid of my disgrace? And what about you? You would be like one of the wicked fools in Israel. Please speak to the king; he will not keep me from being married to you." But he refused to listen to her, and since he was stronger than she, he raped her." (2 Samuel 13:2-5, 9-14, NIV)

"Ahithophel answered, "Sleep with your father's concubines whom he left to take care of the palace."" (2 Samuel 16:21, NIV)

I KINGS

"Because of this, I am going to bring disaster on the house of Jeroboam. I will cut off from Jeroboam every last male in Israel—slave or free. I will burn up the house of Jeroboam as one burns dung, until it is all gone." (1 Kings 14:10, NIV)

2 KINGS

"She answered, "This woman said to me, 'Give up your son so we may eat him today, and tomorrow we'll eat my son.' So we cooked my son and ate him. The next day I said to her, 'Give up your son so we may eat him,' but she had hidden him." (2 Kings 6:28–29, NIV)

"Josiah slaughtered all the priests of those high places on the altars and burned human bones on them... This he did to fulfill the requirements of the law written in the book that Hilkiah the priest had discovered in the temple of the Lord." (2 Kings 23:20, 24, NIV)

ISAIAH

"Who, like you, will have to eat their own excrement and drink their own urine?" (Isaiah 36:12, NIV)

JEREMIAH

"I will make them eat the flesh of their sons and daughters, and they will eat one another's flesh because their enemies will press the siege so hard against them to destroy them." (Jeremiah 19:9, NIV)

LAMENTATIONS

"With their own hands compassionate women have cooked their own children, who became their food when my people were destroyed." (Lamentations 4:10, NIV)

LEVITICUS

"Your male and female slaves are to come from the nations around you; from them you may buy slaves. You may also buy some of the temporary residents living among you and members of their clans born in your country, and they will become your property. You can bequeath them to your children as inherited property and can make them slaves for life, but you must not rule over your fellow Israelites ruthlessly." (Leviticus 25:44-46, NIV)

"You will eat the flesh of your sons and the flesh of your daughters." (Leviticus 26:29, NIV)

"None of your descendants who has a defect may come near to offer the food of his God. No man who has any defect may come near: no man who is blind or lame, disfigured or deformed; no man with a crippled foot or hand, or who is a hunchback or a dwarf, or who has any eye defect, or who has festering or running sores or damaged testicles.... he must not go near the curtain or approach the altar, and so desecrate my sanctuary." (Leviticus 21:17-20, 23 NIV)

Gratuitous Sexual & Other Obscenity

EZEKIEL

"Eat the food as you would a loaf of barley bread; bake it in the sight of the people, using human excrement for fuel." (Ezekiel 4:12, NIV)

"Therefore in your midst parents will eat their children, and children will eat their parents." (Ezekiel 5:10, NIV)

"You also took the fine jewelry I gave you, the jewelry made of my gold and silver, and you made for yourself male idols and engaged in prostitution with them." (Ezekiel 16:17, NIV)

NAHUM

""I am against you," declares the Lord Almighty. "I will lift your skirts over your face. I will show the nations your nakedness and the kingdoms your shame. I will pelt you with filth, I will treat you with contempt and make you a spectacle." (Nahum 3:5-6, NIV)

JUDGES

"And Jephthah made a vow to the Lord: "If you give the Ammonites into my hands, whatever comes out of the door of my house to meet me when I return in triumph from the Ammonites will be the Lord's, and I will sacrifice it as a burnt offering."" (Judges 11:30-31, NIV)

His daughter was the one who came out to greet him.

""My father," she replied, "you have given your word to the Lord. Do to me just as you promised…But grant me this one request," she said. "Give me two months to roam the hills and weep with my friends, because I will never marry."… After the two months, she returned to her father, and he did to her as he had vowed." (Judges 11:36-37, 39, NIV)

"The owner of the house went outside and said to them, "No, my friends, don't be so vile. Since this man is my guest, don't do this outrageous thing. Look, here is my virgin daughter, and his concubine. I will bring them out to you now, and you can use them and do to them whatever you wish. But as for this man, don't do such an outrageous thing."

But the men would not listen to him. So the man took his concubine and sent her outside to them, and they raped her and abused her throughout the night, and at dawn they let her go. At daybreak the woman went back to the house where her master was staying, fell down at the door and lay there until daylight.

When her master got up in the morning and opened the door of the house and stepped out to continue on his way, there lay his concubine, fallen in the doorway of the house, with her hands on the threshold. He said to her, "Get up; let's go." But there was no answer. Then the man put her on his donkey and set out for home.

When he reached home, he took a knife and cut up his concubine, limb by limb, into twelve parts and sent them into all the areas of Israel." (Judges 19:23–29, NIV)

MALACHI

"Because of you I will rebuke your descendants; I will smear on your faces the dung from your festival sacrifices, and you will be carried off with it." (Malachi 2:3, NIV)

3.4 Comparing Narratives in the Qur'an and Bible

One of the benefits of analyzing a text like the Bible is that it can be compared to other writings from the broader Abrahamic tradition. The Qur'an contains narratives about many of the Prophets found in the Bible, enabling us to explore alternative perspectives on similar stories, teachings, and themes.

This section does not aim to promote the Qur'an, but rather to challenge the notion that the Old Testament "needed" to present these disturbing stories with such graphic detail.

To begin with, the Qur'an speaks about many of the same Prophets as the Old Testament, but yet it does not have a single passage that attributes cardinal sins to any of them or blemishes their moral character.

The Prophets are mentioned with adoration and respect. For example, Prophets David and Solomon (Pbut) are said to be faithful to God (Qur'an 27:15–44); Prophet Jacob (Pbuh) as a righteous messenger of God (Qur'an 21:72); and the prophet Abraham (Pbuh) as 'a truthful man' (Qur'an 19:41) as well as 'obedient to Allah' (Qur'an 16:120). It describes Prophets Ishmael and Isaac, both sons of Abraham (Pbut), as 'true to his promise.' (Qur'an 19:54), and Prophet Moses (Pbuh) as *mukhlasan* (Qur'an 19:51), which roughly translates to 'one who has been specially chosen.'

As for Prophet Jesus (Pbuh), the Qur'an gives him a very tender description. "(His) name is Messiah, Jesus son of Mary, distinguished in the world and the Hereafter and one of those brought near [to Allah]." (Qur'an 3:45). Prophet Muhammad (Pbuh) is described as a model for humankind. "There is certainly a good exemplar for you in the Apostle of Allah—for those who look forward to Allah and the Last Day, and remember Allah much." (Qur'an 33:21)

What in the present day would God want us to understand from these scriptures seeing as we live in such different times? We need to look at scripture intertextually, and interpret them through their socio-political and historical contexts (Esposito 1999). What do we find when exploring the two depictions of prophets within the Bible and the Qur'an?

Let us begin by comparing the story of God's promise to Prophet Abraham in both the Bible and Qur'an.

In the Quran, God tells the 12 tribes of Israel to settle in the land among the people:

> "After him We said to the Children of Israel, 'Take up residence in the land, and when the occasion of the other [promise] comes, We shall gather you in mixed company.'" (Qur'an 17:104)

In comparison, the Old Testament says:

> "The Lord appeared to Abram and said, "To your offspring[a] I will give this land."" (Genesis 12:7, NIV)

> "However, in the cities of the nations the Lord your God is giving you as an inheritance, do not leave alive anything that breathes. Completely destroy them—the Hittites, Amorites, Canaanites, Perizzites, Hivites and Jebusites—as the Lord your God has commanded you." (Deuteronomy 20:16-17, NIV)

In both the Qur'an and Bible, God promises land to Abraham (Pbuh) and his descendants then blesses him to build a great nation. However, there is nothing in the Qur'an saying that Abraham must kill everyone on the land in order for it to become his.

Moses

Muslims know Moses (Musa Pbuh) to be a very respected and beloved Prophet because he rescued people from the rule of the Pharaoh. In Islam, God's prophets help those under oppression and teach them to worship and submit to God alone.

> "Thereat the magicians fell down prostrating. They said, 'We have believed in the Lord of Aaron and Moses!'" (Qur'an 20:70)

> "And mention in the Book Moses. Indeed he was exclusively dedicated [to Allah], and an apostle and prophet." (Qur'an 19:51)

How does the Bible depict Moses? It seems as though Moses led his people differently.

> "Now kill all the boys. And kill every woman who has slept with a man, but save for yourselves every girl who has never slept with a man." (Numbers 31:17–18, NIV)

David

The Qur'an depicts the Prophet David (Pbuh) as a loving prophet, reciting beautiful tunes in harmony with the birds.

> "Certainly We gave David our grace: 'O mountains and birds, chime in with him!' And We made iron soft for him, saying, 'Make easy coats of mail, and keep the measure in arranging [the links], and act righteously. Indeed I watch what you do.'" (Qur'an 34:10–11)

Regarding the war with Goliath, the Quran simply says:
> "Thus they routed them with Allah's will, and David killed Goliath, and Allah gave him kingdom and wisdom and taught him whatever He liked…" (Qur'an 2:251)

By contrast, here are the stories the Bible chooses to tell of Prophet David (pbuh).

Saul, the first king of Israel, told David that if he wanted to marry his daughter he would have to bring him one hundred Philistines' foreskins. So David goes and gets Saul, not one hundred but two hundred foreskins to prove his strength:

> "David took his men with him and went out and killed two hundred Philistines and brought back their foreskins. They counted out the full number to the king so that David might become the king's son-in-law. Then Saul gave him his daughter Michal in marriage." (1 Samuel 18:27, NIV)

Gratuitous Sexual & Other Obscenity

Below is another example of David's misbehavior as told by the Bible:

> "One evening David got up from his bed and walked around on the roof of the palace. From the roof he saw a woman bathing. The woman was very beautiful, and David sent someone to find out about her. The man said, "She is Bathsheba, the daughter of Eliam and the wife of Uriah the Hittite." Then David sent messengers to get her. She came to him, and he slept with her. (Now she was purifying herself from her monthly uncleanness.) Then she went back home. The woman conceived and sent word to David, saying, "I am pregnant…" (2 Samuel 11:2-5, NIV)

> "…In the morning David wrote a letter to Joab and sent it with Uriah. In it he wrote, "Put Uriah out in front where the fighting is fiercest. Then withdraw from him so he will be struck down and die." So while Joab had the city under siege, he put Uriah at a place where he knew the strongest defenders were. When the men of the city came out and fought against Joab, some of the men in David's army fell; moreover, Uriah the Hittite died." (2 Samuel 11:14-17, NIV)

Samson

Contrary to the impression made by terrorist suicide bombers, regarding suicide the Qur'an says:

> "…And do not kill yourselves. Indeed Allah is most merciful to you." (Qur'an 4:29)

In comparison, the Bible describes the suicide martyrdom of Samson:
> "Now the temple was crowded with men and women; all the rulers of the Philistines were there, and on the roof were about three thousand men and women watching Samson perform. Then Samson prayed to the Lord, "Sovereign Lord, remember me. Please, God, strengthen me just once more, and let me with one blow get revenge on the Philistines for my two eyes." Then Samson reached toward the two central pillars on which the temple stood. Bracing himself against them, his right hand on the one and his left hand on the other, Samson said, "Let me die with the Philistines!" Then he pushed with all his might, and down came the temple on the rulers and all the people in it. Thus he killed many more when he died than while he lived." (Judges 16:27–30, NIV)

Elijah

In Islam, the mighty Prophet Elijah called people to monotheism to guard against evil.
> "Indeed Ilyas was one of the apostles. When he said to his people, 'Will you not be Godwary? Do you invoke Baal and abandon the best of creators, Allah, your Lord and Lord of your forefathers?'" (Qur'an 37:123–126)

The Bible depicts Elijah (Pbuh) differently, though.
> "Then Elijah commanded them, "Seize the prophets of Baal. Don't let anyone get away!" They seized them, and Elijah had them brought down to the Kishon Valley and slaughtered there."
> (1 Kings 18:40, NIV)

Elisha

The Bible depicts Elisha, Elijah's successor who also raised people from the dead, as a psychopath.

> "From there Elisha went up to Bethel. As he was walking along the road, some boys came out of the town and jeered at him. "Get out of here, baldy!" they said. "Get out of here, baldy!" He turned around, looked at them and called down a curse on them in the name of the Lord. Then two bears came out of the woods and mauled forty-two of the boys." (2 Kings 2:23–24, NIV)

In contrast, the Qur'an says about him:

> "And remember Ishmael, Elisha and Dhu'l-Kifl—each [of whom was] among the elect." (Qur'an 38:48)

Noah

Noah (Pbuh) is one of the righteous prophets in both the Qur'an and Bible. After he was appointed as a Prophet, Noah invited people to worship God but experienced nothing but persecution until God ordered him to make the ark and the flooding began. In the Qur'an, Noah is very truthful, God-fearing, and morally upright. His message pointed towards strict monotheism and righteous character.

> "Descendants of those whom We carried [in the ark] with Noah. Indeed, he was a grateful servant." (Qur'an 17:3)

> "'O my people, worship Allah! You have no other god besides Him. Indeed I fear for you the punishment of a tremendous day.'" (Qur'an 7:59)

In the Bible, Noah (Pbuh) is depicted differently. The Bible says that he made wine, drank it, became drunk, and laid naked in his tent. Is this the type of character required of a prophet? What is the moral lesson from this story? If prophets are role models, are we to imitate the actions of Noah?

"Noah, a man of the soil, proceeded to plant a vineyard. When he drank some of its wine, he became drunk and lay uncovered inside his tent." (Genesis 9:20–23, NIV)

Lot

In Genesis 19:5-8, men of Sodom surrounded the house of Lot and wanted to sexually assault the two guests inside the home. Lot says:

"Look, I have two daughters who have never slept with a man. Let me bring them out to you, and you can do what you like with them. But don't do anything to these men, for they have come under the protection of my roof." (NIV)

This verse is shocking and appalling, as it reveals Lot's willingness to sacrifice his own daughters to protect his guests from the violent mob of Sodom. Prophet Lot is comfortable with his own daughters being raped instead of his guests.

In contrast, about this incident, the Qur'an says:

"Then his people came running toward him, and they had been committing vices aforetime. He said, 'O my people, these are my daughters: they are purer for you. Be wary of Allah and do not humiliate me with regard to my guests. Is there not a right-minded man among you?'" (Qur'an 11:78)

Gratuitous Sexual & Other Obscenity

The key difference is that in the Qur'an, the reference to virginity and rape, is replaced with a reference to purity and obeying God.

Lot (pbuh) is not offering his daughters for rape, he is asking them to become pious men that he can marry to his daughters. Further, his daughters are an analogy for all women, encouraging the men to marry the women of their community rather than continue with their heinous acts.

The Qur'an never portrays Lot or any other prophet/messenger as indecent, sexually immoral, or vulgar. But the Bible tells of Lot taking part in incest with his daughters.

Lot took his two daughters to live in a cave up in the mountains. They then planned to manipulate their father by getting him drunk and then having sex with him each consecutive night. Their plan was successful, and they became pregnant. The older daughter eventually gave birth to Moab—which is Hebrew for 'My Father'—and the younger daughter gave birth to Ben-Ammi—which is Hebrew for 'Son of my Father'.

> "One day the older daughter said to the younger, "Our father is old, and there is no man around here to give us children—as is the custom all over the earth. Let's get our father to drink wine and then sleep with him and preserve our family line through our father."
>
> That night they got their father to drink wine, and the older daughter went in and slept with him. He was not aware of it when she lay down or when she got up. The next day the older daughter said to the younger, "Last night I slept with my father. Let's get him to drink wine again tonight, and you go in and sleep with him so we can preserve our family line through our father."

So they got their father to drink wine that night also, and the younger daughter went in and slept with him. Again he was not aware of it when she lay down or when she got up. So both of Lot's daughters became pregnant by their father." (Genesis 19:31–36, NIV)

After hearing this story, we ask our Christian Brethren, what can we learn from stories like these? Why does the Bible even mentions these disgusting and incestuous scenes?

Solomon

Solomon was the son of David and a mighty prophet of God in Islam. The Qur'an constantly refers to Solomon possessing glory and gifted with majesty.

"Certainly, We gave knowledge to David and Solomon, and they said, 'All praise belongs to Allah, who granted us an advantage over many of His faithful servants.'" (Qur'an 27:15)

In the Qur'an, the prophets all preach against idolatry and the worship of anything/anyone other than God. In the Bible, however, Solomon is depicted quite differently.

According to 1 Kings 11:3–10, Solomon had 700 wives and 300 slave women that were like wives. When he was old, his wives forced him to worship their gods, so he worshipped Ashtoreth, the Canaanite goddess of love and war, and Malkam, the god of the Ammonite people. He also built a place on a hill next to Jerusalem to worship Chemosh, the idol of the Moabite people, and a temple for Molech, the idol of the Ammonite people. Solomon did the same thing for all

Gratuitous Sexual & Other Obscenity

of his wives from other countries. The Lord finally came to Solomon and told him that he must not follow other gods, but Solomon did not follow the Lord's command.

> "He had seven hundred wives of royal birth and three hundred concubines, and his wives led him astray. As Solomon grew old, his wives turned his heart after other gods, and his heart was not fully devoted to the Lord his God, as the heart of David his father had been. He followed Ashtoreth the goddess of the Sidonians, and Molek the detestable god of the Ammonites. So Solomon did evil in the eyes of the Lord; he did not follow the Lord completely, as David his father had done. On a hill east of Jerusalem, Solomon built a high place for Chemosh the detestable god of Moab, and for Molek the detestable god of the Ammonites. He did the same for all his foreign wives, who burned incense and offered sacrifices to their gods." (1 Kings 11:3–8, NIV)

What kind of prophet disobeys God's direct commands and worships anyone other than Him? Again, this begs the question: what are we learning morally, intellectually, and spiritually from these prophets in the Bible?

> "And what more shall I say? I do not have time to tell about Gideon, Barak, Samson and Jephthah, about David and Samuel and the prophets, who through faith conquered kingdoms, administered justice, and gained what was promised…" (Hebrews 11:32–33)

Abraham

The story of prophet Abraham's attempted sacrifice of his son appears in both the Quran and the Bible, with notable differences in how the event unfolds.

In the Bible (Genesis 22:1-19, NIV), God commands Abraham to sacrifice Isaac as a test of faith. Without any consultation or discussion, Abraham takes Isaac to Mount Moriah, binds him, and prepares to kill him until an angel intervenes at the last moment. Isaac is unaware of what is happening. In fact, when Isaac asks "where is the lamb for the burnt offering?", Abraham responds "God himself will provide the lamb for the burnt offering, my son."

Abraham intentionally misleads his son as to what is about to happen, placing no value on his consent.

In contrast, the Quranic account (Qur'an 37:99-111) presents a different approach. Abraham sees a dream about the sacrifice and speaks with Ishmael, his son, about it, saying, "'My son! I see in dreams that I am sacrificing you. See what you think.'" (Qur'an 37:102). His son responds willingly, saying, "'Father! Do whatever you have been commanded. If Allah wishes, you will find me to be patient.'" (Qur'an 37:102).

This exchange shows that both Abraham and his son are aware of the situation, discuss it, and willingly submit together.

The Quranic account presents the event as a shared trial for both father and son, emphasizing understanding, mutual faith, and trust in God. Abraham does not mislead his son and act immediately but rather seeks his son's consent.

3.5 Women in the Bible

In this section, we aim to explore the role of women in the Bible by examining verses that are often not well known or commonly discussed. Some of these passages raise important questions about how women are portrayed in the text. By looking closely at these verses, we aim to evaluate women's presence and roles in biblical narratives.

Below is a list of depictions of women in the Bible.

> "A woman should learn in quietness and full submission. I do not permit a woman to teach or to assume authority over a man; she must be quiet. For Adam was formed first, then Eve. And Adam was not the one deceived; it was the woman who was deceived and became a sinner." (1 Timothy 2:11–14, NIV)

This scripture is a bit difficult for Christian women to read. It clearly suggests that the woman who was deceived in the Garden of Eden and not the man. It therefore places the blame on women. Similarly, in the story of Samson and Delilah, Delilah (the woman) betrays Samson (Judges 16:19).

> "Women should remain silent in the churches. They are not allowed to speak, but must be in submission, as the law says. If they want to inquire about something, they should ask their own husbands at home; for it is disgraceful for a woman to speak in the church." (1 Corinthians 14:34, NIV)

The passage above seems harsh and unfair towards women, who would like to feel equal and be allowed to speak—in both the Church and elsewhere.

> "But every woman who prays or prophesies with her head uncovered dishonors her head—it is the same as having her head shaved. For if a woman does not cover her head, she might as well have her hair cut off; but if it is a disgrace for a woman to have her hair cut off or her head shaved, then she should cover her head. A man ought not to cover his head, since he is the image and glory of God; but woman is the glory of man. For man did not come from woman, but woman from man; neither was man created for woman, but woman for man. It is for this reason that a woman ought to have authority over her own head, because of the angels." (1 Corinthians 11:5–11, NIV)

The imagery here is quite disturbing but consistent with other scripture. It says that a woman must have a sign of authority on her head, showing that she is subordinate to man. Women, according to these verses, are of the man and created specifically for the man.

> "Judge for yourselves: Is it proper for a woman to pray to God with her head uncovered?" (1 Corinthians 11:13, NIV)

> "All wickedness is but little to the wickedness of a woman let the portion of a sinner fall upon her… Of the woman came the beginning of sin, and through her we all die." (Ecclesiasticus 25:19, 24, KJV)

Through the women we all die? I find it very doubtful that a woman reading this passage would feel very inspired by it.

> "And I find more bitter than death the woman who is a snare, whose heart is a trap and whose hands are chains. The man who pleases God will escape her, but the sinner she will ensnare...while I was still searching but not finding, I found one upright man among a thousand but not one upright woman among them all." (Ecclesiastes 7:26, 28, NIV)

> "If a man has sexual relations with an animal, he must be put to death, and you must kill the animal." (Leviticus 20:15, NIV)

What did the animal do to deserve death? Surely, the animal could not have seduced the man.

> "'If a woman approaches an animal to have sexual relations with it, kill both the woman and the animal. They are to be put to death; their blood will be on their own heads." (Leviticus 20:16, NIV)

In the case of a woman, merely approaching the animal is enough to elicit the same punishment.

> "To the woman he said, "I will make your pains in childbearing very severe; with painful labor you will give birth to children. Your desire will be for your husband, and he will rule over you." (Genesis 3:16, NIV)

Because of the supposed sin of one woman in the beginning (Eve), all future generations of women were cursed with the pains of childbearing. Also because of this sorrow, God decreed that women are to be ruled over by man? This, again, is puzzling for women.

"Wives, submit yourselves to your own husbands as you do to the Lord. For the husband is the head of the wife as Christ is the head of the church, his body, of which he is the Savior. Now as the church submits to Christ, so also wives should submit to their husbands in everything." (Ephesians 5:22–24, NIV)

""""If a priest's daughter defiles herself by becoming a prostitute, she disgraces her father; she must be burned in the fire." (Leviticus 21:9, NIV)

"Then the young woman's father and mother shall bring to the town elders at the gate proof that she was a virgin. Her father will say to the elders, "I gave my daughter in marriage to this man, but he dislikes her. Now he has slandered her and said, 'I did not find your daughter to be a virgin.' But here is the proof of my daughter's virginity." Then her parents shall display the cloth before the elders of the town, and the elders shall take the man and punish him… She shall continue to be his wife; he must not divorce her as long as he lives. If, however, the charge is true and no proof of the young woman's virginity can be found, she shall be brought to the door of her father's house and there the men of her town shall stone her to death. She has done an outrageous thing in Israel by being promiscuous while still in her father's house.

You must purge the evil from among you." (Deuteronomy 22:15–21, NIV)

Polygamy

As an additional point, Christians have, at times, criticized Islam for allowing polygamy. Among the arguments against it are that it disrespects women. However, it should be noted that the Old Testament is filled with polygamy.

Many of the important prophets in the Bible had multiple wives, and even at times hundreds of concubines. These are the men who were supposedly great leaders and role models for us.

> "If he marries another woman, he must not deprive the first one of her food, clothing and marital rights." (Exodus 21:10, NIV)

> "After he left Hebron, David took more concubines and wives in Jerusalem, and more sons and daughters were born to him." (2 Samuel 5:13, NIV)

> "He had seven hundred wives of royal birth and three hundred concubines, and his wives led him astray." (1 Kings 11:3, NIV)

> "Rehoboam loved Maakah daughter of Absalom more than any of his other wives and concubines. In all, he had eighteen wives and sixty concubines, twenty-eight sons and sixty daughters." (2 Chronicles 11:21, NIV)

> "If a man has two wives…" (Deuteronomy 21:15, NIV)

David is mentioned as having many sons and wives (1 Chronicles 3:1–9).

Jacob had four wives (Genesis 29:23–28 and Genesis 30:4–9)

Moses had two wives (Exodus 2:21 and Numbers 12:1).

There are many more verses to cite, but these are sufficient to prove the point. The Bible clearly allowed polygamy in the Old Testament. Keep in mind that Jesus did not come in the New Testament to abolish the law, but to fulfill it (Matthew 5:17). There is also no clear verse in the Bible condemning polygamy.

Our Christian friends may respond with Genesis 2:24: "That is why a man leaves his father and mother and is united to his wife, and they become one flesh." (NIV)

In such a case they will have to contend with this being yet another contradiction within the Bible:

> "Do you not know that he who unites himself with a prostitute is one with her in body? For it is said, "The two will become one flesh."" (1 Corinthians 6:16, NIV)

It's no surprise that Marcion, one of the most prominent and controversial Christian thinkers of the 2nd century, concluded that the God of the Old Testament was a fundamentally different being from the God revealed by Jesus. Troubled by the violence, wrath, and horror he saw in the Hebrew scriptures, Marcion ultimately believed that the two testaments reflected two distinct deities (Ehrman 2005).

3.6 Uncomfortable verses from the New Testament

It is not only the Old Testament that contains such verses, the New Testament, including the words of Jesus, can be just as uncomfortable.

When a Canaanite woman came to Jesus crying out for him to help her demon-possessed daughter (Mark 7:24-30 and Matthew 15:21-28), Jesus initially ignored her and did not say a word. It was only after his disciples came and urged him to respond that he said, "I was sent only to the lost sheep of Israel." The woman then began to beg him and knelt before him, saying, "Lord, help me!" Jesus replied, "It is not right to take the children's bread and toss it to the dogs."

Jesus insulted and refused to help the woman because she was not an Israelite. Jesus did eventually heal her daughter, but the insult and rejection was not necessary nor befitting

> Luke 9:57-62 seems to depict a lack of empathy from Jesus.
>
> "As they were walking along the road, a man said to him, "I will follow you wherever you go." Jesus replied, "Foxes have dens and birds have nests, but the Son of Man has no place to lay his head." He said to another man, "Follow me." But he replied, "Lord, first let me go and bury my father." Jesus said to him, "Let the dead bury their own dead, but you go and proclaim the kingdom of God." Still another said, "I will follow you, Lord; but first let me go back and say goodbye to my family." Jesus replied, "No one who puts a hand to the plow and looks back is fit for service in the kingdom of God."" (NIV)

The above seems harsh and unreasonable especially in ancient Jewish culture. Burying a parent, particularly a father, was an important and sacred duty. It was considered a grave responsibility to honor your parents by ensuring they were properly buried, and failure to do so was seen as neglecting family obligations.

Similarly, saying goodbye to family before leaving was a culturally significant part of leaving on a long journey or making a major life decision.

Jesus is depicted here as having no empathy for this man, and suggesting that his attending to his father's burial will prevent him from entering the kingdom of God.

Jesus is also depicted as lacking back hygiene. Mark 7:2-3 reads:

"And saw some of his disciples eating food with hands that were defiled, that is, unwashed. 3 (The Pharisees and all the Jews do not eat unless they give their hands a ceremonial washing, holding to the tradition of the elders." (NIV)

Matthew 15:2:

"Why do your disciples break the tradition of the elders? They don't wash their hands before they eat!" (NIV)

Luke 11:38:

"But the Pharisee was surprised when he noticed that Jesus did not first wash before the meal." (NIV)

Jesus' response seems to downplay an important cultural practice related to cleanliness. Even if Jesus was aiming to expose the hypocrisy of the Jews, washing of the hands before eating is an important part of hygiene. Did Jesus not know this?

> "Do not suppose that I have come to bring peace to the earth. I did not come to bring peace, but a sword. For I have come to turn a man against his father, a daughter against her mother, a daughter-in-law against her mother-in-law— a man's enemies will be the members of his own household.'" (Matthew 10:34-36, NIV)

The idea of causing family divisions over faith seems pretty harsh, especially when family is supposed to be a source of support and unity.

> "If anyone comes to me and does not hate father and mother, wife and children, brothers and sisters—yes, even their own life—such a person cannot be my disciple." (Luke 14:26, NIV)

Telling someone to "hate" their family and even their own life to follow something feels extreme, as it goes against the natural bonds people have with those closest to them.

Earlier we discussed uncomfortable verses regarding women in the Bible. From the New Testament we mentioned:
> "A woman should learn in quietness and full submission. I do not permit a woman to teach or to assume authority over a man; she must be quiet." (1 Timothy 2:11-12, NIV)

> "Wives, submit yourselves to your own husbands as you do to the Lord. For the husband is the head of the wife as Christ is the head of the church." (Ephesians 5:22-23, NIV)

"Women should remain silent in the churches. They are not allowed to speak, but must be in submission, as the law says. If they want to inquire about something, they should ask their own husbands at home; for it is disgraceful for a woman to speak in the church." (1 Corinthians 14:34-35, NIV)

We also have verses such as Matthew 19:9:
"I tell you that anyone who divorces his wife, except for sexual immorality, and marries another woman commits adultery." (NIV)

The prohibition against divorce unless for sexual immorality might be tough for Christians or others to believe, but according to scripture this is the only way to be divorced, nothing else is specified.

Luke 19:27 states:
"But those enemies of mine who did not want me to be king over them—bring them here and kill them in front of me." (NIV)

Often Christians would like to respond by saying this is a parable. Even if it's "just a parable", it's pretty harsh language for a parable. It raises red flags about what kind of "love" and "justice" are really being preached.

Ephesians 6:5 reads:
"Slaves, obey your earthly masters with respect and fear, and with sincerity of heart, just as you would obey Christ." (NIV)

The call for slaves to obey their masters and serve them as they would serve Christ is unsettling, especially since it can sound like it justifies the institution of slavery instead of pushing for freedom and dignity for all.

> 1 Peter 2:18 says:
> "Slaves, in reverent fear of God submit yourselves to your masters, not only to those who are good and considerate, but also to those who are harsh." (NIV)

This verse seems to justify enduring unjust treatment instead of challenging or changing it. Is this what Christianity is about?

Chapter 3 Gratuitous Sexual & Other Obscenity

References:
Bruce Metzger, A Textual Commentary on the Greek New Testament (Stuttgart, 1971).

Deedat, A., 1985. *Is the Bible God's Word?*. Adam Publishers.

Ehrman, B.D., 2005. Lost Christianities: The battles for scripture and the faiths we never knew. Oxford University Press, USA.

McKinsey, C.D., 1995. *The encyclopedia of biblical errancy*. Prometheus Books.

Whitlark, J.A. and Parsons, M.C., 2006. The 'Seven' Last Words: A Numerical Motivation for the Insertion of Luke 23.34 a. New Testament Studies, 52(2).

4

"Fellow Israelites, listen to this: Jesus of Nazareth was a man accredited by God to you by miracles, wonders and signs, which God did among you through him, as you yourselves know"

(Acts 2:22, NIV)

Jesus' (Pbuh) Divinity in the Bible?

"It does not behoove any human that Allah should give him the Book, judgement and prophethood, and then he should say to the people, 'Be my servants instead of Allah.' Rather [he would say], 'Be a godly people, because of your teaching the Book and because of your studying it.' And he would not command you to take the angels and the prophets for lords. Would he call you to unfaith after you have submitted [to Allah]?" (Qur'an 3:79–80)

Jesus' (Pbuh) Divinity in the Bible?

4.1 Is the Trinity in the Bible?

"For God is not the author of confusion, but of peace…" (1 Corinthians 14:33, KJV)

The belief or idea of a triune God is one of the fundamental differences between Christianity and the other Abrahamic religions. While many non-Trinitarians often misquote the actual doctrine, it seems that not all Trinitarian Christians understand it either. Not only do Muslims have a hard time with the idea, Christians do as well. Laymen have difficulty with it but so do scholars. This can be seen in the book *Two views on the doctrine of the Trinity* (Holmes et al. 2014).

The idea of the Trinity may be summed up in the following words (*Hastings' Dictionary of the Bible*, ed. James Hastings, Trinity, by W. H. Griffith Thomas, p. 949):

> "The Father is God, the Son is God, and the Holy Ghost is God. And yet they are not three Gods, but one God. The Godhead of the Father, and of the Son, and of the Holy Ghost is all one, the Glory equal, the Majesty co-eternal. And in this Trinity none is afore or after other: none is greater or less than another, but the whole three Persons are co-eternal together and co-equal."

The Old Testament does not explicitly lay out a Trinitarian doctrine. Sophisticated Trinitarians claim that God revealed the Trinity later in the New Testament. Accompanied with this idea comes the argument of scattered, unclear verses about the co-working of the Father, Son, and Holy Spirit.

The New Testament also contains no explicit Trinitarian itself. However, many Christian theologians and philosophers hold that the doctrine is inferred from what the New Testament teaches about God. The questions remain. How is this doctrine inferred—deductively or reasonably? Or is it incorrect?

The term 'Trinitas' for the concept of the Trinity was first credited to Tertullian. Tertullian (AD 155–220) was a lawyer and presbyter of the third-century Church in Carthage (Interpreter's Dictionary of the Bible, V4, p. 711). The doctrine of the Trinity briefly states that God is fully existent in three distinct ways (White 1998).

Trinitarian Christians emphasize that the reason they believe in the doctrine of the Trinity is because they believe it is a Biblical doctrine. Trinitarian Christians hold that they are forced to the doctrine of the Trinity by three Biblical truths: 1) there is only one true God, 2) there are three divine persons revealed to be God, and 3) these three persons (Father, Son, and Holy Spirit) are equal.

However, the history suggests there was a forced acceptance of the Trinity. It is known to have evolved over time and developed into what we know it as today. You can refer to the many different councils held in history that relate to vital questions and debates about the Trinity. These include interrelationship within Trinity, different phases or aspects of one single person, different persons sharing eternity, and different persons with distinctly different characters.

By comparison, notice how concisely the Qur'an is able to summarise monotheism in Islam:

> "Say, 'He is Allah, the One. Allah is the All-embracing. He neither begat, nor was begotten, nor has He any equal." (Qur'an 112:1-4)

Jesus' (Pbuh) Divinity in the Bible?

It has been made clear that Allah (God) in Islam is one and not two, three, or more. Similar verses are not only found all throughout the Quran, but also within the Bible. As we shall see, the same cannot be said about the doctrine of Trinity.

> "Hear, O Israel: The Lord our God, the Lord is one...." (Deuteronomy 6:4–5, ESV)

> "To the King of the ages, immortal, invisible, the only God, be honor and glory forever and ever. Amen." (1 Timothy 1:17, ESV)

> "I made the earth and created man on it" (Isaiah 45:12, ESV)

> "Have we not all one Father? Has not one God created us?" (Malachi 2:10, ESV)

It is a sad fact that in the course of Church history, Christians deviated increasingly from the monotheism of the Old Testament. By mixing Christian and pagan elements, worshipping the Virgin Mary came into existence. The mother of Jesus was exalted to the position of a cult object. She received titles that are not due to her and above what is evident from the New Testament.

A clear example of this is in the third ecumenical council of Ephesus (AD 431). The council met at the Church of Mary in Ephesus in Anatolia, declaring that Mary was *theotokos*. The term *theotokos* refers to and should be translated as 'bearer of God' (Price 2007). This same *theotokos* is found in the discovered papyrus (AD 250) as the earliest known prayer to the *theotokos* (Mary).

So why then do Christians believe in the Trinity? What arguments and verses lead them down this road? One must ensure whenever discussing such issues with anybody that we remain respectful and gracious however incorrect a position may seem to us.

> "...always being prepared to make a defense to anyone who asks you for a reason for the hope that is in you; yet do it with gentleness and respect." (1 Peter 3:15, ESV)

According to the concise encyclopedia of Christianity by Geoffrey Parrinder (1998), Jesus was born during the reign of Herod the Great, who would have died around the year 4 BC. Jesus lived on and exercised a ministry for approximately three years in the location of Galilee (North Palestine and South Lebanon).

He is described as a mighty man (Acts 2:22) and a charismatic prophet of God sent to preach his message to the people about the kingdom of God. Along the way, he healed the sick, socialized and ate with the people, and preached in parables with messages from God Almighty. Soon after the crucifixion, an abundance of Christian writings developed.

The letters of Paul to churches that he himself founded or desired to be an advocate for, were followed by more writings, specifically the four Gospels. These Gospels outlined the life and teachings of Jesus as they appeared to the authors (Matthew, Mark, Luke, and John).

Fast tracked further in time, Christianity was scattered throughout the Roman Empire, Egypt, and North Africa, and eastwards from Syria to Persia, India, and even China (Parrinder, 1998).

Jesus' (Pbuh) Divinity in the Bible?

As Christianity separated from Judaism, the idea of the Trinity began to take shape, but not all Christians agreed on the specifics.

Arianism was a form of Christological teaching differing from the orthodox Trinitarian perspective. Arius was a priest of Alexandria (250–336AD) whose idea of monotheism made him incapable of accepting the equality of the Logos (word) with the Father. For Arius, Christ was not an eternal being; rather, he was a created being. Unfortunately, only fragments of his writings still survive. Furthermore, frustration for and against his teachings caused the emperor of the time, Constantine, to call for the council of Nicaea (325AD).

Athanasius at the time was the opponent of Arius who championed the view of Christ being co-eternal and of one substance with the Father. His ideas won out at the council of Nicaea, and Arianism was declared a heresy.

Although Arianism was defeated, it returned for a time and Constantine's successors embraced it. Athanasius became the bishop of Alexander in (328AD) and eventually insisted that the salvation for people depended on the complete humanity and divinity of Jesus Christ. This teaching later won again at the council of Constantinople (381AD).

The argument between Arius (non-Trinitarian) and Athanasius (Trinitarian) was more political than it was theological. There existed a power struggle between Arius and Athanasius. The moment Christianity became the official state religion of the Romans, the church became a political power. Both Christian leaders had momentous followings and support, and both wanted to be in control. There is no denying the followers of the two groups fought each other in battles in the centers of the empire. Eventually, state law under Theodosius the 2nd enforced the Trinity doctrine.

This edict condemned all other Christian beliefs as heresy, punishable by both the Roman state and, Theodosius claimed, by God's condemnation (Freeman, 2002). The council of Nicaea was responding to Arius and the Gnostics at the time. This council determined Christ and God were unified, being each fully God. This was a statement of belief rather than evidence based on theology.

When we hear of the Trinity concept, the Holy Spirit is always included. But The Holy Spirit was missing from the council of Nicaea. The controversy related to this council was specifically the nature of Christ and his relationship to God. They did not address the Holy Spirit's nature. So even at the time of Nicaea, this did not produce a Trinity but, at best, a 'duality'.

The historian Charles Freeman argues at length that this edict brought about confusion and an end to external Christianity (Freeman 2002). All bible studies, theology classes, and preaching were now implemented within the framework of the Trinitarian dogma, as there existed this fear of being accused of heresy. At this time, the state had power over the Church, and the Roman Empire became a one-church state as it did a one-party state.

Before this period, the theory of the three-person Godhead was never formally introduced into the church. This was introduced after the 'apostolic age' and Nicene council. Slowly but surely, theologians had made this theory a problem. Eventually, this caused divisions within the Christian communities' arising small denominations. The history behind the council can be found detailed in *Eerdman's Handbook to the History of Christianity, Councils, and Creeds.*

Jesus' (Pbuh) Divinity in the Bible?

Furthermore, Professor David F. Wright, a senior lecturer in Ecclesiastical history in his *Formation of the Doctrine of the Trinity* (2001) states:

> "Arius was a senior presbyter in charge of Baucalis, one of the twelve 'parishes' of Alexandria. He was a persuasive preacher, with a following of clergy and ascetics, and even circulated his teaching in popular verse and songs. Around 318AD, he clashed with Bishop Alexander. Arius claimed that Father alone was really God; the Son was essentially different from his father. He did not possess by nature or right any of the divine qualities of immortality, sovereignty, perfect wisdom, goodness, and purity."

In 325AD, when Emperor Constantine called for a meeting of all the Bishops of the 'organized' church to settle the dispute. Despite the large number of people present rejecting the idea, the Nicolaitanes (formal clergy) organized Christianity according to their beliefs. According to Obstat (1909), the Catholic Encyclopedia states:

> "...It is difficult in the second half of the twentieth century to offer a clear, objective, and straightforward account of the revelation, doctrinal evolution, and theological elaboration of the Mystery of the Trinity. Trinitarian discussion, Roman Catholic as well as other, present a somewhat unsteady silhouette...There is also the closely parallel recognition on the part of historians of dogma and systematic theologians that when one does speak of an unqualified Trinitarianism, one has moved from the period of Christian origins to, say, the last quadrant of the fourth century. It was only then that what might be called the definitive Trinitarian dogma, 'One God in three Persons', became thoroughly assimilated into Christian life

and thought... it was the product of three centuries of doctrinal development (emphasis added)."

Trinitarian Christians usually argue that early Christian writers such as Ignatius of Antioch spoke and preached the doctrine of the Trinity along with everyone else at that time. However, the Ignatius of Antioch letters we possess never mention the doctrine of the Trinity specifically, as a Trinitarian would want them to be. There is no explicit teaching of the concept of the Trinity found therein.

This is not to be misconstrued with finding supposed parts that may correspond with the Trinitarian concept. That is a different matter.

Even the famous Justin Martyr cannot be said to have conveyed the Trinity doctrine explicitly. Nor has he ever referred to this concept in any Gospel by name. The names of the Gospels were simply unknown to him. These Gospels were referred to as "Memoirs of the Apostles", the names specifically are not mentioned. In fact, according to Segal (1977) he conveys Justin Martyr's speak of a concept of 'two higher powers'. The ideas in which he would have taught could not be accepted under the Athanasius Creed or the agreed Trinitarian language.

During the Apostolic Age of the early Church, the Doctrine of the Trinity was unheard of. The early church did not believe in three persons in the Godhead. They believed in the Father, the Son, and the Holy Spirit. Simply accepting that each was a dispensation, force of God, or plain manifestation of one and the same God.

Jesus' (Pbuh) Divinity in the Bible?

Paul, for example, says in 1 Corinthians 11:3, "But I want you to realize that the head of every man is Christ, and the head of the woman is man, and the head of Christ is God." Notice that there is a separation between Jesus and God being an external being other than Jesus himself. This is clear and self-evident.

Furthermore, we read in Acts 2:22:

"Men of Israel, hear these words: Jesus of Nazareth, a man attested to you by God with mighty works and wonders and signs that God did through him in your midst, as you yourselves know." (ESV)

Jesus of Nazareth is a man according to the bible. If Peter, writing Acts of the Apostles, were under the impression of a Trinitarian Godhead, he would never have begun the verse in such a way. He would have and could have easily said 'Jesus of Nazareth was God', but he never said this, nor did anyone else make such a claim.

We read on in Acts 2:36, "…God has made him both Lord and Christ…" (ESV). Jesus is seen to be made into something. In this case, it is Lord and Messiah. Simple logic dictates that in order to be made into something, you must have had a beginning. Jesus therefore had a beginning. He was born via his mother Mary and was never preexistent.

Act 3:26 states "God, having raised up his servant, sent him to you first…" (ESV). This verse does not say special God or divine son. This is not the language of a Trinitarian but of a strict monotheistic Unitarian. The entire book of Acts never describes Jesus as God or God incarnate. There is no denying, however, that later Christians did accept and call Jesus God, especially after the idea of Jesus being resurrected.

When we ask our Trinitarian-believing Christian brothers about how they rationalize this concept, there arises some difficulties. For example, let us define the 'Father', 'Son', and 'Spirit' as consisting of the Trinity in fullness of God. There now is a totality of divinity in the Trinity. This divinity is expressed as one God. There is only One God and this One God only exists when three persons are active.

But does the father, for example, have 100 percent divinity individually? If we take the Father out of the equation, is He still one God or does the father then account as a percentage or amount of that one God? These questions pose difficulties for Trinitarians.

They sometimes lead Christian Trinitarians to believe in heretical ideas, such as each person in the Trinity being 1/3 of the Godhead. The Athanasius and Chalcedonian Creed reject such views.

These are only some examples of the incoherence of the Trinity, which we find to be internally illogical when attempting to rationalize it. Christians often fall into heresy in the attempt of doing so although God is not the author of confusion (1 Corinthians 14:33, KJV).

Here is one of the immensely influential philosophers and theologians of Christianity Thomas Aquinas speaking about the Trinity in *Summa Theologica: Translated by Fathers of the English Dominican Province (*Aquinas, T., 2010):

"We cannot come to the knowledge of the Trinity by reason alone, that is, by the natural and unaided efforts of the human mind. By our natural reason, we can know that God exists; that he is the First Cause of all; that he is one, infinite, simple, immutable, etc. But that the one God subsists in three really distinct Persons is a truth that can be known only by supernatural means. That is a truth beyond the reach of human reason to know, to prove, or to disprove. We know this truth by divine revelation, and accept it by supernatural faith; we take it upon the authority of God himself."

St. Thomas Aquinas accepts that we cannot use reason to come to understand the Trinity, or at least not reason alone. The Trinity is something beyond our reasoning. In other words, the concept of the Trinity seems to be unexplainable and impossible to comprehend fully. The Trinity cannot be proven or disproven and must be accepted by supernatural faith.

If true, it is unfortunate that God could not have told us about his nature in the Bible plainly. The fact that the Trinity is not found in the Bible directly should give us pause.

Among the attempts to resolve this rational issue is Gregory Boyd, a theologian who has written extensive in favour of the Trinity, states that one must make a careful distinction between a contradiction and a paradox.

He defines a paradox as something that is beyond our reason but not against it, and a contradiction as something simply going against reason. Boyd then gives an example of a contradiction, such as asserting something like a round triangle. Obviously, a circle by definition is round and is logically incompatible with the definition of a triangle. He goes on to argue that the Trinity is a paradox not a contradiction.

Boyd here makes perfect sense, but what he fails to realize is that within the doctrine of the Trinity, there exists an internal contradiction—not a paradox. This contradiction is that a man (Jesus) (by definition being limited) is also God (unlimited) simultaneously. That is synonymous with saying I have a round triangle.

There are further questions we can also raise. Was Jesus (Pbuh) God from Genesis through to Revelations? Is the alleged Trinity limited to only three persons throughout any of the Biblical texts? The answer to both of these questions is No.

The Trinity's incompatibility with the Bible

We can summarise the discussion illustrating that the Trinity is not in the Bible in 6 main points. Finnegan (2011) shows these similar points in detail, as well as Buzzard (1999).

1. Jesus affirmed the theology of a non-Trinitarian Jew
2. The Trinity is not explained in Scripture
3. There is a lack of controversy of it in the first century
4. Countless singular pronouns
5. Jesus was not omniscient
6. Defies the laws of logic / weak arguments for Trinity

1. Jesus was a Jew

The strict Unitarian monotheism of Deuteronomy (4:35–39) and the Shema (Deuteronomy 6:4–5) are clear. Jews maintain a Unitarian understanding of God. As Jesus was a Jew, he should agree with Judaism's core creed, and he does so.

In Mark 12:28-29, Jesus has a conversation with a Jewish scribe, regarding God's identity. This particular scribe intends to test Jesus, asking him which of the commandments is the most important. Reciting the Shema, Jesus answers: "The most important is, 'Hear, O Israel: The Lord our God, the Lord is one." (ESV)

Notice that Jesus did not change the Shema (Creed), nor did he break it down to mean a complex or compound one-in-three-persons.

Jesus' (Pbuh) Divinity in the Bible?

The Jewish scribe understood it as a Unitarian creed, not Trinitarian. So if Jesus were part of a triune God, that moment would have been a good time to introduce that fact, but he instead remained silent and potentially misleads the scribe in his understanding of God. Jesus then highly praises the scribe by saying, "You are not far from the kingdom of God." (Mark 12:34, ESV).

2. Where is the Trinity taught?

There is no verse in the Bible that describes the Trinity explicitly. Instead, what most Trinitarian Christians do is use ambiguous, enigmatic verses here and there to support their position. We will discuss this in the next section.

If a non-Christian were to read the Bible, they would not produce the idea of a Trinity. Instead, they would see all the Unitarian monotheistic statements that the Qur'an redirects us to.

Some Christians may respond that Trinity is not taught in one place but throughout scripture, or that post-biblical Christians developed the doctrine to correctly explain all the biblical data. They would also claim that God led these Fathers of the Church to the truth. In that case, then, they are in agreement that the Trinity was not taught in scripture but that Christian thinkers highly influenced by Greek philosophy later superimposed it into scripture.

The Trinity doctrine was clearly developed over time, just as the Gospel writings.

3. Lack of controversy over the Trinity in the first century

Imagine if a Jew were to learn a new definition of God—or even just a change or different understanding of God. Would you not expect some form of controversy or resistance? If someone confessed the *Shema* multiple times a day his or her whole life and someone told them that this needs to be replaced by a three-in-one (or Trinitarian) confession, wouldn't that at least cause some questioning? Where, then, is the controversy over the three-in-one God?

Rather than finding such controversy amongst the earliest Christian writings, such controversies are not addressed until almost three hundred years after the life of Jesus.

Councils that were held leading to the Trinity
325: Nicaea I (Is the son eternal?)
381: Constantinople I (Is the Holy Spirit the third person?)
431: Ephesus (Was Mary the bearer of Christ's divine nature?)
451: Chalcedon (Did Christ have one or two natures? If two, How?)
553: Constantinople II (How can we interpret the dual natures without dividing Christ?)
681: Constantinople III (Did Christ have one or two wills?)
787: Nicaea II (Can icons of Christ be worshiped? How?)

4. Countless singular pronouns

Is God a singular person or multiple persons? If God is a *he* and not a *they*, that would make him a singular person, not multiple persons. God is always addressed in the second person (you) and spoken of in the third person (He). When God speaks, he says 'I' (with few exceptions when he uses 'us' (Genesis 1:26; 3:22; 11:7).

Jesus' (Pbuh) Divinity in the Bible?

If this us is understood as plural, does this not mean that there is more than one God? Or rather, is it the royal "we", indicating that God only has one person.

Many Trinitarians would agree that God is one substance with three persons. But why stop at three persons? Why not keep going to 33? If God is complex, 1x1x1x1x1x.... still equals one.

Christians would argue that it is a revelation, which is why they stop at three. But what about Revelation 1:4? "...Grace to you and peace from him who is and who was and who is to come, and from the seven spirits who are before his throne." (ESV)

So why not seven persons? How do you know there isn't an eighth hovering over the planet Neptune? Why didn't the authors of the Bible speak about God as if he was three persons in their use of pronouns?

5. Jesus was not omniscient

Jesus said he did not know the day or hour of his return—only his Father knew it (Mark 13.32). "But concerning that day or that hour, no one knows, not even the angels in heaven, nor the Son, but only the Father." (ESV)

Simply put, if somebody does not know something, they are not omniscient, a necessary attribute of an infinite God. Does this rule not apply to Jesus? Omniscience is a necessary property of divinity; if Jesus were God, he would have been omniscient.

Trinitarians will usually argue that in his human nature, he was limited in knowledge, but in his divine nature, he did know when he would return. In response, wasn't there only one person subsisting in the two natures? How can he have two minds both contradicting each other? We ask our Trinitarian friends, was Jesus lying about not knowing the hour? God cannot lie (Titus 1:2).

A very common response to this question comes from Philippians, which says Jesus emptied himself of divine qualities. This presents a new problem, though. If he humbled himself of divine qualities, how were we supposed to take him as divine? Did Jesus just stop being God? It seems as though this line of questioning is problematic for the Trinitarian Christian.

6. Weak arguments for Trinity

The 'orthodox' Trinitarian church has always admitted openly that the doctrine of the Trinity is a mystery and beyond reason (Sproul 2011). However, this "mystery", according to Oneness Pentecostals, Unitarians, Muslims, and other true monotheists is illegitimate, unreasonable, and unnecessary.

Not only is the doctrine impossible to understand or sufficiently explain, but Trinitarians expect others to accept it, even though they themselves cannot fully comprehend it.

Oneness Pentecostals (believers of Pentecostalism who adhere to a non-Trinitarian doctrine) argue against the Trinity, saying that three persons in one God is a self-contradictory concept and essentially meaningless. Gregory Boyd in his book Oneness Pentecostals and the Trinity mentions there are certain weak arguments regularly used to substantiate the doctrine of the Trinity.

One particular example Boyd mentions is the use of the word for God in the Old Testament—*Elohim*—which is the plural of the word *El,* implying some sort of plurality in a Godhead.

Jesus' (Pbuh) Divinity in the Bible?

Most Hebrew scholars find this invalid because when a numerical plurality is intended, the corresponding verbs in the context should also be plural, which is not the case with *Elohim*. Moreover, Boyd argues that the word *one* in Hebrew (Echad) is a unified *one*, not an absolute *one*. Many Trinitarian argue that God is a complex *one*, which doesn't realistically apply in the world.

For example, if I wanted to buy a three-dollar coffee at a cafe, could I buy it for one dollar? No, of course not. That would not be acceptable. What if I were to explain that the dollar as a complex, unified dollar, divided into three coequal dollars? This would just make matters worse. It might escalate to the manager, who most likely would ask me to leave the cafe or send me to the nearest mental health center.

Boyd concludes by stressing that we should look into the strongest arguments and not the weaker arguments for the trinity doctrine. However, as we have covered, there are six solid points against the Trinity. You can be the judge of what sounds reasonable.

A popular verse often used as evidence for the mysterious concept of the Trinity is Matthew 28:19. "Go therefore and make disciples of all nations, baptizing them in the name of the Father and of the Son and of the Holy Spirit." (ESV)

Does this verse prove the Trinity? No. This verse never says these three are 'one'. In other words, Jesus did not say, 'Go and baptize people in my name (Jehovah) or (Yahweh).' He mentioned God first, then himself (God's messenger), and then God's inspiration or power (the Holy Spirit). Where in the bible can we find the baptism put into practice? Furthermore, as William Barclay states in his commentary *Daily Study Bible:*

"He (Jesus) sent them out to make all the world his disciples. It may well be that the instruction to baptize (Father, Son, and Holy Spirit) is something which is a development of the actual words of Jesus. The Roman exegete and historian Eusebius informs us of the actual words Jesus spoke to his disciples in Matthew 28. This is found in Eusebius, Proof of the Gospel, Book III, Chapter 7, 138 (c), p.159. "…He said to His disciples: "Go, and make disciples of all the nations in my Name.""

Harold Brown makes it very clear in his work *Heresies* (1984) that:
"It is a simple fact and an undeniable historical fact that several major doctrines that now seem central to the Christian faith—such as the doctrine of the Trinity—were not present in a full and self-defined, generally-accepted form until the fourth and fifth centuries."

Analogies

Some Trinitarians go even further into the trap of bad analogies for this mysterious doctrine. You may have heard some of them before. For example, the analogy of the Trinity as an egg. In one egg, there is the white, the yoke, and the shell. This analogy fails because the white, yolk, and shell are different substances. This in fact promotes tritheism.

A more popular analogy is the water analogy, which states that water has three states: solid, liquid, and gas, and although the water changes forms, it is still H_2O. Again, this analogy fails, as no one molecule of H_2O can actually exist as solid, liquid, and gas at the same time. This analogy would actually promote the heresy of modalism—

that is to say, a common theological error concerning the nature of God according to Trinitarians, such as James White (1999).

Modalism states that God is a single person who, throughout Biblical history, revealed himself in three modes or forms. This view states that the Father, the Son, and the Holy Spirit never all exist at the same time—only one after another.

Another analogy that is used is the comparison of the Trinity to a man who is a father, husband, and son. This analogy does not stand because one person alone can simultaneously be a father, husband, and son at once, but only to different people. Furthermore, I can also be a grandson, worker, nephew, and cousin all at the same time.

Similarly, if we look at the components of soil, we find four main elements; water, air, mineral matter, and organic matter. Does this now prove a quadrinity?

An even more desperate attempt to explain this doctrine is the appeal to time. As time consists of the past, present, and future, Trinitarians use this concept to suggest that the Godhood of the Trinity is one whole in three sections or frames.

This is refuted because these three individual sections of time are not time themselves, but rather all together, they are time. The past itself is not time, nor is the present or future. They are all part of time. Trinitarians do not call Jesus *part* of God; quite the opposite, they claim Jesus to be fully God—one hundred percent.

Eventually, Trinitarians may conclude their arguments by stating that the Trinity is a mystery that no person can fully comprehend. As mentioned before, this giving-up mentality represents a lack of critical thought, leading to blind acceptance. But we must prove all things (1 Thessalonians 5:21).

According to Buzzard (2012), Trinitarian Christians are unable to provide a logical explanation of how three beings who are each called God can, in fact, be one God. The Swiss Protestant theologian very powerfully states in his *Dogmatics*, Brunner (1950) that:

> "...We must honestly admit that the doctrine of the Trinity did not form part of the early Christian New Testament...It was never the intent of the original witnesses to Christ...There is no trace of such an idea in the New Testament. This *mysterium logicum*... It is a mystery which the Church places before the faithful in her theology... but which has no connection with the message of Jesus and the Apostles."

Rabbi Apple (2016, p.82) states:

> "He may have thought of himself as the Messiah, who for Jews was a human who would bring earthly redemption..." This earthly redemption does not involve any divinity part of a Trinity whatsoever.

4.2 Indirect Proofs used by the Church

Of all the books in the Bible (both Old and New Testament), proof texts (or scripture supporting the concept of Jesus' divinity) often come from the last Gospel of John and from passages in Saint Paul's letters. These are the main sources used, though not the only ones.

If Jesus were in fact divine, we should expect to see scripture supporting that idea all throughout the Bible. So why is it that most proof texts come from John? (Buzzad 2007).

Christians may argue that there is support throughout the Bible and that we just need to read it holistically. This is a fair point; however,

Jesus' (Pbuh) Divinity in the Bible?

as you may now be aware, the development of the Gospel narratives was an evolutionary process, and John was the last to have been written.

It doesn't make a lot of sense that the last Gospel should be the best scripture to use for support. Keep in mind this development was not necessarily a linear regression advancing upwards, the development of Christology could have been somewhat sporadic.

We discussed how Jesus never claimed to be God. But did he at least tell anyone in secret? Did he tell his mother? If the account of Jesus' life is truly authentic, his family must have guarded the secret about his divinity.

However, Jesus said he spoke openly in this world and never in secret (John 18:29). Additionally, his immediate family and disciples never referred to him as God. Their conversations with him indicate they considered him a human like themselves, a man.

The following sources from the New Testament indicate this:

Mark 6:3:
> "Is not this the carpenter, the son of Mary and brother of James and Joses and Judas and Simon? And are not his sisters here with us?" (ESV)

Matthew 13:55-56:
> "Is not this the carpenter's son? Is not his mother called Mary? And are not his brothers James and Joseph and Simon and Judas? And are not all his sisters with us?" (ESV)

Acts 2:22:

> "Men of Israel, hear these words: Jesus of Nazareth, a man attested to you by God with mighty works and wonders and signs that God did through him in your midst, as you yourselves know." (ESV)

Mark 8:27-28:

> "And Jesus went on with his disciples to the villages of Caesarea Philippi. And on the way he asked his disciples, 'Who do people say that I am?' And they told him, 'John the Baptist; and others say, Elijah; and others, one of the prophets.'" (ESV)

Matthew 16:13-14:

> "Now when Jesus came into the district of Caesarea Philippi, he asked his disciples, 'Who do people say that the Son of Man is?' And they said, 'Some say John the Baptist, others say Elijah, and others Jeremiah or one of the prophets.'" (ESV)

Many will respond by saying we need to read what the Bible says. So let us investigate the alleged proof texts Christians use.

> "And I tell you, ask, and it will be given to you; seek, and you will find; knock, and it will be opened to you. For everyone who asks receives, and the one who seeks finds, and to the one who knocks it will be opened." (Luke 11:9–10, ESV)

Jesus' (Pbuh) Divinity in the Bible?

Gospel of John

My Christian friends often tell me Jesus himself was called God in the Bible. I am frequently referred to John 20:28: "Thomas answered him, "My Lord and my God!"" (ESV)

In this chapter we have Thomas, one of the 12 disciples, doubting the resurrection of Jesus, but eventually 'seeing and believing'. Thomas here is responding in surprise to the resurrection of Jesus.

While this could be Thomas addressing Jesus as God, he could also just be exclaiming his surprise, similar to someone saying "Oh my God!"

However, if, in fact, this is the only Gospel to have someone call Jesus God, why isn't this mentioned in any of the other earlier Gospels? One would think such a tremendously important fact would be mentioned throughout the entire Bible.

There are also issues with the accuracy of this section. For comparison, in Luke 24, Jesus (Pbuh) appears to the eleven remaining disciples in the upper room, including Thomas. In John 20, Thomas was not there, only appearing to Jesus afterwards.

The gospel writer must have intended to convey a particular viewpoint he felt important and changed the resurrection story to do so. Furthermore, since this passage is found only in John and not in the Synoptics, the snowball effect becomes more apparent.

Further supporting the idea that John 20:28 is not Thomas calling Jesus God, here are some of the other verses throughout John. John 12:44-45 reads:

> "And Jesus cried out and said, "Whoever believes in me, believes not in me but in him who sent me. And whoever sees me sees him who sent me."" (ESV)

John 14:9 seems to imply Jesus' divinity:

> "Jesus said to him, "Have I been with you so long, and you still do not know me, Philip? Whoever has seen me has seen the Father. How can you say, 'Show us the Father?'" (ESV)

However, John 14:10, the next verse clarifies:

> "Do you not believe that I am in the Father and the Father is in me? The words that I say to you I do not speak on my own authority, but the Father who dwells in me does his works." (ESV)

John 5:30 states:

> "I can do nothing on my own. As I hear, I judge, and my judgment is just, because I seek not my own will but the will of him who sent me." (ESV)

A further point to note is that even if Thomas was referring to Jesus as God, that is not equivalent to Jesus saying that he is God. My Christian friends often respond to this saying, "Well, why didn't Jesus correct Thomas if he really wasn't God?" This kind of reasoning is slightly flawed.

If we look at Matthew 9:32–35, we see Jesus healing a demon-possessed, mute man. Eventually, the mute man spoke, and the demons were cast out. The Pharisees said Jesus cast out "demons by the prince of demons." This was not true, but did Jesus correct them? No.

> "And Jesus went throughout all the cities and villages, teaching in their synagogues and proclaiming the gospel of the kingdom and healing every disease and every affliction." (ESV)

Jesus' (Pbuh) Divinity in the Bible?

The Jews were mocking Jesus and he never corrected them, the fact that he didn't correct them does not in any way support their claims.

Another important aspect to consider is the Greek language. In the Greek language, one would speak a certain way in reference to a single person, and another way in reference to two persons. This is known as the *Granville Sharp Rule,* which centers on the construction grammar and how nouns connect with words. The Greek language uses the word *theos* ('God', or 'god') with a broader meaning than today's customary meaning.

In the Greek language within the culture of that time, 'God' was a descriptive title applied to a range of authorities, including the Roman governor and even the devil (Bruce 1988). In Acts 12:22 we read "And the people were shouting, "The voice of a god, and not of a man!"" (ESV) This verse is referring to an incident involving King Herod, where the people of Tyre and addressed him as a 'god'. In 2 Corinthians 4:4, Satan is referred to as the "god of this world," which implies a certain dominion or power over earthly matters,

It was not limited to its literal definition of a name for the supreme deity, as we use it today. Given the language of the time and knowing that Jesus did represent the Father and had divine authority, the expression used by Thomas is certainly understandable. It could have been used as an honorific title and not divine at all. It was also common to call God's representatives 'God,' and the Old Testament contains quite a few examples.

When Jacob wrestled with 'God', Christians might argue that he was actually wrestling with an angel as a representative of God. We read in Hosea 12:4 "Yes, he struggled with the angel and prevailed; he wept and sought his favor. He found him at Bethel, and there God spoke with us." We could look at it from another angle here and consider Jesus to be God's representative. Similarly, below we see an example of God's representative:

> "And Manoah said to his wife, "We shall surely die, for we have seen God." (Judges 13:22, ESV)

The word 'God' in this passage does not indicate the absolute Almighty God rather, Manoah saw an angel that was God's representative, just as we see in John 20:28.

> "In their case the god of this world has blinded the minds of the unbelievers." (2 Corinthians 4:4, ESV)

This refers to Satan, even with a definite article in the Greek. Does this then mean Satan is divine? If we look into the Gospel of John, in John 20:17, Jesus implied that he is not divine.

> "I am ascending to my Father and your Father, to my God and your God." (John 20:17, ESV)

Here, Jesus says that he will ascend to the Father. He is also saying that he has a Father and a God. If Jesus had or has a God to ascend to, how can he be the one and only God? Is he ascending to himself?

In the Gospels, Jesus never states explicitly that he is the Almighty supreme God, or anywhere in the Bible for that reason. Jesus never referred to himself as 'God' in the absolute sense, nor did he intend to do so.

When the New Testament applies the term 'God' in its Greek *'ho theos'* ('the one God'), it is never applied to Jesus with certainty. The

Jesus' (Pbuh) Divinity in the Bible?

passage of Thomas describing Jesus did indeed use the term *'theos'*. Jesus himself recognized the Old Testament usage of judges being called gods (John 10:30, Psalm 82:6). The word was used by early Christians in a broader sense.

> "And this is eternal life, that they know you, the only true God, and Jesus Christ whom you have sent." (John 17:3, ESV)

Jesus had already denied any form of divinity in John 10:34–36, and he was also distinguished from the one true God (John 17:3). Readers of the Bible often are not aware that the word 'God' can be applied to a representative of God, as we covered previously. It is very plausible that John had incorporated this concept into his portrait of Jesus. The question remains, though, why the story of Thomas is not mentioned in any other Gospel besides John.

John 1:1

> "In the beginning was the Word, and the Word was with God, and the Word was God." (ESV)

Again, it is important here to understand the entire context and framework of the Gospel of John. We must not let John contradict himself. We should not isolate John 1:1 from John's entire message. "…But these are written so that you may believe that Jesus is the Christ, the Son of God." (John 20:31, ESV). John's Gospel is building on the framework of Jesus as the Messiah.

Notice the verse does not say, "so that you may believe Jesus is God," or "that he's a part of the Trinity with a divine and human nature." It is so that we may know that Jesus is the Messiah, the anointed one of God.

In the Greek version of the text, there was no editorializing or no capitalized words. The addition of these can be a little misleading. The text does not say, "In the Beginning was the Son..." In Hebrew, the word 'word' meant *plan, design, expression of our minds* and intention. For example, in the beginning, God "spoke." Then we read, "The word was with God."

Christians automatically jump to the idea of Jesus as God because he was 'the word'. But we ask when was Jesus ever called 'the word' in the Bible?

If we examine the books of Job and Proverbs, 'Wisdom' was with God. This is not another person but a personification. And then that Word was "fully expressive of God". The word was God-like, if you will. God is His word, a you-are-what-you-think expression. John 1:1 does not necessarily need to be interpreted as being God but as expressing God. Keep in mind that this form of approach to the gospels is a Unitarian Christian perspective (Buzzard 1999).

Another thing to consider is that in all of the eight translations of the Greek language before the King James Version, it did not say all things were made through HIM, but instead all things were made through IT. 'Jesus' is what the word became and is not a one-to-one equivalent with the word.

If we continue reading from John 1:1 until we get to verse 17, the word is in the category of being expressive of God. The word is what God spoke referring to the Genesis account. The word ends up becoming flesh, this doesn't need to refer to Jesus becoming flesh or the son. It is first in a category of God's expression.

Jesus' (Pbuh) Divinity in the Bible?

Then after verse 17 comes another category of Jesus as the son or as the synoptic Gospels depict hm. So as the word became flesh, when Jesus was born, that Word, plan or expression became realized and dwelt among us. John 1:1 could also be an evolutionary development, introducing Jesus not as God almighty, but rather as a lesser God or intermediary God.

It does not make any sense to take the word 'word' in this verse to be equivalent with 'God.' If this were the case, we would have to replace 'word' with 'God,' which would make its meaning nonsensical.

"…In the beginning was the *God* and the *God* was with God and the *God* was God…"

Trinitarians often interpret the term "God" here to refer only to the Father, while applying it differently to other parts of the verse. If we were to consistently interpret "God" as "Father," we would read it as "In the beginning was the Word, and the Word was with Father," and so on.

The assertion about the Word doesn't necessarily claim that Jesus is the supreme God but suggests He possesses godlike qualities. John had a straightforward way of conveying that Jesus is divine, and he could have simply stated it as "Jesus is God".

It makes more sense to suggest that John was presenting the Logos (Word) as some kind of intermediary between God, just as Jesus is said to have a God in John 20:17 and Revelation 1:6.

As a final point, the New World Translation interprets John 1:1 to say "…the word was a god."

John 5:16–18

> "...not only was he breaking the Sabbath, but he was even calling God his own Father, making himself equal with God." (ESV)

The peoples in the time and culture of the Bible knew that children often carried the authority of the family. For example, the son of a king had authority. An example of this can be seen in Genesis 25:31, where Esau is asked to sell his birthright. This birthright would mean leadership of the family, inheritance (Deuteronomy 21:17) and a spiritual blessing.

Take Augustus for example, the first Roman emperor. Augustus' adoptive son, Tiberius, had the authority to represent Augustus in matters of the Roman Empire, even before he became emperor himself. When Christ said that God was his Father, the Pharisees correctly interpreted that to mean that he had God's authority on Earth, which is what Jesus was in fact saying.

The statement, "making himself equal with God," is the Jews reason for wanting to kill Jesus, not the narrator's comment on Jesus' nature. This is seen clearly by the full verse which says, "This was why the Jews were seeking all the more to kill him, because not only was he breaking the Sabbath, but he was even calling God his own Father, making himself equal with God." (John 5:18, ESV).

So, the author is simply recording the reason why the Jews wanted to kill him, because they thought he was making himself equal with God. This was not actually what Jesus was doing.

This verse is actually unsupportive of the Trinity. It accurately records that Jesus was saying that God was his father, not that he was

Jesus' (Pbuh) Divinity in the Bible?

himself God, or that he was 'God the Son.' Jesus' authority came from the fact that he was the Son of God, not God Himself.

The concept of people being equal is found in several places in the Bible. For example, when Joseph was ruling Egypt under Pharaoh, Judah said to him, "for you are like Pharaoh himself." (Genesis 44:18). Paul wrote about men who wanted to be considered "equal with us" (2 Corinthians 11:12, NIV). No Christian believes that Joseph and Pharaoh or Paul and his opponents are "of one substance," and make up "one being" simply because they are called "equal." John 5:18 should not be isolated but handled just as the other verses that mention equality.

John 8

"I told you that you would die in your sins, for unless you believe that I am he you will die in your sins." (John 8:24, ESV)

Trinitarians occasionally cite this verse to try to show the necessity of believing their doctrine and, unfortunately, sometimes even to intimidate those who doubt it. They supply the word 'God' after 'I am,' not from the text, but from their doctrine. This is a distortion of the biblical text and of the Gospel of John in particular.

The purpose of the Gospel is stated in John 20:31: "But these are written so that you may believe that Jesus is the **Christ**..." (ESV). The verse is clear, you shall believe he is the Christ, it does not say to believe that he is God! The true meaning of the text is that if one does not believe that Jesus is the Christ, he will die in his sins. This teaching can be found in a number of scriptures in the New Testament.

"Before Abraham was, I am." (John 8:58, ESV)

If Jesus wanted to say "I am God", he could have said that. But he doesn't. This could be taken as another divine passage, or proof text. However, this verse is mistranslated.

The correct translation of the verse should be, "Before Abraham was born I am he" (Craig 2005) In short, Abraham was looking forward to the Messiah to come, as Abraham precedes Jesus (Pbut). We see a similarity in Jeremiah 1:5. "Before I formed you in the womb I knew you." (ESV)

Trinitarians argue this verse states that Jesus said he was the "I am (*Yahweh* of the Old Testament)", so he must be God. Saying, "I am" does not make a person God. The blind man that Jesus healed was not claiming to be God when he said, "I am the man." The Greek translation reads exactly like Jesus' statement, "I am."

Most Bible translators are Trinitarian, so their bias often appears in various places of their translation. Paul also used the same phrase when he said that he wished all men were as "I am." (Acts 26:29, ESV)

The phrase 'I am' occurs many other times in the New Testament, and is often translated as "I am he" or some equivalent.

"I am he" (Mark 13:6; Luke 21:8; John 13:19; 18:5, 6 and 8, ESV).

"It is I" (Matthew 14:27; Mark 6:50; John 6:20, ESV).

"I am he" (John 8:24 and 28, ESV).

In order for the Trinitarian argument that Jesus' "I am" statement in John 8:58 makes him God, it must be equivalent with God's "I am" statement in Exodus 3:14. However, the two statements are very different. While the Greek phrase in John does mean, 'I am,' the Hebrew phrase in Exodus actually means *to be* or *to become*.

John 10

"I and the Father are one." (John 10:30, ESV)

Considering the evolution of the Gospels, one could potentially take this verse to mean that Christ was saying that he and the Father make up 'one God', as in the divinity. However, one could also understand it as a pretty commonly used phrase.

Even today, if someone used it, people would know that it means he and his father are very much alike. When Paul wrote to the Corinthians about his ministry there, he said that he had planted the seed and Apollos had watered it. Then he said, "he who plants and he who waters are one." (1 Corinthians 3:8, ESV)

The concept of 'being one' is used in other places to mean 'one purpose'. John 11:52 says Jesus was to die to make all God's children 'one'. In John 17:11, 21 and 22, Jesus prayed to God that his followers would be 'one' as he and God were 'one'. I think it is obvious that Jesus was not praying that all his followers would become one being or substance just as he and his Father were supposedly one being or substance. Rather, Jesus was praying that all his followers be one in purpose just as he and God were one in purpose.

The context of John 10:30 helps us understand that Jesus was referring to the fact that he had the same purpose as God. Jesus was speaking about his ability to keep the 'sheep' (the believers), who came to him. He said that no one could take them out of his hand or his Father's hand. Then he said that he and the Father were 'one' (*i.e.*, had one purpose), which was to keep and protect the sheep.

> "For this reason the Father loves me, because I lay down my life that I may take it up again. No one takes it from me, but I lay it down of my own accord. I have authority to lay it down, and I have authority to take it up again. This charge I have received from my Father." (John 10:17-18, ESV)

We need to take into consideration the words that are used here in order to understand what Jesus is saying. Reasonably speaking, if Jesus had the ability and authority to raise himself from the dead, but this command and ability was given to Jesus, how does this make the man divine? If something is given to someone, this generally implies that the person at one stage did not have it. Thus, at one stage Jesus was not divine? Did divinity duplicate itself?

> "I and the Father are one." The Jews picked up stones again to stone him. Jesus answered them, "I have shown you many good works from the Father; for which of them are you going to stone me?" The Jews answered him, "It is not for a good work that we are going to stone you but for blasphemy, because you, being a man, make yourself God.'" (John 10:30-33, ESV)

When Jesus prays, "And I am no longer in the world, but they are in the world, and I am coming to you. Holy Father, keep them in your

Jesus' (Pbuh) Divinity in the Bible?

name, which you have given me, that they may be one, even as we are one." (John 17:11, ESV), Trinitarians understand that being "one" refers to a unity of purpose and mission, not to being one God.

This concept is clarified in John 10:30, where Jesus states that he is one with the Father in the same way that believers are called to be one with each other. There is no implication of consubstantiality in this context; it emphasizes relational unity.

Assuming the Pharisees' interpretation of Jesus' statements poses a significant issue. The Pharisees often sought to entrap Jesus, and their accusation of blasphemy—claiming he called himself God—cannot be taken as a sincere assessment of his words.

Importantly, the Greek text does not say, "you, being a man, make yourself God," but rather, "you, being a man, make yourself a god." (Craig 2005). This distinction matters. Their accusation suggests that Jesus was elevating himself to a divine status, not claiming equality with the Father, as Trinitarians often assert. Jesus' response highlights their hypocrisy and clarifies his identity as a prophet of God. He then points out their hypocrisy in calling themselves "gods," thus Jesus is showing that they are not saying that they are equal with God.

> "Jesus answered them, "Is it not written in your Law, 'I said, you are gods'?"" (John 10:34, ESV)

In John 10:24, the Pharisees ask Jesus to "If you are the Christ, tell us plainly." (ESV) If Trinitarians argue that Jesus explicitly claimed to be God in John 5 and identified as the "I AM" of Exodus in John 8:58, then their inquiry about whether he is the Messiah—a lesser title meaning "the anointed one of God"—raises questions. If he were indeed God, why would they seek confirmation of a title that implies a distinct role within God's plan?

Gospel of Mark

Mark 2:7

> "Why does this man speak like that? He is blaspheming! Who can forgive sins but God alone?" (ESV)

On several occasions, Jesus told the Pharisees that their doctrine was wrong. Mark 2:7 records an instance where this was the case. There is no verse of scripture that says only God can forgive sins. That idea came from their tradition. The truth is that God grants the authority to forgive sins as He pleases. He granted that authority to the prophets and to the apostles.

John 20:23 records Jesus saying to them, "If you forgive the sins of any, they are forgiven them." (ESV) If the Pharisees were right and only God can forgive sins, then God, Jesus, and the apostles were all God, because they all had the authority to forgive sins. There is no claim of divinity here. God can simply allow Jesus to forgive sins just as he allowed him to perform miracles (Acts 2:22). Jesus makes it very clear that "authority" was given to him (Matthew 28:18-20).

Mark 14: 61–65

A common proof text used by Trinitarians is Mark 14, which refers to the trial in front of the Jewish council. Christians claim that Jesus claimed to be 'Yahweh' (Exodus 3:14) and also the 'Son of man' (Daniel 7:13 and Psalm 110:1) by sitting at the right hand of the Lord.

Jesus' (Pbuh) Divinity in the Bible?

"Again the high priest asked him, "Are you the Christ, the Son of the Blessed?" And Jesus said, "I am, and you will see the Son of Man seated at the right hand of Power, and coming with the clouds of heaven." And the high priest tore his garments and said, "What further witnesses do we need? You have heard his blasphemy. What is your decision?" And they all condemned him as deserving death." (Mark 14:61-64, ESV)

Matthew 26 has a similar idea:
"Tell us if you are the Christ, the Son of God." Jesus said to him, "You have said so. But I tell you, from now on you will see the Son of Man seated at the right hand of Power and coming on the clouds of heaven." (Matthew 26:63-64, ESV)

It is important to highlight the fact that nobody in the trial asked Jesus if he was God; rather, they asked him, "Are you the Messiah?" Firstly, being the Messiah or even the son of Man does not equate to being God.

Secondly, sitting at the right hand of the Mighty one means you are not actually the Mighty one. Thirdly, Daniel 7:13-14 specifically mentions "came one like a son of man" and says, "And to him was given dominion." (ESV) What kind of God or divine figure is given authority?

"I saw in the night visions, and behold, with the clouds of heaven there came one like a son of man, and he came to the Ancient of Days and was presented before him. And to him was given dominion and glory and a kingdom, that all peoples, nations, and languages should serve him." (Daniel 7:13-14, ESV)

"And Jesus came and said to them, "All authority in heaven and on earth has been given to me."" (Matthew 28:18, ESV)

Where has this authority come from? The Christian may respond and say God or the Father. In that case, it logically follows that Jesus was given authority, as opposed to infinitely possessing it, and therefore lacked the divine characteristic of omnipotence.

Our Christian friends also point to the question of blasphemy. Why was he, according to the Bible, worthy of death? Jesus was accused of blasphemy during his trial before the Sanhedrin after he affirmed his identity as the Messiah.

The Jewish leaders interpreted this as a violation of God's sovereignty. In Mark 14:61-65, Jesus responds, "I am," to the question of whether He is the Messiah, and further claims, "you will see the Son of Man sitting at the right hand of the Mighty One and coming on the clouds of heaven." The Jews took those words to mean he was breaking the third commandment, taking God's name in vain by assuming God's character and majesty.

The fact that Jesus was accused of blasphemy does not prove that He was God, as the charge was rooted in the religious leaders' misunderstanding and rejection of his identity. Nor does it prove that he actually blasphemed, just because he was accused of doing so. Jewish and Christian scholars have throughout history struggled with such passages of Jesus being accused of blasphemy here as it isn't quite clear what Jesus violated to be accused of blasphemy.

In Jewish law, blasphemy in the broadest sense, is any act contrary to the will of God or derogatory to his power. This can include things like cursing God or a false claim to divine authority, especially if it was perceived as challenging God's unique sovereignty (Leviticus 24:10–23 & Exodus 22:27).

However, this accusation does not equate to a divine declaration by Jesus himself. In fact, Jesus consistently distinguished himself from God, as seen in John 17:3, where he prays "And this is eternal life, that they know you, the only true God, and Jesus Christ whom you have sent" (ESV), clearly distinguishing the Father as the "only true God" and himself as the one sent by God.

Romans 9:5

Another common proof text raised from Trinitarians is from Paul's letter to the Romans:

> "To them belong the patriarchs, and from their race, according to the flesh, is the Christ, who is God over all, blessed forever. Amen." (Romans 9:5, ESV)

We need to be cautious of the translation and punctuation used. The real question here should be whether Paul says that Jesus is God over all.

The original text had no punctuation. So, as you can see, there are some instances when there is more than one way a verse can be translated without violating the grammar of the text.

Romans 9:5 is a verse that can be translated in different ways, so the context and scope of the surrounding scripture will help us determine the correct interpretation. You can see in the examples below that translators and translating committees vary greatly in their handling of Romans 9:5.

NRSV: "To them belong the patriarchs, and from them, according to the flesh, comes the Messiah, who is over all, God blessed for ever. Amen"

KJV: "Whose are the fathers, and of whom as concerning the flesh Christ came, who is over all, God blessed for ever. Amen."

NIV: "Theirs are the patriarchs, and from them is traced the human ancestry of the Messiah, who is God over all, forever praised! Amen."

Even Trinitarians such as R.S. Franks (1953) do not believe this passage can be used to prove Paul thought Jesus was God. Franks mentions that Paul never left the grounds of Judaist monotheism. Rather, there is evidence to indicate this verse as a doxology or eulogy.

"Because they exchanged the truth about God for a lie and worshiped and served the creature rather than the Creator, who is blessed forever! Amen." (Romans 1:25, ESV)

This sounds a bit like what Trinitarian Christians are doing today.

Philippians 2:6-8

"Who, though he was in the form of God, did not count equality with God a thing to be grasped, but emptied himself, by taking the form of a servant, being born in the likeness of men. And being found in human form, he humbled himself by becoming obedient to the point of death, even death on a cross." (ESV)

Jesus' (Pbuh) Divinity in the Bible?

First, many Trinitarians argue that the term "form," derived from the Greek word *morphe*, signifies Christ's inner nature as God. While Christ was fully human and had the outward form of a human, he consistently did the Father's will and exhibited a godly representation, giving him an outward appearance of Gods work.

The passage doesn't depict a God-man who is beyond our understanding; instead, it presents a man similar to us—someone who grew and aged, yet was wholly focused on God, perfectly reflecting the Father.

Moreover, after stating that Christ was in the form of God, Philippians 2:6 notes that Christ "did not count equality with God a thing to be grasped". This statement is a strong argument against the concept of the Trinity. If Jesus were God, it would be illogical to say he did not "grasp" at equality with God, as no one seeks equality with themselves. It makes sense to commend someone for not pursuing equality only if they are not actually equal.

Colossians 1:15–17

> "He is the image of the invisible God, the firstborn of all creation. For by him all things were created, in heaven and on earth, visible and invisible, whether thrones or dominions or rulers or authorities—all things were created through him and for him. And he is before all things, and in him all things hold together." (ESV)

Although written by Paul, these verses do not affirm the Trinity because they open with Christ being described as "the image (*eikon*) of the invisible God." If Christ were God, then the verse would simply say so.

The Father is plainly called 'God' in dozens of places, so this would have been a good place to say that Jesus was God. Instead, we are told that Christ is the image of God. If one thing is the image of another thing, then the 'image' and the 'original' are not the same thing.

Calling Jesus the image of God squares beautifully with his statement that, "Whoever has seen me has seen the Father." (John 14:9–10, ESV). Being firstborn does not make you God as there were many firstborns before Jesus (Exodus 4:22; Jeremiah 31:9; Psalm 2:7), and some were even gods. (Psalm 82:6)

Many people think that because Colossians 1:16 says, "For by him all things were created," Christ must be God. The entire verse must be read carefully, though, with an understanding of word usage and figures of speech. When the words *all* or *every* or *everything* are used, they are often used in a limited sense.

People use them this way in normal speech all over the world. For example, one day I felt like eating some popcorn, so I asked my parents if there was any popcorn. They said, "The kids ate all the popcorn." Obviously, the kids didn't eat all the popcorn in the world, right? But the context is referring to the popcorn in the house. Similarly, the Bible uses the word *all* in that way, too.

When Absalom was holding a council against his father David, 2 Samuel 17:14 (ESV) says that "all the men of Israel" agreed on advice. 'All' the men of Israel were not there, but the verse refers to 'all' who were there.

Jesus' (Pbuh) Divinity in the Bible?

Colossians 2:9

"For in him the whole fullness of deity dwells bodily." (ESV)

God granted Jesus authority on earth to heal, cast out demons, forgive sins, and more. Therefore, it is logical for Scripture to state that Christ had the fullness of the "divine nature" dwelling in him.

Interestingly, this same description applies to every Christian as well (2 Peter 1:4).

The assertion that Christ possesses "all the fullness" of God does not imply that he is God. Ephesians 3:19 encourages Christians to be filled with "all the fullness of God," yet no one claims that this means each Christian is God.

If Christ were indeed God, it would be contradictory to say that the fullness of God dwelt in him, since, as God, he would inherently possess the fullness of God at all times. The fact that the fullness of God could dwell in Christ suggests that he is not God. Moreover, 2 Peter 1:4 states that through God's great and precious promises, we "may participate in the divine nature."

Hebrews 7:3

"He is without father or mother or genealogy, having neither beginning of days nor end of life, but resembling the Son of God he continues a priest forever." (ESV)

Some Trinitarians propose that Melchizedek was actually Jesus Christ, citing the description of him as being without father or mother, beginning or end of life, etc. However, this interpretation misses the central point of this passage.

Understanding the Old Testament, particularly the Law of Moses, reveals why the Jews did not view Jesus as a legitimate high priest. According to the Law, only descendants of Aaron and the tribe of Levi could serve as priests, whereas Jesus came from the tribe of Judah. Hebrews addresses this issue directly: "For it is evident that our Lord was descended from Judah, and in connection with that tribe Moses said nothing about priests" (Hebrews 7:14, ESV). Therefore, Jesus cannot be Melchizedek.

Hebrews 7:3 states that Melchizedek was without father or mother and without genealogy, meaning he does not have a genealogy recorded in Scripture. In contrast, Jesus had both a father, God, and a mother, Mary, along with two genealogies—one in Matthew and one in Luke. Additionally, the passage describes Melchizedek as being "like the Son of God." If he is "like" the Son, then he cannot be the Son of God himself.

2 Peter 1:1

"...Our God and Savior Jesus Christ." (2 Peter 1:1, ESV)

It should be noted first and foremost that the books of 1 and 2 Peter are considered by scholarly consensus not to have actually been written by Peter the apostle – most specifically 2 Peter.

Even Acts 4:13 (ESV) states that Peter was "uneducated", and, considering his location and its statistics of literacy, he was most likely very poor. While Peter being a fisherman does not exclude him from writing, taking into account the historical information, it seems doubtful. Some Trinitarians try to use this verse to prove the Trinity using the Granville Sharp Rule of Greek grammar. But this verse is generally translated one of two ways:

"Our God and Savior Jesus Christ" (ESV)
"God and our Savior Jesus Christ" (KJV)

Although it is possible that the word 'God' (*theos*) here is being used in its lesser sense (i.e., in reference to a man with divine authority, (Hebrews 1:8), it is more likely that it is referring to the true God as distinct from Jesus Christ. This seems to be the context, as the next verse speaks of them separately.

Again, we are yet to find any evidence of Jesus claiming to be divine, which is quite strange. Notice the proof texts used so far do not hold up to scrutiny.

Revelation 1:8

""I am the Alpha and the Omega," says the Lord God, "who is and who was and who is to come, the Almighty."" (ESV)

These words apply to God and not to Christ. The one, "who is, and who was and who is to come" is clearly identified in the context.

"Grace to you and peace from him who is and who was and who is to come, and from the seven spirits who are before his throne, and from Jesus Christ the faithful witness, the firstborn of the dead, and the ruler of kings on earth." (Revelation 1: 4-5, ESV)

The separation between "the one who was, is and is to come" and Christ is clear. The one "who is, and who was and who is to come" is God.

This verse is made slightly more ambiguous in the King James Version because the word "God" is left out of the Greek text from which the KJV was translated. Nevertheless, modern textual research shows that it should be included, and modern versions such as the NIV do include the word "God."

Another reason why we know that this verse is in reference to God, and not to Christ is that the word "almighty" is only used of God in scripture (2 Corinthians 6:18; Revelation 4:8; 15:3; 16:7; 19:15; 21:22). In these verses, he is the only "almighty" one, there is no other.

Revelation 22:13

"I am the Alpha and the Omega, the first and the last, the beginning and the end." (ESV)

The title "the First and the Last" appears five times in the Bible: twice in Isaiah referring to God (Isa. 44:6; 48:12) and three times in Revelation concerning Jesus (Revelation 1:17; 2:8; 22:13). Trinitarians often assume that because this title is used for both the Father and Jesus, they must both be God. However, there is no biblical basis for this assumption.

A comprehensive study of Scripture shows that the same titles can apply to God, Christ, and even humans. For instance, terms like "Lord" (Romans 10:9), "Savior" (Luke 1:47), and "King of kings" (Ezra 7:12; 1 Timothy 6:14-16) are used for all three without

Jesus' (Pbuh) Divinity in the Bible?

suggesting that they are all one God. Therefore, there is no reason to conclude that the title "the First and the Last" implies they are the same God, unless Scripture explicitly states so, which it does not.

Titles like "Alpha and Omega" and "First and Last" indicate uniqueness and singularity within a category. It's also noteworthy that Jesus does not include the phrase that Trinitarians often highlight; he does not say, "there is no other God besides me," but rather states, "I am the First and the Last."

Simply claiming the title "First and Last" does not inherently make someone God. However, the phrase "there is no other God besides me" would indeed suggest divinity, yet Jesus does not assert this. He is claiming a uniqueness of being the Messiah and all the above that which no one else can be. Thus, the phrase "I am the First and the Last" signifies uniqueness within a category.

As an example, consider Hakeem Olajuwon, a renowned Muslim athlete who was the first player to win both the NBA MVP and the NBA Finals MVP in the same season (1994) while leading the Houston Rockets to their first championship. His extraordinary achievements in basketball could rightfully earn him the title "the First and the Last" in that context, as it is a remarkable feat that sets him apart in the history of the sport.

Additionally, it's inappropriate to automatically apply everything from an Old Testament passage to a New Testament context.

For example, in Hebrews 1:9, which quotes Psalm 45:7 regarding Jesus, we wouldn't apply the entire Psalm to him, as it describes a king who has a wife (Psa. 45:9). Therefore, we have no justification to do the same in Revelation 22:13. Jesus does not claim to be God in this verse, so we should not read that assumption into the text.

Isaiah 9:6

"His name shall be called Wonderful Counselor, Mighty God, Everlasting Father, Prince of Peace...." (ESV)

Jesus is not called the 'Everlasting Father' anywhere else in the Bible. Trinitarians themselves deny that Jesus is the "Everlasting Father." It is a basic tenet of Trinitarian doctrine that Christians should neither confound the Persons nor divide the Substance (Athanasius Creed).

If this is a correct translation of the scripture, then Trinitarian Christians have a real problem. However, the word *everlasting* should have been translated as *age*, and the correct translation (if this is in fact referring to Jesus as Messiah to come) would be 'father of the [coming] age.'

In the culture of the Bible, anyone who started anything or played a vital role in something was called its 'father.'

For example, because Jabal was the first one to live in a tent and raise livestock, the Bible says, "...He was the father of those who dwell in tents and have livestock." (Genesis 4:20, ESV) Because Jubal was the first inventor of musical instruments, he is called "the father of all those who play the lyre and pipe." (Genesis 4:21, ESV)

The phrase 'Mighty God' can also be better translated. As we discussed, the word *God* in the Hebrew culture had a much wider range of application than it does in ours.

Although English makes a clear distinction between 'God' and 'god,' the Hebrew language, which has only capital letters, cannot. A better translation for the English reader would be 'mighty hero.'

Our Christian friends insist there are prophecies fulfilled in the New Testament that were told in the Old Testament. But New

Jesus' (Pbuh) Divinity in the Bible?

Testament writers actually took clues and details from the Old Testament rather than actual facts and applied them to Jesus, based on their predisposed ideas and beliefs. One example of this is the suffering servant in Isaiah 53. But when studied closely, many of these supposed prophecies do not work consistently (Helms 1986).

Was Jesus Worshipped?

> "Jesus heard that they had cast him out, and having found him he said, "Do you believe in the Son of Man?" He answered, "And who is he, sir, that I may believe in him?" Jesus said to him, "You have seen him, and it is he who is speaking to you." He said, "Lord, I believe," and he worshiped him." (John 9:35–38, ESV)

It is sometimes stated that since we are to worship *only* God and we are also to worship Jesus, Jesus must be God. This argument is not valid because, although there is a special worship that is reserved just for God, we can 'worship' certain people as well. We must understand what is being said here.

In the biblical culture, the act of worship was not directed only to God. It was very common to worship, or pay homage to, men of a higher status.

This is hard to see in the English translations of the Bible. The translators usually used the same word to describe the worship of God as to bow before or pay homage to a man. The term 'worship' was used more widely then. We must reflect on the language of worship to help clarify what the central question means.

The Greek term 'proskynein' and the Hebrew word 'Shachah' is the basic meaning of 'bow down', 'prostrate', or 'obey' (Dunn 2010).

This is more clearly established in the Hebrew and Greek texts. For example, depending on which translation you are reading:

Lot 'worshipped' two strangers that came to Sodom. (Genesis 19:1)

Abraham 'worshipped' the pagan leaders of the land in which he lived. (Genesis 23:7)

Jacob 'worshipped' his older brother when they met after being apart for years. (Genesis 33:3)

Joseph had a dream that his parents and brothers 'worshipped' him. (Genesis 37:10)

Joseph's brothers 'worshipped' him. (Genesis 43:26)

Joshua fell down and 'worshipped' an angel. (Joshua 5:14)

David 'worshipped' Jonathan. (1 Samuel 20:41)

Abigail 'worshipped' David. (1 Samuel 25:41)

These scriptures sufficiently show that the word 'worship' was a part of the culture and a way of showing respect or reverence. Due to the theological stance that only God should be worshipped, translators have avoided the English word 'worship' in spite of the fact that it is clearly in the original text. It is very clear in the biblical text that men 'worshipped' men.

Danker (2011) defines '*proskynein*' as to express in attitude or gesture a submission to a high authority figure. Another close parallel to *proskynein* is the phrase to 'fall down.'

For example, the wise men "fell down and worshipped him," (Matthew 2:11, ESV) and "the elders fell down and worshipped." (Revelation 5:14, ESV) Another near synonym is '*latreuein*,' which means 'to serve.' "It is the Lord your God you shall fear. Him you shall serve and by his name you shall swear." (Deuteronomy 6:13, ESV)

Characteristic worship language includes the term *doxazein*, meaning to glorify and give glory to. This again can be used in the context of honoring someone else, such as in Matthew 6:2. as the hypocrites do in the synagogues and in the streets, that they may be praised by others." (ESV)

There is a sense, of course, in which there is a very special worship (homage, allegiance, reverent love, and devotion) to be given only to God. But there is no unique word that represents that special worship. Scripturally, this must be determined from context.

Even words like *proskuneo*, which are usually used of God, are occasionally used for showing respect to other men (Acts 10:25). But when Jesus said, "You shall worship the Lord your God, and him only shall you serve" (Luke 4:8, ESV) he was speaking of the special worship of God.

The Hebrew word *shachah* and the Greek word *proskuneo* account for more than 80 percent of the appearances of the word 'worship' in most English versions of the Bible, so these are the two words with which we want to concern ourselves with (Dunn 2010). A study of the Hebrew word *shachah* and the Greek word *proskuneo* reveals that both words mean 'to bow down'. The Hebrew word *shachah* is used to mean bowing or prostrating oneself, often before a superior or before God.

In the King James Version, a number of English words are used as translations, including: *worship* (ninety-nine times), *bow* (thirty-one times), *bow down* (eighteen times), *obeisance* (nine times), and *reverence* (five times). The Greek word *proskuneo* comes from the Greek words *pros*, (to or toward), and *kuneo* (to kiss).

> "Abraham rose and bowed [*shachah*] to the Hittites, the people of the land." (Genesis 23:7, ESV)

> "He himself [Jacob] went on before them, bowing [*shachah*] himself to the ground seven times, until he came near to his brother [Esau]." (Genesis 33:3, ESV)

> "…And Joseph's brothers came and bowed [*shachah*] themselves before him with their faces to the ground." (Genesis 42:6, ESV)

> "So the servant[a] fell on his knees, [*proskuneo*] imploring him, 'Have patience with me, and I will pay you everything.'" (Matthew 18:26, ESV)

A study of the Greek and Hebrew words and how they are translated shows something else that has misled many Christians. The three examples below are typical.

> "Then he said to Moses, "Come up to the Lord, you and Aaron, Nadab, and Abihu, and seventy of the elders of Israel, and worship [*shachah*] from afar."" (Exodus 24:1, ESV)

> "…All the people would rise up and worship [*shachah*], each at his tent door." (Exodus 33:10, ESV)

Jesus' (Pbuh) Divinity in the Bible?

> "God is spirit, and those who worship him must worship [*proskuneo*] in spirit and truth." (John 4:24, ESV)

The verses above reveal a pattern that has caused many Christians to misunderstand the word *worship*. When the Hebrew or Greek words for worship refer to men worshipping other men, the translators use the English words bow down.

However, when the act of worship is toward God or Jesus, then the translators use the English word "worship" in their Bibles. This way of translating leads the English reader to believe that only God and Jesus are worshipped. How can a person reading the English Bible be expected to know that biblical worship is not just for God and Jesus when the word *worship* is only used in reference to them? This is difficult for many readers to distinguish.

> "And they told the king, "Here is Nathan the prophet." And when he came in before the king, he bowed [*shachah*] before the king, with his face to the ground." (1 Kings 1:23, ESV)

Nathan was a prophet of God, yet he had no problem worshipping King David—that is, bowing down before him. It is perfectly appropriate to bow down (in worship) for a king.

Likewise, when Jesus met the women who had come to his tomb, they worshipped him and were correct in doing so because he was their king and they honored and respected him. The act of placing oneself facedown at the feet of the king showed respect and honor and was not polytheistic.

Jesus himself makes it very clear for us who is to be worshipped.

> "And Jesus answered him, "It is written, 'You shall worship the Lord your God, and him only shall you serve.'"" (Luke 4:8, ESV)

Here, Jesus distinguished himself from God and emphasized the oneness of the one true Lord to be worshipped.

> "And Joab fell on his face to the ground and paid homage [*shachah*]..." (2 Samuel 14:22, ESV)

> "Afterward David also arose and went out of the cave, and called after Saul, "My lord the king!" And when Saul looked behind him, David bowed [*shachah*] with his face to the earth and paid homage." (1 Samuel 24:8, ESV)

Old Testament Prophecies

In regards to Old Testament prophecies of Jesus (Pbuh), I submit there is no such explicit verse stating the name of Jesus nor his divinity as Messiah. Rather there are reasons to suggest the contrary. There are many messiahs in the Old Testament itself, as well as Sons. (Romans 8:14)

Many verses are used by Christians which usually provide no specific details of Jesus, in particular Micah 5:2, Isaiah 53, and Isaiah 7:14. Micah does not show anything specific. Zechariah 4:14 even calls him "two anointed ones." Isaiah 53 speaks of a servant eventually able to "see his offspring; he shall prolong his days."(ESV)

After studying these verses, they do not seem befitting for Jesus. There is no good reason to suggest that Jesus is prevalent throughout the Old Testament or that he was predicted as the suffering servant.

Jesus' (Pbuh) Divinity in the Bible?

The Old Testament may have predicted Jesus as the coming Messiah; however, this does not make him God.

According to Randel Helmes in his book *"Gospel Fictions"* 1988, New Testament writers looked back at passages like Isaiah 53, took it to be a prediction about Jesus and then wrote the details about Jesus to match the prediction. This is not a prophecy being fulfilled, rather the history being written as though it is fulfilling the prophecy.

Jesus has the attributes of God?

We can see that based on the above definitions of God, this cannot apply to Jesus. Jesus was unaware of things. He was ignorant of the hour to come (Mark 13:32). He was ignorant of the season for figs (Luke 8:46; Mark 11:13). If we are then told that this is only the man part or human nature of Jesus and that he has humbled himself, allowing himself to be unaware, this becomes confusing. Keep in mind God is not the author of confusion (1 Corinthians 14:33, KJV).

Jesus cannot do what God does, as Jesus was simply created. Jesus was born and had limitations. He was given authority from God in the first place (Matthew 28:18). When Jesus for example, forgave people's sins, he was given the ability and authority by God to do so (Acts 2:22), just as he has been given the power, signs, and wonders to perform miracles.

Without going into the doctrine of the Trinity, we must understand that if we define God as possessing certain qualities which then go against the qualities in which Jesus possessed, are we not unreasonable in claiming that Jesus is God?

4.3 Church Fathers on the Trinity

If the Trinity is indeed in the Bible, one would expect early Christian scholars, otherwise known as Church Fathers, to have spoken about the Trinity. Further, we would expect that Christians would hold a belief in the Trinity before the Council of Nicaea in 325AD, which defined Jesus Christ as sharing one substance (*homoousios*) with the Father?

In this section, I will examine the views of significant Christian figures from the 2nd and 3rd centuries to address this question.

As Tuggy (2016) has pointed out, there isn't a single doctrine of "the" Trinity; rather, there are various interpretations of the creedal language established by the Constantinopolitan Council of 381AD. However, as noted previously, the idea of the Trinity may be summed up in the following words (*Hastings' Dictionary of the Bible*, ed. James Hastings, Trinity, by W. H. Griffith Thomas, p. 949):

> "The Father is God, the Son is God, and the Holy Ghost is God. And yet they are not three Gods, but one God. The Godhead of the Father, and of the Son, and of the Holy Ghost is all one, the Glory equal, the Majesty co-eternal. And in this Trinity none is afore or after other: none is greater or less than another, but the whole three Persons are co-eternal together and co-equal."

Theologian Dale Tuggy (2013) has repeatedly pointed out, there is no one doctrine of "the" Trinity. Rather, there are several competing ways of interpreting the creedal language of the Constantinopolitan Council of 381. For my purpose here, when I use the phrase, "the Trinity," I'm referring to what Christian author Matt Slick specifies in the following paragraph:

Jesus' (Pbuh) Divinity in the Bible?

"God is a trinity of persons: the Father, the Son, and the Holy Spirit. The Father is not the same person as the Son; the Son is not the same person as the Holy Spirit; and the Holy Spirit is not the same person as Father [sic]. They are not three gods and not three beings. They are three distinct persons; yet, they are all the one God. Each has a will, can speak, can love, etc., and these are demonstrations of personhood. They are in absolute perfect harmony consisting of one substance. They are coeternal, coequal, and copowerful [sic]. If any one of the three were removed, there would be no God. Jesus, the Son, is one person with two natures: Divine and Human. This is called the Hypostatic Union. The Holy Spirit is also divine in nature and is self aware [sic], the third person of the Trinity."

Let us look at some of the most used quotes and sources of evidence from early church fathers which Trinitarians argue for.

1. Polycarp (70-155/160)

"O Lord God almighty... I bless you and glorify you through the eternal and heavenly high priest Jesus Christ, your beloved Son, through whom be glory to you, with Him and the Holy Spirit, both now and forever" (Ehrman, B.D. ed., 2003. The Apostolic Fathers (Vol. 2). Harvard University Press.)

First, Polycarp explicitly identifies the "Lord God Almighty" as the Father of Jesus Christ. Second, he primarily views Christ as the mediator through whom we can know God. There is no mention of concepts like person, substance, Trinity, co-equality, or co-eternity in his writings.

Ultimately, Polycarp provides no evidence of a Trinitarian belief. While he may have acknowledged the personality of the Spirit, this remains ambiguous at best.

2. Justin Martyr (100-165?)

> "For, in the name of God, the Father and Lord of the universe, and of our Savior Jesus Christ, and of the Holy Spirit, they then receive the washing with water" (First Apology 61)

This clearly references the baptismal formula from Matthew 28:19, where Jesus instructs his disciples to baptize "in the name of the Father and of the Son and of the Holy Spirit." (ESV) However, Justin adds a few phrases that elevate the Father above both Jesus and the Spirit, referring to God as "the Father and Lord of the universe." This choice of words suggests that Justin does not view the Father and Son as equal.

Furthermore, his description of "the Father and Lord of the universe" serves to distinguish God from Christ and the Holy Spirit. In the next paragraph, Justin uses a similar phrase and explicitly equates God with the Father, reinforcing the idea that he does not support a fully equal Trinitarian view.

Additionally, Eusebius of Caesarea, an early Church Father, presented a shortened version of this statement, which some scholars suggest reflects a corruption of the original context, further complicating the understanding of early Christological beliefs.

> "[T]here is pronounced over him who chooses to be born again, and has repented of his sins, the name of God the Father and Lord of the universe; he who leads to the laver the person that is to be washed calling him by this name alone. For no one can utter the name of the ineffable God…And in the name of Jesus Christ, who was crucified under Pontius Pilate, and in the name of the Holy Ghost, who through the prophets foretold all things about Jesus, he who is illuminated is washed." (First Apology 61)

Notice the distinction Justin makes between "God the Father and Lord of the universe" and Jesus Christ. He describes the former's name as ineffable, while he speaks of the latter's name without hesitation. This aligns with Justin's other writings, where he explicitly states that Jesus is "in the second place" next to God, clearly indicating a subordinate view (First Apology 8).

Given this, it's not surprising that many patristic scholars such as Dr H. R, Boer (1976) conclude that Justin did not hold a Trinitarian perspective.

3. Ignatius of Antioch (died 98/117)

> "In Christ Jesus our Lord, by whom and with whom be glory and power to the Father with the Holy Spirit for ever" (n. 7; PG 5.988).

This quotation is not actually from Ignatius himself, but from the Martyrdom of Ignatius, which scholars typically consider a later forgery and thus exclude from the Apostolic Fathers collection. Even so, this quote doesn't provide much insight into the author's beliefs. Simply mentioning Jesus, the Father, and the Holy Spirit does not necessarily prove that the author embraced the concept of the Trinity. In fact, "Ignatius" contradicts the idea of the Trinity earlier in the same work when he states:

> "Thou art in error when thou callest the daemons of the nations gods. For there is but one God, who made heaven, and earth, and the sea, and all that are in them; and one Jesus Christ, the only-begotten Son of God, whose kingdom may I enjoy."

This statement is exclusive. He identifies the one God as someone apart from the one Jesus Christ (cf. John 17.3).

> "But our Physician is the only true God, the unbegotten and unapproachable, the Lord of all, the Father and Begetter of the only-begotten Son. We have also as a Physician the Lord our God, Jesus the Christ, the only-begotten Son and Word, before time began, but who afterwards became also man, of Mary the virgin." (Ignatius to the Ephesians 7.22 (Long Recension))

The contrast is striking. The Father is described as the "only true God, the unbegotten and unapproachable, the Lord of all, the Father and Begetter", titles that are not attributed to the Son in this context. Once again, there's no mention of the Trinity, equality, essence, or eternality. In fact, this text emphasizes the differences between the Father and the Son rather than suggesting any form of unity or equality.

Jesus' (Pbuh) Divinity in the Bible?

4. Irenaeus (115-190)

"The Church, though dispersed throughout the whole world, even to the ends of the earth, has received from the apostles and their disciples this faith:... one God, the Father Almighty, Maker of heaven, and earth, and the sea, and all things that are in them; and in one Christ Jesus, the Son of God, who became incarnate for our salvation; and in the Holy Spirit, who proclaimed through the prophets the dispensations of God, and the advents, and the birth from a virgin, and the passion, and the resurrection from the dead, and the ascension into heaven in the flesh of the beloved Christ Jesus, our Lord, and His manifestation from heaven in the glory of the Father 'to gather all things in one,' and to raise up anew all flesh of the whole human race, in order that to Christ Jesus, our Lord, and God, and Savior, and King, according to the will of the invisible Father, 'every knee should bow, of things in heaven, and things in earth, and things under the earth, and that every tongue should confess; to him, and that He should execute just judgment towards all... '" (Against Heresies X.l)

While Irenaeus does refer to Jesus as God, there is no mention of the Trinity in this text. In fact, this is one of Irenaeus' strongest Unitarian statements! He identifies the one God as the Father and discusses Jesus in a separate category. The Father is portrayed as the Almighty Creator, while the Son is described as having become incarnate for our salvation.

Like Justin before him, Irenaeus sees Jesus as a lesser divinity who existed prior to his incarnation. Yet he cannot be considered a

Trinitarian, as he consistently emphasizes the Father's superiority over Jesus.

> "Both the Lord [Jesus], then, and the apostles announce as the one only God the Father, Him who gave the law, who sent the prophets, who made all things; and therefore does He say [in the parable in Matthew 22], "He sent his armies," because every man, inasmuch as he is a man, is His workmanship, although he may be ignorant of his God. For He gives existence to all; He, "who maketh His sun to rise upon the evil and the good, and sendeth rain upon the just and unjust." [Luke 15:11]" (Against Heresies IV.36.6, p. 517)

5. Tertullian (160-215)

> "We define that there are two, the Father and the Son, and three with the Holy Spirit, and this number is made by the pattern of salvation... [which] brings about unity in trinity, interrelating the three, the Father, the Son, and the Holy Spirit. They are three, not in dignity, but in degree, not in substance but in form, not in power but in kind. They are of one substance and power, because there is one God from whom these degrees, forms and kinds devolve in the name of Father, Son and Holy Spirit."
> (Adv. Prax. 23; PL 2.156-7).

By the third century, we finally see the term "trinity". While this quote may seem to strongly position Tertullian as a full-fledged Trinitarian, especially if we read it with later Trinitarian theology in mind, it's important to remember that this brief statement isn't the entirety of Tertullian's thoughts on the subject. He wrote extensively about the "trinity," so we should consider this quote in the context of his other writings.

As it turns out, Tertullian maintained a classic subordinationist view, despite giving considerable elevation to the Son and Spirit.
In another quote from the same work, it becomes clear that Tertullian sees a significant difference in substance between the Father and the Son, effectively denying the idea that they share the same substance.

> "[T]he Father is not the same as the Son, since they differ one from the other in the mode of their being. For the Father is the entire substance, but the Son is a derivation and portion of the whole, as He Himself acknowledges: "My Father is greater than I." In the Psalm His inferiority is described as being "a little lower than the angels." Thus the Father is distinct from the Son, being greater than the Son, inasmuch as He who begets is one, and He who is begotten is another; He, too, who sends is one, and He who is sent is another; and He, again, who makes is one, and He through whom the thing is made is another." (Against Praxeas 9)

Tertullian sees the Father as greater than the Son because of his origin. While Trinitarians often interpret subordinationist texts in Scripture as functional necessities arising from the incarnation, Tertullian does not view it that way.

He considers the Son to be inferior to the Father in both origin and substance. Although Tertullian does refer to the Father and the Son as being of one substance elsewhere, this is not in a Nicene sense. Instead, he means that they are both made of the same divine essence, similar to how two people share the same human nature.

6. Arius of Alexandria

I want to offer one more historical corrective, this time regarding Nicaea in 325. The typical narrative goes like this: Christians always believed in the Trinity, but when the radical innovator Arius began preaching that the Son was created rather than eternal, a great controversy erupted.

Arius is depicted as an outsider attacking the body of Christ, while heroic figures like Alexander, Athanasius, and the Cappadocians valiantly defended the faith against "Arianism." Today, when someone questions the validity of the Trinity, they're often dismissed and looked at as heretics. However, history cannot remain buried under centuries of dust, especially in our information age, where we can access the records and uncover what truly happened in the early fourth century.

Regardless of the specifics of Arius's teachings, it's clear that he was advocating a perspective that fundamentally conflicted with the views of Athanasius and other proponents of Trinitarian doctrine. Arius's belief that Christ was a created being, subordinate to God the Father, directly challenged the notion of the co-equality of the Father, Son, and Holy Spirit that would later become central to mainstream Christian theology.

While a person may disagree with Arius's conclusions, it's important to recognize that the early Church was marked by a diversity of beliefs.

According to Barnes (2019) in his work on Athanasius, states that many of the early church fathers had differing views and beliefs. Some, such as Origen, taught that Jesus was subordinate to the father. Eusebius of Caesarea believed the son was distinct from the father.

Jesus' (Pbuh) Divinity in the Bible?

Ignatius of Antioch taught that Christ was both begotten and unbegotten, using a surprising expression 'the blood of God' (Schoedel 1987).

David Gwynn, 1982, says that the issue of Christ's deity was a genuinely undecided one even after Nicaea, which explains that even after all the centuries of debates and conflicts we still have Christians with differing beliefs on who Jesus is and was.

Non-Trinitarian Church Father Quotes

To further illustrate this point that the Trinity is not readily apparent in the Bible, I have provided a short list of non-trinitarian Church Father Quotes:

Didache 9:2-3, 10:2-3 (100-200sAD)
> "We thank you, our Father, for the holy vine of David, your **CHILD**, which you have revealed through Jesus, your **CHILD**. To you be glory forever... We thank you, our Father, for the life and knowledge which you have revealed through Jesus, your **CHILD**. To you be glory forever... We thank you, holy Father, for your sacred name which you have lodged in our hearts, and for the knowledge and faith and immortality which you have revealed through Jesus, your **CHILD**. To you be glory forever. Almighty Master, 'you have created everything' for the sake of your name, and have given men food and drink to enjoy that they may thank you. But to us you have given spiritual food and drink and eternal life through Jesus, your **CHILD**."

Clement of Rome, 1 Clement 42:1-2 (80s-90sAD)
"The Apostles received the Gospel for us from the Lord Jesus Christ; Jesus Christ was sent forth from God. So then Christ is **FROM** God, and the Apostles are **FROM** Christ. Both therefore came of the will of God in the appointed order".

Clement of Rome, 1 Clement 59:4 (80s-90sAD)
"Let all the Gentiles know that You, [Father, Lord and Master, the Creator of the Universe] are the God **ALONE**, and Jesus Christ is Your Son, and we are Your people and the sheep of Your pasture."

Justin Martyr, Dialogue with Trypho, Chapter 56 (150-160sAD)
"…they [the Jews] said they had understood them [the scriptures], but that the passages adduced brought forward no proof that there is any other god or lord… **besides the Maker of all things**…"

Justin Martyr, Dialogue with Trypho, Chapter 48 (150-160sAD)
"Now assuredly, Trypho, [the proof] that this man is the Christ of God does not fail, though I be unable to prove [to you] that he **EXISTED FORMERLY** as Son of the Maker of all things, being [a] god, and was born a man by the Virgin. But since I have certainly proved that this man is the Christ of God, whoever he be, even **if I do not PROVE that he PRE-EXISTED**,"

Irenaeus, Against Heresies, Book 2 Chapter 6 (175-189AD)
"How, again, could either the angels, OR the creator of the world [Jesus Christ], have been ignorant of the Supreme God, seeing THEY were **His PROPERTY and His CREATURES**, and were

contained by Him? He might indeed have been invisible to them on account of His superiority, but He could by no means have been unknown to them on account of His providence".

Irenaeus, Against Heresies, Book 2 Chapter 30 (175-189AD)
"...there is one only God, the Creator — He who is above every Principality, and Power, and Dominion, and Virtue; He is the Father, He is God, He the Founder, He the Maker, He the Creator, who made those things by Himself, that is, through His Word and His Wisdom.... **He is the Father of our Lord Jesus Christ**..."

Clement of Alexandria, The Stromata, Book 5, Chapter 13 (180-215AD)
"They were misled by what is said in the book of Wisdom; "He pervades and passes through all by reason of His purity", since they did not understand that this was said of Wisdom, which was the first of the **CREATION of God**".

Tertullian, Against Praxeas, Chapter 4
"...we have been already able to show that the Father and the Son are two separate Persons, not only by the mention of their separate names as Father and the Son, but also by the fact that He who delivered up the kingdom, and he to whom it is delivered up — and in like manner, He who subjected (all things), and he to whom they were subjected — must necessarily **be two different Beings**".

Tertullian, Against Praxeas, Chapter 12

"…I ask you how it is possible for a Being who is merely and absolutely One and Singular, to speak in plural phrase, saying, 'Let us make man in our own image, and after our own likeness;' whereas He ought to have said, 'Let me make man in my own image, and after my own likeness,' as being a unique and singular Being? …He is either deceiving or amusing us in speaking plurally, if He is One only and singular… **was it because He was AT ONCE the FATHER, THE SON, AND THE SPIRIT, that He spoke TO HIMSELF in plural terms, making HIMSELF PLURAL on that very account? NO**, it was because He had already His Son close at His side, as a second Person, His own Word, and a third Person also, the Spirit in the Word, that He purposely adopted the plural phrase, 'Let us make;' and, 'in our image;' and, 'become as one of us'".

Origen, Against Celsus, Book 8, Chapters 26-27 (200-250s AD)

"…our duty is to pray to the Most High **God Alone, AND to the Only-begotten**, the First-born of the whole creation, and to ask him as our High Priest to present the prayers which ascend to him from us, to his God and our God, to his Father and the Father of those who direct their lives according to His word".

Hippolytus of Rome, Apostolic Tradition (200s AD)

"We give you thanks, O God, through your beloved Servant Jesus Christ, whom at the end of time **you did send to us** [as] a Saviour and Redeemer and the Messenger of your counsel".

"Thus God the Father, the Founder and Creator of all things, who **ONLY** knows no beginning, invisible, infinite, immortal, eternal, is one God; ... **WHEN He WILLED** it, the Son, the Word, was born... in the substance of the power put forth by God... since he was begotten of the Father, is always in the Father..."

Ignatius of Antioch, Epistle to the Philadelphians (longer version), Chapter VI

"If anyone confesses Christ Jesus the Lord, but denies the God of the law and of the prophets, saying that the Father of Christ is not the Maker of heaven and earth, he has not continued in the truth any more than his father the devil, and is a disciple of Simon Magus, not of the Holy Spirit."

Ignatius of Antioch, Epistle to the Philippians, Chapter II.

"**There is then one God and Father, and not two or three**; One who is; and there is no other besides Him, the only true [God]. For "the Lord thy God," saith [the Scripture], "is one Lord." And again, "Hath not one God created us? Have we not all one Father?""

Irenaeus of Lyons, Against Heresies, Book I. Chapter X. 1.

"The rule of truth which we hold, is, that there is one God Almighty, who made all things by His Word, and fashioned and formed, out of that which had no existence, all things which exist. Thus saith the Scripture, to that effect: "By the Word of the Lord were the heavens established, and all the might of them, by the spirit of His mouth." And again, "**All things were made by Him, and without Him was nothing made.**""

Theophilus of Antioch, Theophilus to Autolycus, Book II. Chapter XXXIV.

"But God at least, the Father and Creator of the universe, did not abandon mankind, but gave a law, and sent holy prophets to declare and teach the race of men, that each one of us might awake and understand that **there is one God**."

Hippolytus of Rome, Against the Heresy of One Noetus, 3.

"For it is right, in the first place, to expound the truth that **the Father is one God**, "of whom is every family," "by whom are all things, of whom are all things, and we in Him.""

Lactantius, The Divine Institutes, Chapter VII.

"I have, as I think, sufficiently taught by arguments, and confirmed by witnesses, that which is sufficiently plain by itself, that there is **one only King of the universe, one Father, one God**."

Cyril of Jerusalem, The Father (Lecture VIII)

"But worship thou **One God** the Almighty, the Father of our Lord Jesus Christ."

Maximinus, Debate with Augustine

"**I believe that there is one God the Father** who has received life from no one **AND** that there is **one Son who has received from the Father his being and his life so that he exists** and that there is one Holy Spirit, the Paraclete, who enlightens and sanctifies our souls. I state this on the basis of the scriptures."

Eusebious of Caesarea, Letter on the Council of Nicaea
[In his letter on the Council of Nicaea, Eusebious indicates that a simi-Arian could still affirm the creed. He also indicates that you could also believe the expressed logos was not eternal and still be in conformance with the creed. The purpose of the Council of Nicaea was to determine whether or not the son is of the same essence as the Father and in what way the son was begotten. Eusebious makes no mention of the creed teaching a tri-personal God while suggesting that it is inclusive of Semi-Arianism.]

Church Fathers on Jesus being Created

In this section, I present some Church Fathers who, despite differing views, expressed beliefs that align with the notion of Jesus as a creation of God. While some early church fathers acknowledged the pre-existence of Christ, they maintained that Jesus was a distinct and subordinate being, challenging the core tenets of Trinitarianism.

Similarly, other church fathers' teachings suggested a hierarchy within the Godhead, where the Son was not fully equal to the Father. These perspectives, though nuanced and varied, collectively oppose the traditional Trinitarian view of Jesus as eternally begotten and fully divine.

This variety among early Christian thinkers shows just how complex the debates about who Jesus were. Some of their beliefs really line up with Unitarian views, focusing on the idea that Jesus was created by God rather than being fully divine like the Trinitarian perspective suggests.

Clement of Alexandria

"Now being differs from becoming, as the cause from the effect, the father from the son. For the same thing cannot both be and become at the same instant; and consequently it is not the cause of itself. Things are not causes of one another, but causes to each other. For the splenetic affection preceding is not the cause of fever, but of the occurrence of fever; and the fever which precedes is not the cause of spleen, but of the affection increasing." **(Stromata, 8.9)**

Hippolytus

"And thus there appeared another beside Himself. But when I say another, **I do not mean that there are two Gods**, but that it is only as light of light, or as water from a fountain, or as a ray from the sun. For there is but one power, which is from the All; and **the Father is the All, from whom comes this Power, the Word. And this is the mind which came forth into the world, and was manifested as the Son of God. All things, then, are by Him, and He alone is of the Father.** Who then adduces a multitude of gods brought in, time after time? For all are shut up, however unwillingly, to admit this fact, that the All runs up into one." **(Against Noetus, 11)**

Justin Martyr

"For I would not say that the dogma of that heresy which is said to be among you is true, or that the teachers of it can prove that [God] spoke to angels, or that the human frame was the workmanship of angels. **But this Offspring, which was truly brought forth from the Father, was with the Father before all the creatures, and the Father communed with Him**; even as the Scripture by Solomon has made clear, that He whom Solomon calls Wisdom, was begotten as a Beginning before all His creatures and as Offspring by God." **(Dialogue with Trypho, Ch 62)**

Origen

"**For the Son of God, the First-born of all creation**, although He seemed recently to have become incarnate, is not by any means on that account recent. For the holy Scriptures know Him to be the most ancient of all the works of creation; for it was to Him that God said regarding the creation of man, "Let Us make man in Our image, after Our likeness."" **(Commentary on John, 2.6)**

Hippolytus

"**God, subsisting alone, and having nothing contemporaneous with Himself, determined to create the world**. And conceiving the world in mind, and willing and uttering the word, He made it; and straightway it appeared, formed as it had pleased Him." **(Against Noetus, 10)**

Hypostatic Union

According to New Testament scholar James White, Jesus had to be fully man in order for the atonement to have any meaning and fully God because God cannot cease to be God.

This is theologically known as the hypostatic union—Jesus being one person, with two natures: fully divine and fully human. Trinitarianism presents an internal inconsistency by asserting that two persons besides the Father are also infinite, uncreated, and absolutely eternal, diminishing the perfection and supremacy of the God.

Moreover, this hypostatic union Christians speak of having the second person of the Trinity united with human nature in the person of Christ also conflicts with the concept of Divine immensity.

Scripture frequently describes Jesus as a man, distinct from and subordinate to God (Rees 1823). Yet Trinitarians assert that divine names, attributes, works, and worship are equally ascribed to him.

Thus, they claim that at the incarnation, Christ assumed human nature into union with his divine nature, forming one person with two natures: fully God and fully man. This also challenges the coherence of God's unchanging nature and absolute unity.

Emergence of Later Christologies

The evolution of Christology shows a gradual shift away from the original Unitarian beliefs of the 1st century, where Jesus was seen mainly as a prophet and a created being, focusing on his humanity.

By the 2nd century, Subordinationist views started to emerge, introducing the idea of a hierarchy within the Godhead and suggesting that Jesus was subordinate to the Father, which complicated the earlier understanding.

Then, in the 4th century, the formal doctrine of the Trinity took shape, pushed by figures like Athanasius, who insisted on Jesus' full divinity and equality with the Father. This marked a big departure from those earlier, simpler beliefs.

By the 7th century, the orthodox Trinitarian view became firmly established, reflecting a corruption of the initial Unitarian perspective and introducing complexities that strayed from the original teachings about Jesus' true nature.

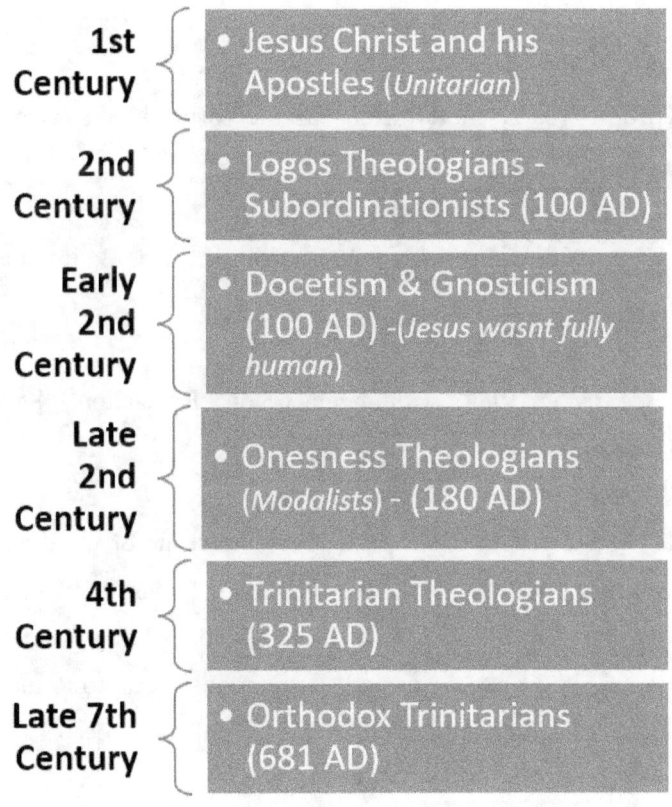

Chapter 4 Jesus' (Pbuh) Divinity in the Bible?

References:

Aquinas, T., 2010. Summa Theologica: Translated by Fathers of the English Dominican Province.

Barnes, P, 2019. Athanasius of Alexandria: His Life and Impact (Early Church Fathers). Christian Focus Publications

Biblical Unitarian (n.d.) Biblical Unitarian. Available at: http://www.biblicalunitarian.com/ (Accessed: 10 January 2025).
Boyd, G., 1992. Oneness Pentecostals and the Trinity. Baker Books.

Boer, H.R., 1976. A short history of the early church. Wm. B. Eerdmans Publishing.

Bruce, F.F., 1988. The book of Acts (Vol. 5). Wm. B. Eerdmans Publishing.

Bullinger, E.W., 1984. Commentary on Revelation. Kregel Publications.

Buzzard, A. and Hunting, C.F., 1999. The doctrine of the Trinity: Christianity's self-inflicted wound. Intl Scholars Pubns.

Buzzard, A.F., 2007. Jesus was not a Trinitarian: A Call to Return to the Creed of Jesus. Restoration Fellowship.

Jesus' (Pbuh) Divinity in the Bible?

Charles Freeman, The Closing Of The Western Mind (London: Heinemann, 2002) and also AD381: Heretics, Pagans And The Christian State (London: Pimlico, 2008).

Danker, F.W., 2000. A Greek-English lexicon of the New Testament and other early Christian literature. Biblical Interpretation (ed. JH Hayes; 2 vols.; Nashville: Abingdon, 1999), 2.

Dunn, J.D., 2010. Did the first Christians worship Jesus?: the New Testament evidence. Westminster John Knox Press.

Ehrman, B.D. ed., 2003. The Apostolic Fathers (Vol. 2). Harvard University Press

Finnegan, S 2011, Five major problems with the Trinity, 28 August, online video, https://www.youtube.com/watch?v=HPOQp3f9XMo.

Michael Holmes, The Apostolic Fathers: Greek Texts and English Translations, Third Edition (Grand Rapid: Baker Academic, 2007).

Helms, R., 1986. Fiction in the Gospels. RJ Hoffman and G. A. Larue (Eds.), Jesus in myth and history.

Holmes, S., Molnar, P., McCall, T., Fiddes, P. and Sexton, J. (n.d.). Two views on the doctrine of the Trinity.

Kirk, J. R. D. 2016. A Man Attested by God: The Human Jesus of the Synoptic Gospels, William B. Eerdmans Publishing Company.

Klein, W.W., 2010. How on Earth Did Jesus Become a God. Agenda.

Obstat, N., 1909. The Catholic Encyclopedia.

Lamson, A., 2022. The Church of the First Three Centuries. BoD–Books on Demand.

Milavec, A., 2016. The Didache: Text, translation, analysis, and commentary. Liturgical Press.

Osiek, C., 1987. Ignatius of Antioch: A Commentary on the Letters of Ignatius of Antioch.

Price, R., 2007. Theotokos: The Title and its Significance in Doctrine and Devotion. Mary: The Complete Resource.

R. S. Franks, The Doctrine of the Trinity, (Gerald Duckworth and Co., London, 1953).

Rees, Thomas. *Objections to the Doctrine of the Trinity*. LL.D. F.A.S. London, 1823.

Roberts, A. ed., 2007. The Ante-Nicene Fathers: The Writings of the Fathers Down to AD 325 Volume I-the Apostolic Fathers with Justin Martyr and Irenaeus (Vol. 1). Cosimo, Inc..

Ross, C.R., 1989. Common Sense Christianity. Occam Pub.

Segal, A.F., 1977. Two powers in heaven: Early Rabbinic reports about Christianity and Gnosticism (Vol. 25). Brill Archive.

Slick, Matt, "Early Trinitarian Quotes," carm.org/early-trinitarian-quotes, accessed on March 3, 2019.

Slick, Matt, "The Trinity Chart," carm.org/trinity, accessed on March 26, 2019.

Stenschke, C.W., 2005. Review of *The Gospel of John: A Commentary* by Craig Keener. *Jahrbuch für evangelikale Theologie* 19.

Sproul, R. (2011). What is the Trinity?. Orlando, Fla.: Reformation Trust Pub.

For Tuggy's taxonomy, see Tuggy, Dale, "Trinity," The Stanford Encyclopedia of Philosophy (Winter 2016 Edition), Edward N. Zalta (ed.), plato.stanford.edu/archives/win2016/entries/trinity.

Tuggy, D., 2013. Trinity. Lulu. com.

White, J.R., 1998. The Forgotten Trinity. Baker Books.

Wright, D.F., 2001. The Formation of the Doctrine of the Trinity in the Early Church. Reformation and Revival, 10.

5

"Paul, a servant of Christ Jesus, called to be an apostle and set apart for the gospel of God." (Romans 1:1, NIV)

Paul, an Apostle?

"O you who have faith! Be Allah's helpers, just as Jesus son of Mary said to his disciples, 'Who will be my helpers for Allah's sake?' The Disciples said, 'We will be Allah's helpers!' So a group of the Children of Israel believed, and a group disbelieved. Then We strengthened the faithful against their enemies, and they came to prevail [over them]." (Qur'an 61:14)

Paul, an Apostle?

5.1 Who is Paul?

Formerly known as Saul, Paul was a Jew from the tribe of Benjamin in Tarsus near today's modern Turkey. We do not know his exact birth; however, the scholarly consensus suggests he was born around the same time as Jesus (Pbuh), with his death around 62–64AD (Sanders 2011).

He grew up in a Greco-Roman culture, and, as a Roman citizen, was often capable of moving from place to place. He would have possibly been able to speak Hebrew, Aramaic, and Latin. Paul would have definitely spoken the international language at the time, which was Koine Greek. He was for a long time a very strong Pharisee, according to Tabor and Dean (2012).

The Pharisees were one of the three major religious movements of Judaism—Saducees, Pharisees, and Essenes. Pharisees believed in the resurrection (1 Corinthians 15), as did Paul, and observed "extremely zealous" traditions (Galatians 1:14). The most extraordinary title ascribed to Paul was that of persecutor.

Comparing Paul and Jesus allows for such drastic differences evident throughout both of their lives. Paul is definitely one of the most influential people in the history of Christianity after Jesus himself.

Paul was once an active persecutor of early Christians until, on his way to Damascus in Syria, was called into a 'vision' or spiritual encounter with Jesus and reconsidered (Acts 9). He ultimately converted from a persecutor to follower/apostle of Christ. This would likely have been in the year 33AD (Tabor and Dean 2012).

Paul often wrote letters that were later collected, edited, and published. Not all were published, but many were. These letters provide great insight into Paul's characteristics during his life. In the New Testament, Paul's letters are quite predominating (Sanders 2001).

Of the twenty-seven books, thirteen are thought to have been written by Paul despite the forgery and pseudonymous claims. Whether this is true or false, he remains an integral part of the New Testament and Christianity historically. He saw himself as a spokesperson for Jesus and thought this stage of his life to be 'Gods plan for humanity.' Having said all that, we must ask some important questions in respect to the divine light Paul experienced.

We often refer to Paul as 'Apostle Paul', but what or who gave Paul the authority to be claimed an apostle? Did he really see Jesus on the road to Damascus?

"And no wonder, for Satan himself masquerades as an angel of light." (2 Corinthians 11:14, NIV).

Interestingly, Paul warned that even the devil is able to appear as light to be deceitful. In order to determine if Paul was indeed an apostle, we can begin with the question of whether Paul was in agreement with Jesus.

Paul, an Apostle?

5.2 Paulianity or Christianity?

Timeline of major events

Major Event	Time Period
Rule of Herod the Great	4 BC
Rule of Augusts, first emperor of Rome	AD 14
Birth of John the Baptizer, Jesus and Paul	3–5 BC
Rule of Tiberius, second emperor of Rome	AD 14–37
Execution of John the baptizer	AD 29
Execution of Jesus	AD 30
Rule of Caligula emperor of Rome	AD 37–41
Paul Converts to the sect of the Nazarenes	AD 37
Rule of Claudius	AD 41–54
Rule of Nero, fifth emperor of Rome	AD 54–68
Paul's execution	AD 65

The world of the New Testament was the world of the Roman Empire, the Greek language (Hellenism) and civilization, and the Jewish religion and culture. Hellenism, comes from the Greek word *hellenismos* which means imitation of the Greeks. This 'Hellenistic' period can be dated from 323 BC, the death of Alexander the Great, to the end of the New Testament period of 150AD (Telford 2002).

Understanding the political and cultural backgrounds is vital, as these worlds are the background of the New Testament, beginning with the Roman Empire.

At its very peak, the Roman Empire had encompassing areas, such as Spain, France, Greece, the Middle East, and the North African coastal regions totaling 2.75 million square kilometers. Founded, according to legend, by Romulus in 753 BC, this little city of Rome slowly but dominantly influenced the Mediterranean world (Ehrman 2000).

After the death of Augustus in 14AD, Augustus' adopted son, Tiberius, became his successor until 37AD. Under this reign, Pontius Pilate was elected governor of Judaea in 26AD. Pontius Pilate was the governor in the time of Jesus (Pbuh). Son and nephew of Tiberius, Gaius Caligula, succeeded him in 37AD. After him, Caligula's uncle Claudius, the conqueror of Britain, took over from 41–54AD.

Fast forward to the most famous emperor of the New Testament period, Nero—the nephew, stepson, and adopted son of Claudius. Initiating the first officially sanctioned Roman persecution against the Christians, Nero reigned from 54–68AD. It was under the rule of the Emperor Nero that Paul went under trial in Rome and was ultimately executed, around 65AD (Telford 2002).

More than just understanding his life, it is important to understand not only who Paul was, but also who Paul *thought* he was.

Paul envisioned himself in God's plan fulfilling the prophets' and perhaps Jesus' expectations (Romans 1:5)—a minister of Jesus to the Gentiles (Romans 15:6). However, it seems as though Apostolic Christianity, which predates Paul, came to be and developed independently of him, by those who were not only familiar with Jesus but spent time with him personally.

This kind of Christianity was in sharp contrast to Paul's ideas or version of Christianity (Tabor and Dean 2012). Paul's lost and distorted Christianity faded slowly during Paul's own time.

It was not until the death of James and subsequently the destruction of Jerusalem (AD 70) that Jerusalem began to lose its influence as the center of the Jesus movement (Dunn 1991). Interestingly, the production and final editing of the New Testament itself in the second century supported Paul's version of Christianity, ensuring the marginalization and near death of the original Christianity within orthodoxy (Tabor 2013).

By the fourth century, the Roman Church declared any surviving forms of Jewish Christianity as heresy, forbidding citizens to follow any kind of observances (Brown 2012). But it was this Jewish Christianity that Jesus was born into and fulfilled (Matthew 5:17).

The modified version of Christianity that emerged in the late Roman Empire was heavily based upon and influenced by the experiences of Paul. Put simply, Christianity as we know it, is Paul, and Paul, as we know him, is Christianity (Tabor and Dean 2012). In fact, the bulk of the New Testament is dominated by his theological visions and ideas. The main factors that Paul expresses in his letters are as follows (Wilson 2008):

- Forgiveness of sins through the blood of Christ
- Jesus as God's divine son
- Jesus' sacrificial death on the cross
- Jesus' resurrection from the dead

Attempting to envision a Christianity before Paul is extremely difficult without those factors. Nonetheless, the evidence indicates that Christianity's most crucial doctrines were introduced by Paul. So what did Christianity look like before Paul?

The original followers of Jesus—led by James, Peter, and John, son of Zebedee—continued to live as Jews. They observed the Torah and worshipped in the Temple at Jerusalem. They remembered and honored their Teacher Jesus, the Messiah.

They neither worshipped nor divinized Jesus as the Son of God nor as a sacrificial savior who died for our sins on the cross as the perfect being. They did not accept any of these ideas.

By contrast, their message was simple and mainly focused on the expectation of the kingdom soon to come (as proclaimed by John the Baptist). In the meantime, Jews and gentiles were to repent for their sins and turn to God righteously, as instructed in Ezekiel 18:20 and Isaiah 43:25 (Dunn, 2003).

Paul had no physical contact with the historical Jesus. In fact, although possible, he probably never heard him preach. He was not part of the twelve disciples whom Jesus chose, which undermines Paul's claim to authority.

Furthermore, Paul expressed he had little contact with the successors of Jesus in Jerusalem. By reading Paul's letters, we come to understand that he was up against agents from Jerusalem who were confident and convinced that he was spreading deviant messages.

"You foolish Galatians." (Galatians 3:1, NIV)

"For if someone comes to you and preaches a Jesus other than the Jesus we preached…" (2 Corinthians 11:4, NIV)

"I do not think I am in the least inferior to those "super-apostles."" (2 Corinthians 11:5, NIV)

Paul, an Apostle?

It is evident that Paul had some adversaries, and Paul and those adversaries thought of each other as deviant. Unfortunately, all we have remaining are Paul's writings, but none of his opponents' writings. Paul was the winner, and all we have are references from Paul to the agents against him.

But why should we put Paul above the others? Paul very rarely cites or refers to Jesus' teachings when defending his arguments against his opponents. This leads to an important question: What would we know of Jesus if we only had Paul's letters?

5.3 Peter, John, James, and the thirteenth Apostle

To the surprise of many, the link between the teachings of Paul and historical Jesus is weak. In his letters, Paul focuses on the post-death Jesus, communicating with him through visions. This reinforces the idea of Paul founding a separate Christianity not centered on Christ's original teachings.

According to Paul, the movement of Jesus included James (Galatians 1:19), the brother of Jesus, as well as Peter and John (Hengel 2010). In Matthew 16:18, Jesus mentions Peter as the rock on which he will build his Church.

Peter, John, and James knew Jesus best, were around Jesus throughout his ministry, spending personal time with him, and understood his values, teachings, and practices.

According to Paul, he only contacted these followers of Jesus years later, and even then, only briefly, which is strange behavior for a recent convert via a spiritual encounter (Galatians 1 & 2).

This should cause us to pause and consider whether Paul was an authentic apostle.

Paul is attempting to argue that his Gospel comes from Jesus directly. However, in the process of arguing this he is actually admitting that his Gospel is different to the gospel of the disciples (Galatians 1:6-10). He claims his Gospel is directly from Jesus, yet his teachings are different to the teachings of Jesus' actual students.

Below is a list of some of the letters associated with Paul. We have seven genuine letters of Paul, the Pauline authorship of three additional writings disputed by scholars, and three others that are most likely pseudonymous—that is, falsely attributed to Paul.

Letters of Paul		
Undisputed Pauline epistles	**Deutero-Pauline** (possibly pseudonymous)	**Pastoral Epistles** (likely pseudonymous)
Roman 1 Corinthians 2 Corinthians Galatians Philippians 1 Thessalonians Philemon	Ephesians Colossians 2 Thessalonians	1 Timothy 2 Timothy Titus

Of the twenty-seven books that finally came to comprise the New Testament, traditionally about fourteen were attributed to Paul or his

Paul, an Apostle?

admirers. The Pauline corpus includes the seven letters widely accepted as authentic by New Testament scholars: Romans, 1 and 2 Corinthians, Galatians, Philippians, 1 Thessalonians and Philemon.

Then there are the disputed letters of Ephesians, Colossians, 2 Thessalonians, 1 and 2 Timothy, and Titus. Their claim to authenticity is widely challenged in New Testament scholarship. In addition, there is the letter to the Hebrews, long ascribed to Paul in popular tradition even though it is actually anonymous (Bray, 2019).

Finally, there are the two volumes of Luke – Acts. This influential account of the life of Jesus and of the early church is usually considered to have been written by someone wishing to affirm the validity and the providential character of the Pauline mission.

As mentioned previously, Paul rarely mentions anything about the historical Jesus. In total, Paul provided us with five main points of information about Jesus.

1. He was born of a woman. (Galatians 4:4)

2. He was a Jew under the law. (Galatians 4:4)

3. He was a descendant of David. (Romans 1:3)

4. He had brothers. (1 Corinthians 9:5)

5. He was crucified and he died. (1 Corinthians 15:3)

Every man was born of a woman, so that is not exactly fascinating. By Paul's account, Jesus was a Jewish male, human, and descendant of King David. His writings, however, fail to tell us anything else about the specific aspects of Jesus' life. For example, he made no mention of the circumstances of his birth, his upbringing, or the geographical location of Jesus' ministry.

Paul made no mention of Jesus' extended family other than his brothers—not his parents, sisters, cousins, or close associates like Mary Magdalene, who helped fund the Jesus mission—nor does he trace Jesus' movements from Galilee to Jerusalem, his dramatic last week in Jerusalem, or the circumstances surrounding his death.

Goulder (1995) in his book *St Peter vs. St Paul* demonstrates that there was never a single united church. In fact, from 30AD, there were two missions: one run from Jerusalem with Peter, John, and James, and the other run by Paul from various centers. They of course agreed about the significance of Jesus, but they disagreed about many other issues such as Jesus' divinity and his resurrection from the dead. We see this tension in the following scripture:

> "Then after fourteen years, I went up again to Jerusalem, this time with Barnabas. I took Titus along also. I went in response to a revelation and, meeting privately with those esteemed as leaders, I presented to them the gospel that I preach among the Gentiles. I wanted to be sure I was not running and had not been running my race in vain. Yet not even Titus, who was with me, was compelled to be circumcised, even though he was a Greek. This matter arose because some false believers had infiltrated our ranks to spy on the freedom we have in Christ Jesus and to make us slaves." (Galatians 2: 1–4, NIV)

The 'false brethren' were Christians from Jerusalem who traveled to see if the Church in Antioch was observing the Jewish Law, something Jesus held up most importantly. They raised an objection, and Paul refused to change his ways, calling them false brethren. Paul

Paul, an Apostle?

also saw John, James, and Peter and spoke of them in a sarcastic way (Goulder 1995), as we see in Galatians 2: 6, 9:

> "As for those who were held in high esteem—whatever they were makes no difference to me; God does not show favoritism—they added nothing to my message... James, Cephas and John, those esteemed as pillars". (NIV)

Not only was there tension between Paul and Peter, but according to Acts, Paul seems to have engaged in hypocrisy near the end of his career. Paul arrived in Jerusalem and appeared before James and the elders of the church. James heard a rumor that Paul was teaching Jews that they could ultimately disregard the Torah, so James wanted to confront him about it:

> "You see, brother, how many thousands of Jews have believed, and all of them are zealous for the law. They have been informed that you teach all the Jews who live among the Gentiles to turn away from Moses, telling them not to circumcise their children or live according to our customs. What shall we do? They will certainly hear that you have come, so do what we tell you. There are four men with us who have made a vow. Take these men, join in their purification rites and pay their expenses, so that they can have their heads shaved. Then everyone will know there is no truth in these reports about you, but that you yourself are living in obedience to the law." (Acts 21:20–24, NIV)

James subsequently went on to say the rumor was false and that Paul himself was aligned with the elders in understanding and participated in the purification ceremony in the Temple, which involved an offering of sacred areas for the Jews. Paul was surprisingly silent at this, and neither confirmed nor denied the rumor; however, it seems as though he denied it, as he went along with the purification.

So, we must ask our Christian brethren the following; If a new covenant was made with Jesus no longer requiring the Old Testament laws and regulations, why did Paul himself perform sacrifices after Jesus died on the cross?

> "The next day Paul took the men and purified himself along with them. Then he went to the temple to give notice of the date when the days of purification would end and the offering would be made for each of them." (Acts 21:26, NIV)

According to Kelhoffer, 2014 in his work 'Conceptions of "Gospel" and legitimacy in early Christianity' states on page 321:

> "The author of James objects to some type of, or a misunderstanding of, Pauline theology in regard to "faith and works" (James 2:14-26)."

Several theological differences between Paul and "James" notwithstanding, the latter can be interpreted as not only opposing but also extending and refining several aspects of Paul's theology in Galatians and Romans.

Christians usually respond that Paul maintained situational ethics according to his circumstances, but that seems to contradict what he stood for. Paul seemed to be double-sided depending on the circumstances. For instance, Paul would be under the Torah, but when he was with Gentiles, he lived as a Gentile (1 Corinthians 9:20–21).

Paul, an Apostle?

James and the rest of the Jewish followers of Jesus were zealous for the Torah, but the author of Acts seems to harmonize the image of Paul and the close followers of Jesus throughout the episodes.

Barrie Wilson, a professor of Humanities and Religious Studies at York University Toronto, goes to show that Paul often contradicted Jesus' teachings (2008).

"To the married I give this command (not I, but the Lord)..." (1 Corinthians 7:10, NIV)

"To the rest I say this (I, not the Lord)..." (1 Corinthians 7:12, NIV)

Paul's teachings really have to be scrutinized given how passionately he claims to be conveying the word of God.

"I think that it is good..." (1 Corinthians 7:26, NIV)

"In my judgment..." (1 Corinthians 7:40, NIV)

Are these the inspired words of God, or are they Paul's opinions and thoughts? Could they be both? Take for example 1 Corinthians 1:14-16:

"I thank God that I did not baptize any of you except Crispus and Gaius, so no one can say that you were baptized in my name. (Yes, I also baptized the household of Stephanas; beyond that, I don't remember if I baptized anyone else.)" (NIV)

Paul appears to have made a mistake but then corrected it by mentioning who he also baptized. Even though the mistake was corrected, it remains in the Bible. So, is this mistake and correction also inspired by God?

The aim here is not to belittle the Christian faith. The objective is to know whether the Christianity we know today is really based upon the authentic teachings of Jesus (Pbuh) himself, or if it has been changed into a different religion by Paul.

We must understand that Jesus (Pbuh) was a Jew and lived under Mosaic law. He did not come to abolish the law but to fulfill it.

"For truly I tell you, until heaven and earth disappear, not the smallest letter, not the least stroke of a pen, will by any means disappear from the Law until everything is accomplished. Therefore anyone who sets aside one of the least of these commands and teaches others accordingly will be called least in the kingdom of heaven, but whoever practices and teaches these commands will be called great in the kingdom of heaven." (Matthew 5:18–20, NIV)

Paul on the other hand seemed to claim that Jesus had abolished the law:

"For he himself is our peace, who has made the two groups one and has destroyed the barrier, the dividing wall of hostility, by setting aside in his flesh the law with its commands and regulations." (Ephesians 2:14-15, NIV)

Paul, an Apostle?

In his letters, Paul seemed to suggest Christians were no longer required to follow the Law of Moses, which completely contradicts earlier statements by Jesus, which can be found in Matthew 23:2–3:

"The teachers of the law and the Pharisees sit in Moses' seat. So you must be careful to do everything they tell you." (NIV)

To that same effect, he said in Matthew 28:20 "...And teaching them to obey everything I have commanded you." (NIV)

Jesus stated that we should obey the law and *not* abolish it as Paul indicated. We must take into question Paul's authority, as there was a difference between him and the early disciples of Jesus.

Interestingly, if we ignore Paul's writings, we find that Muslims are closer to Jesus' biblical teachings than Christians are. It goes without saying that Jews would also be closer to Jesus than Christians are.

General Commands	Christian	Muslim	Jesus
Drinking alcohol/drunkenness (Leviticus 10:9, Qur'an 2:219)	Yes	No	No
Eating swine (Leviticus 11:7, Qur'an 2:173)	Yes	No	No
Circumcision (Luke 2:21)	No	Yes	Yes
Halal/Kosher (Leviticus 11, Qur'an 16:115)	No	Yes	Yes
Ablution / Prostrate prayer (2 Samuel 12:20, Matthew 26:39)	No	Yes	Yes
Head covering / clothing (1 Timothy 2:9, Qur'an 24:31)	No	Yes	Yes

Greeting of peace (Matthew 10:12, Luke 24:36)	No	Yes	Yes
Usury (Deuteronomy 23:19, Qur'an 2:275)	Yes	No	No
Pilgrimage (Luke 2:41, Qur'an 22)	No	Yes	Yes
Strict Monotheistic Unitarianism (Mark 12:29, Qur'an 112)	No	Yes	Yes

5.4 Lost Paulitics

Paul's significant influence on the development of Christian doctrine has led some scholars to argue that Christianity, as it evolved, reflects more of Pauline theology—or "Paulianity"—than the original teachings of Jesus (Tabor, 2012).

Paul introduced and expanded theological concepts such as justification by faith, the universality of salvation, and the abolition of certain Jewish laws. He shifted the focus from the Jewish roots of Jesus' message to a more universalist, Gentile-oriented framework.

Jesus was adhering to the Mosaic laws and, for example, never ate pork as he himself stated very clearly in Matthew 5:17, 18 "Do not think that I have come to abolish the Law... not the smallest letter, not the least stroke of a pen, will by any means disappear from the Law". (NIV)

This seems to be a very different perspective from traditional Christian belief, which holds that Jesus fulfilled the Law through his death on the cross, thus removing the need to follow it anymore.

Paul, an Apostle?

However, if Jesus truly believed that the Law no longer applied, why didn't he demonstrate this by eating pork, for example? Why is it Paul who supports this view, rather than Jesus himself?

These shifts marked a dramatic transformation in early Christian beliefs, often prioritizing Paul's interpretations over the historical teachings and practices of Jesus.

While seven of the 13 letters traditionally attributed to Paul are undisputed and likely genuine (Romans, 1 Corinthians, 2 Corinthians, Galatians, Philippians, 1 Thessalonians, and Philemon), the remaining six are either disputed or widely regarded as pseudonymous.

Letters like Ephesians, Colossians, and 2 Thessalonians show differences in style and theology, suggesting they may have been written by someone else in Paul's name, while the pastoral letters (1 Timothy, 2 Timothy, and Titus) are often seen as later forgeries addressing second-century concerns about church organization.

Despite this, it is evident from references within his letters and early church writings that Paul wrote more than the seven undisputed letters that survive today. For instance, in 1 Corinthians 5:9, Paul mentions, "I wrote to you in my letter not to associate with sexually immoral people," (NIV) referring to a previous letter that is now lost (Keener 2005).

In 2 Corinthians 2:4, Paul says:

"For I wrote you out of great distress and anguish of heart and with many tears, not to grieve you but to let you know the depth of my love for you." (NIV)

Scholars believe this refers to a letter between 1 Corinthians and 2 Corinthians, often called the "tearful letter" or "severe letter." In Colossians 4:16, Paul instructs:

> "After this letter has been read to you, see that it is also read in the church of the Laodiceans and that you in turn read the letter from Laodicea." (NIV)

It is also hypothesized by some scholars that 2 Corinthians is a composite of multiple letters Paul sent to the Corinthians, with particular focus on chapters 10–13 (Keener 2005).

Roetzel, for instance, divides 2 Corinthians into distinct sections based on this theory: Letter C (2 Corinthians 8), Letter D (2 Corinthians 2:14-7:4), Letter E (2 Corinthians 10:1-13:10), Letter F (2 Corinthians 1:1-2:13; 7:5-16; 13:11-13), and Letter G (2 Corinthians 9). Altogether, Roetzel proposes that Paul sent a total of seven letters to the Corinthians, with 2 Corinthians being a compilation of several of these.

Similarly, Melissa Sellew, in her work "'Laodiceans' and the Philippians Fragments Hypothesis," argues that Philippians is also a composite of multiple letters.

For argument's sake, let us assume Paul wrote 50 letters in total—a modest estimate considering the scope of his ministry and influence. If only seven of these letters have survived, that constitutes just 14% of his total writings. This raises theological and philosophical difficulties: Were the lost letters not "God-breathed" or inspired by the Holy Spirit?

If they were, why would God allow them to be lost, depriving generations of believers of potentially critical insights into his divine plan? Conversely, if they were not divinely inspired, how do we distinguish between what was truly inspired and what was not?

If some of Paul's lost letters were ever found, would they instantly be considered sacred and added to the Bible? Would they change Christian theology or challenge the beliefs that have been built on the letters we have now? The fact that only a handful of his writings survived—while the rest were lost to time—makes it hard to trust the completeness of the Bible as the definitive "Word of God."

It also raises bigger questions: how much of what we call Christianity today is based on just a small slice of Paul's thoughts? If the rest of his letters had survived, would Christianity look completely different?

5.5 Paul's Contradictions and Misquotations

When critiquing the Bible, it's important to recognize that it was written by numerous authors at different times, in various parts of the world, for diverse audiences, and with differing understandings of significant matters. Consequently, it's natural to find errors, inconsistencies, and contradictions.

But are these contradictions still understandable when they come from just one person? Some of these contradictions even concern significant issues, such as the identity of Jesus. Let's briefly examine some of these alleged contradictions, starting with Paul's perspective on salvation in comparison to the Gospel authors.

How do we attain salvation?

In Matthew's account of the rich young ruler (Matthew 19:16-26), Jesus engages in a dialogue that highlights the importance of following the law to attain eternal life. When the young man asks Jesus what good deed he must do to inherit eternal life, Jesus initially responds by listing commandments from the Mosaic law.

However, when we look at Galatians 2:15-21, Paul argues that justification comes through faith in Christ rather than through observing the law.

Did Timothy accompany Paul?

The book of Acts states that when Paul went to Athens he left Timothy and Silas behind in Berea (Acts 17:10–15) and did not meet up with them again until after he left Athens and arrived in Corinth (18:5).

In 1 Thessalonians Paul himself narrates the same sequence of events and indicates just as clearly that he was not in Athens alone, but that Timothy was with him. (1 Thess 3:1–3).

Did Paul go to Jerusalem and meet the apostles?

Paul is quite emphatic in the epistle to the Galatians that after he had his vision of Jesus and came to believe in him, he did *not* go to Jerusalem to consult with the apostles (Galatian 1:17):

> "**I did not go up to Jerusalem** to see those who were apostles before I was, but I went into Arabia." (NIV)

The book of Acts, of course, provides its own narrative of Paul's conversion.

Paul, an Apostle?

In this account, Paul does exactly what he claims not to have done in Galatians:

> "When he came to Jerusalem, he tried to join the disciples, but they were all afraid of him, not believing that he really was a disciple." ((Acts 9:26, NIV)

Was Paul against the law?

Paul appears to have no problems violating the Jewish Law when the situation required him to do so. In Paul's own words, he could adapt his behavior not only to 'live like a Jew' when advantageous but also 'like a Gentile,' particularly when converting Gentiles (1 Corinthians 9:21). He even confronts Cephas for failing to do so himself (Galatians 2:11–14).

According to Acts, especially in the early chapters, Paul is portrayed as observant of Jewish customs and practices. For example, he participates in purification rituals (Acts 21:26), observes Jewish festivals (Acts 18:21, Acts 20:6), and circumcises Timothy (Acts 16:3).

Did Christ die for our sins?

Deuteronomy 24:16 says:

> "Parents are not to be put to death for their children, nor children put to death for their parents; each will die for their own sin." (NIV)

1 Corinthians 15:3 Paul says "Christ died for our sins according to the Scriptures." (NIV)

Original Sin

In Romans 5:12-19 Paul repeatedly states that we are all sinners because of Adam's sin.

In Ezekiel 18:20 (NIV) it states:
> "The one who sins is the one who will die. The child will not share the guilt of the parent, nor will the parent share the guilt of the child. The righteousness of the righteous will be credited to them, and the wickedness of the wicked will be charged against them."

Did God lie?

In Hebrews 6:18 Paul says, "It was impossible for God to lie," (NIV) and in Titus 1:2 he says God cannot lie.

Kings 22:23 says, "Lord hath put a lying spirit in the mouth of all these thy prophets." (KJV)

What did the men with Paul hear or see?

Acts 9:7 says, "The men traveling with Saul stood there speechless; **they heard the sound but did not see anyone.**" (NIV)

Acts 26:14 says "We all fell to the ground, and I heard a voice saying to me…" (NIV)

In Acts 22:9 Paul says: "My companions **saw the light**, but they **did not understand the voice of him** who was speaking to me." (NIV)

Paul, an Apostle?

Should we abstain from meats offered to idols?

In Acts 15:29 Paul says , "You are to abstain from food sacrificed to idols, from blood..." (NIV)

But in 1 Corinthians 10:25, 27 Paul says, "Eat anything sold in the meat market without raising questions of conscience... If an unbeliever invites you to a meal and you want to go, eat whatever is put before you without raising questions of conscience." (NIV)

The coming of the Lord

Paul says in Romans 13:12 "The night is nearly over; the day is almost here." (NIV)

Jesus says in Luke 21:8: "Watch out that you are not deceived. For many will come in my name, claiming, 'I am he,' and, 'The time is near.' Do not follow them." (NIV)

On forgiveness

Paul says in Ephesians 1:7, "In him we have redemption through his blood, the forgiveness of sins, in accordance with the riches of God's grace" (NIV) and Romans 4:25, "He was delivered over to death for our sins and was raised to life for our justification." (NIV)

Jesus says in Matthew 6:14-15, "For if you forgive other people when they sin against you, your heavenly Father will also forgive you. But if you do not forgive others their sins, your Father will not forgive your sins." (NIV)

On being justified

Paul says in Romans 5:9, "Since we have now been justified by his blood, how much more shall we be saved from God's wrath through him!" (NIV)

Jesus says in Matthew 12:37, "For by your words you will be acquitted, and by your words you will be condemned." (NIV)

Keeping the commandments

Paul says in Romans 7:9-10, "Once I was alive apart from the law; but when the commandment came, sin sprang to life and I died. I found that **the very commandment that was intended to bring life actually brought death.**" (NIV)

Jesus says in Matthew 19:17, "Why do you ask me about what is good?" Jesus replied. "There is only One who is good. **If you want to enter life, keep the commandments.**" (NIV)

To be sacrificed?

Paul says in 1 Corinthians 5:7, "For Christ, our Passover lamb, has been **sacrificed.**" (NIV)

Jesus says in Matthew 9:13, "But go and learn what this means: 'I desire mercy, **not sacrifice.**'" (NIV)

Paul, an Apostle?

Misquotations and non-quotes

Acts 20:35, Paul says "we must help the weak, remembering the words the Lord Jesus himself said: '**It is more blessed to give than to receive.**'" (NIV)

Nowhere in the New Testament did Jesus ever make such a statement.

1 Corinthians 2:9 Paul says, "However, as it is written: "What no eye has seen, what no ear has heard, and what no human mind has conceived" the things God has prepared for those who love him" (NIV)

Paul is misquoting Isaiah 64:4 "Since ancient times no one has heard, no ear has perceived, no eye has seen any God besides you, who acts on behalf of those who wait for him." (NIV)

Hebrews 10:7 "Then I said, 'Here I am—it is written about me in the scroll— I have come to do your will, my God.'" (NIV)

Paul distorts Psalms 40:7-8 "Then I said, "Here I am, I have come— it is written about me in the scroll. I desire to do your will, my God; your law is within my heart.""" (NIV) Paul leaves out the last phrase, **"thy law is within my heart,"** because that would have shown God's will is the Law.

Romans 10:11 Paul says, "As Scripture says, "Anyone who believes in him will never be put to shame.""" (NIV)

No such statement exists in Scripture.

Paul comments in 1 Corinthians 15:4-6, "He was raised on the third day according to the Scriptures, and that he appeared to Cephas, and then to the Twelve. After that, he appeared to more than five hundred of the brothers and sisters at the same time." (NIV)

No gospel says that Peter saw Jesus before the twelve.

This also clashes with Matthew 27:5. Judas was dead after the Resurrection and only eleven apostles remained. Judas' replacement, Matthias, was not elected until after the Ascension.

1 Thessalonians 2:3 Paul says, "For the appeal we make does not spring from error or impure motives, **nor are we trying to trick you.**" (NIV)

In 2 Corinthians 12:16 he says, "Yet, crafty fellow that I am, **I caught you by trickery!**" (NIV)

Romans 12:14 he says, "Bless those who persecute you; bless and do not curse." (NIV)

In Acts 23:3 he says "God will strike you, you whitewashed wall!" (NIV)

In 1 Thessalonians 4:15, 17 Paul says, "**We who are still alive,** who are left until **the coming of the Lord,** will certainly not precede those who have fallen asleep… we who are still alive and are left will be caught up together with them in the clouds to meet the Lord in the air. And so we will be with the Lord forever." (NIV)

Both verses reasonably suggest that Paul was confident the end of the world was coming in the lifetime of his contemporaries.

Paul, an Apostle?

Looking at Paul's writings above, we can see contradictions and misquotations that don't always match with what Jesus or other scriptures say. Whether it's about salvation, the law, or Paul's own actions, there's a lot that doesn't quite line up.

While Paul's teachings have had a huge impact on Christianity, these differences make us question how his ideas fit into the bigger picture of Christian belief.

Given these inconsistencies, it's worth questioning Paul's authority in shaping Christian doctrine. If Paul himself made mistakes in his interpretations, actions, and teachings, can we fully rely on his writings as the foundation for key Christian beliefs? This uncertainty calls into question the extent to which his authority should be accepted without critical reflection, especially when considering his quarrels with some of Jesus' disciples.

Chapter 5 Paul, an Apostle?

References:
Bray, G.L., 2019. The Pastoral Epistles (ITC). Bloomsbury Publishing.

Brown, H.O., 1984. Heresies: The Image of Christ in the Mirror of Heresy and Orthodoxy from the Apostles to the Present. Doubleday.

Brown, P., 2012. The rise of Western Christendom: triumph and diversity, AD 200-1000. John Wiley & Sons.

Brunner, E., 1950. Dogmatics: The Christian Doctrine of God (Vol. 1). Westminster Press.

Dunn, J.D., 1991. The partings of the ways: between Christianity and Judaism and their significance for the character of Christianity. scm Press.

Dunn, J.D., 2003. Jesus Remembered: Christianity in the Making, Volume 1 (Vol. 1). Wm. B. Eerdmans Publishing.

Goulder, M.D., 1995. St. Paul versus St. Peter: a tale of two missions. Westminster John Knox Press.

Hengel, M. and Trapp, T., 2010. Saint Peter: The Underestimated Apostle. Wm. B. Eerdmans Publishing.

Kelhoffer, J.A., 2014. Conceptions of "Gospel" and legitimacy in early Christianity (Vol. 324). Mohr Siebeck.

Sanders, E. (2001). Paul. Oxford: Oxford University Press.

Stenschke, C.W., 2005. Review of *The Gospel of John: A Commentary* by Craig Keener. *Jahrbuch für evangelikale Theologie* 19.

Tabor, J. and Dean, R., 2012. Paul and Jesus.

Tabor, J.D., 2013. Paul and Jesus: How the apostle transformed Christianity. Simon and Schuster.

Wilson, B.A., 2008. How Jesus Became Christian. Macmillan.

6

"The God of our ancestors raised Jesus from the dead—whom you killed by hanging him on a cross." (Acts 5:30, NIV)

Crucifixion and Resurrection

"and for their saying, 'We killed the Messiah, Jesus son of Mary, the apostle of Allah'—though they did not kill him nor did they crucify him, but so it was made to appear to them. Indeed those who differ concerning him are surely in doubt about him: they do not have any knowledge of that beyond following conjectures, and certainly, they did not kill him." (Qur'an 4:157)

6.1 Original Sin?

Original Sin is one of the major tenets of mainstream Christianity. It is generally understood as the sin that Adam and Eve committed by disobeying God. Consequently, this original sin was transmitted to all of their descendants. It is only through the grace of God, whose son, Jesus Christ, died on the cross to save us, that we may be redeemed. As noted earlier, the origin of this belief is Paul (Romans 5:12-21).

Is the idea of original sin honestly a fair one? Is it logical? Is it reasonable?

Putting aside these questions, further investigation reveals that this idea may even be non-Biblical (Haag 1969).

"God made man upright..." (Ecclesiastes 7:29, ESV)

If we were made upright, how can we be born in a sinful state? This is an important doctrine of original righteousness, as opposed to original sin. It is not the 'erectness of their bodies but the disposition of their minds,'" as John Gill's exposition of the Bible states.

Although many Biblical commentators suggest this is referring to the first Man, it does not necessarily have to be interpreted that way. According to Matthew Henry's commentary, "...Man, whom God made upright, has found out so many ways to render himself wicked and miserable" (Henry 1991).

"The son shall not suffer for the iniquity of the father, nor the father suffer for the iniquity of the son. The righteousness of the righteous shall be upon himself, and the wickedness of the wicked shall be upon himself. But if a wicked person turns away from all his sins that he has committed and keeps all my statutes and does what is just and right, he shall surely live; he shall not die." (Ezekiel 18:20-21, ESV)

Henry (1991) interprets this passage as follows:
"All souls are in the hand of the great Creator. He will deal with them in justice or mercy; nor will any perish for the sins of another, who is not in some sense worthy of death for his own."

If Adam erred, why should that affect later generations? Should it not remain with Adam himself, since the son shall not bear the iniquities of the father?

"God said, Let us make man in our image, after our likeness... And God saw everything that he had made, and behold, it was very good." (Genesis 1:26, 31, ESV)

"Fathers shall not be put to death because of their children, nor shall children be put to death because of their fathers. Each one shall be put to death for his own sin." (Deuteronomy 24:16, ESV)

"Far be it from you to do such a thing, to put the righteous to death with the wicked, so that the righteous fare as the wicked! Far be that from you! Shall not the Judge of all the earth do what is just?" (Genesis 18:25, ESV)

"But he did not put their children to death, according to what is written in the Law, in the Book of Moses, where the Lord commanded, "Fathers shall not die because of their children, nor children die because of their fathers, but each one shall die for his own sin.""" (2 Chronicles 25:4, ESV)

The Bible passages usually cited as 'proof texts' for the doctrine of Original Sin have much debate concerning them, stemming all the way from the second or third century.

The Bible verses most frequently quoted as proof texts for the doctrine of Original Sin are: Romans 5:19, Ephesians 2:3-5, and Psalms 58:2–3.

"For as by the one man's disobedience the many were made sinners, so by the one man's obedience the many will be made righteous." (Romans 5:19, ESV)

"Among whom we all once lived in the passions of our flesh, carrying out the desires of the body and the mind, and were by nature children of wrath, like the rest of mankind. But God, being rich in mercy, because of the great love with which he loved us, even when we were dead in our trespasses, made us alive together with Christ—by grace you have been saved." (Ephesians 2:3-5, ESV)

"No, in your hearts you devise wrongs; your hands deal out violence on earth. The wicked are estranged from the womb; they go astray from birth, speaking lies." (Psalms 58:2–3, ESV)

If you believe that these verses support the doctrine of original sin, do you then see them as contradicting the earlier passages? Given that two of these verses are from Paul, we also need to reconsider our earlier questions about his relationship to the historical Jesus.

Even if you're able to reconcile these issues, do you find the idea of an innocent Christ redeeming a sinful humanity to be reasonable? How do you make sense of such a concept?

As you'll discover, this very question was one that many of the early Church Fathers struggled to answer.

6.2 Human Sacrifice for the Redemption of Sin?

What kind of God would require the death/human sacrifice of his beloved 'Son' for the redemption of sin? This seems gravely cruel and unjust, and the deeper we delve into the concept of atonement, the worse it seems. Many Christians have debated this topic and continue to differ on it (Finlan 2005).

Christianity inherits a number of its central doctrines from Judaism, such as monotheism and final judgment, but a central doctrine unique to Christianity is the incarnation. Although borrowed by features from various places, it is void of any Jewish or Gentile sources.

For many centuries, sacrificial practices in Israel resembled those of its neighbors—the Canaanites, Moabites, and Babylonians. On a basic level, the sacrificial meat is 'the food for the deity'. The priests called it "a food offering to the Lord" (Leviticus 3:11, ESV).

The Incarnation is difficult to interpret without some concept of the divinity of Christ. Though Trinitarians would suggest otherwise, his sacrifice is no different from that of anybody else. But what does this atonement mean? Is it the idea of blood purifying, as mentioned in Leviticus? Does it mean the death of Jesus was a payment to God?

Did he die as a substitutive victim? Let us look at what scholars and historical figures made of it.

> "For even the Son of Man came not to be served but to serve, and to give his life as a ransom for many." (Mark 10:45, ESV)

The development of the doctrines of the Atonement can vary in their understandings. For example, Bishop Irenaeus accepted Christ's death as a ransom paid to the devil (AD 202), but this idea was not fully developed.

In the eleventh century, Anselm formed a theory based on the social structure of his time, giving a feudal structure to salvation (1098). In the generations after Anselm, a professor of theology, Peter Abelard (who lived from 1079–1142), rejected all theories of ransom and satisfaction.

Abelard stated, "How cruel and wicked it seems that anyone should demand the blood of an innocent person as the price for anything, or that it should in any way please him that an innocent man should be slain."

For the last 250-plus years, popular ideas of atonement have caused embarrassment amongst Christians who move away from the idea that the Son's death was either a kind of payment or a divinely demanded penalty.

Either defenders of this idea do not recognize the violence implicit within it or they choose not to see it. Some may be aware but still have their reasons to support it, so they spiritualize it and improve it with a modern, more humane spin. Ultimately, they redefine the atonement as a metaphor, meaning something different than it initially did.

Crucifixion and Resurrection

The problem with this idea of atonement is not necessarily with Jesus himself but with the character of God. If God wanted to save humanity, why use such an atrocious method? Why should Jesus need to suffer and die? Could God not have simply forgiven the world? If God is so loving and just, why did the blood of his Son Jesus need to be spilled? Is God not powerful enough to forgive? These are some of the questions even Christians ask.

Despite the heroic image painted, this is all washed away if God himself is sadistic. If my son were in front of a speeding bus, I would put myself in his position in order to save him, not the other way around. This also rightly points out the absurdity of God having a son.

The purpose of offspring is to replace their parents' generation. The parents sacrifice for their children and do everything they can to make their lives easier. A father certainly does not allow his son to be killed because he is angry with the people killing him!

Does the Christian God need to be replaced? Does He want Jesus to be killed so He can forgive his killers?

Our Christian brethren also claim that Jesus was the perfect sacrifice according to the Old Testament (Hebrews 10:14). But according to Old Testament rules, an altar with the sacrificial animal would need to be provided (Leviticus 4).

Moreover, Malachi 1:8 states that sacrificial animals were not to be blind, injured, or diseased. Jesus was clearly injured before his crucifixion. So was Jesus really a perfect sacrifice?

It may sound strange to speak about Jesus like a sacrificial animal, but this is unfortunately what the concept of a sacrificial son leads us to. Below are a few theories regarding the alleged atonement of Jesus (Pbuh).

Recapitulation theory

The Recapitulation Theory of atonement is a theological concept most notably associated with Irenaeus of Lyons (c. 130–202AD), one of the early Church Fathers (Finlan 2005).

This theory has it that the atonement of Christ has reversed the course of humankind from disobedience to obedience. This theory claims Jesus has reversed the sin initiated by Adam in the Garden of Eden. Irenaeus believed that Christ is the "new Adam" who reverses the damage done by the first Adam.

Why did God create a system where every child is sinful from birth, and the only solution is the sacrifice on the innocent and beloved son of God?

Ransom to Satan

Origen of Alexandria (c. 185–254AD) is one of the earliest Christian theologians to explicitly teach a version of this "ransom" theory (Demarest 2006).

This theory sees Christ as a ransom paid to Satan for the purchase of man's freedom, releasing man from Satan's enslavement. Why did God need to bargain with Satan?

Satisfaction theory of atonement

Anselm of Canterbury (1033–1109) developed the satisfaction theory of atonement, focusing on the idea that Christ's death satisfied the demands of God's justice (Finlan 2005). Jesus Christ suffered crucifixion as a substitute for human sin, satisfying God's just wrath against man's transgression due to Christ's infinite merit. Why is God satisfied with the murder of His beloved son?

Example theory

The Example Theory was popularized by some of the early Christian thinkers such as Peter Abelard (1079–1142), a medieval scholar and theologian (Finlan 2005).

This theory holds that Christ was providing an example of faith and obedience to inspire man to be obedient to God. Christ's death was a demonstration of God's love, which would lead humans to repentance.

What kind of example is it for anybody to have the all-loving, all-just God crucify his beloved and innocent son?

Penal substitution theory

John Calvin (1509–1564) is widely recognized for formulating the idea of penal substitution theory (Finlan 2005).

This theory sees the atonement of Christ as a vicarious sacrifice that satisfied the demands of God's justice upon sin. This would mean that with Jesus' sacrifice, Christ paid the penalty of man's sin. Did God penalize the innocent for the crimes of the guilty?

Again, these theories do not hold a just position. The best way to understand these evolved theories over the decades is to approach the subject from a developmental perspective. The theories above have developed over time, ultimately to the point of Jesus being a part of something that was never truly intended.

When Christians claim that they know Jesus died for their sins and that they will be going to heaven and how so exactly, I wonder if that same belief in atonement would have existed during an earlier period of Christianity.

Since atonement theories evolved over time, Christians in the 2nd to 4th centuries held diverse views, emphasizing cosmic restoration, moral transformation, and victory over death, rather than later legalistic or substitutionary models.

6.3 Atonement Dilemma

The early Church's understanding of salvation and the scope of Christ's redemptive work was marked by significant theological struggles and divergent views. In the second century, Irenaeus challenged the Gnostic division of humanity into the "saved" and the "damned," insisting that Christ's salvation was available to all, but this was countered by the Gnostic's fatalistic view of humanity.

Similarly, in the third century, Origen struggled with the implications of Greco-Roman fatalism and determinism, particularly regarding passages like Romans 9:18; "So then he has mercy on whomever he wills, and he hardens whomever he wills." (ESV) Yet his insistence on human free will over divine predestination raised questions about the compatibility of human autonomy with divine grace.

In the fourth century, the Apollinarian heresy sparked further debate, with Apollinaris denying Christ's full humanity and proposing a diminished view of Christ's redemptive role. Meanwhile Gregory of Nyssa firmly rejected the notion that God's will was divided or that Christ's redemptive act was limited to a select few (Bounds 2012).

However, the most contentious debate came in the fifth century with Augustine's doctrine of predestination, where he argued that God's will to save was limited to the elect, with others destined for damnation (Wetzel 2000).

Crucifixion and Resurrection

Figures like Justin Martyr and Clement of Alexandria insisted that God wills all to be saved, but the real issue lay in human refusal to accept salvation (First Apology 1948).

Ultimately, these debates showed a deep tension between divine justice and human free will, with each view—whether Gnostic, Apollinarian, or Augustinian—struggling to reconcile the universality of Christ's atonement with the harsh reality that not all are saved.

The result was a fractured understanding of salvation that has continued to haunt Christian theology. It left unresolved questions about the justice and mercy of God, the nature of divine will, and the role of human agency in salvation by having an innocent beloved son die for the sins of humanity.

Origen was the first to propose that Christ's death was a ransom paid to Satan, suggesting that the devil was deceived into accepting Christ's death, believing he would maintain control over Him. Origen had his ideas condemned by the church, leading to a weak foundation for the Ransom Theory (Demarest 2006).

About 150 years later, in the late 4th century, Gregory of Nyssa revisited and modified Origen's theory, but it was not widely accepted at the time. Gregory of Nazianzus, a contemporary, rejected it, arguing that since the devil was a thief, he had no legal claim to receive payment for what he had taken, and it would be absurd for God the Son to be given as a ransom (Browne, 1894).

Christians today have a mixed acceptance of various atonement theories, such as Example, Ransom, and Penal Substitution, each attempting to explain the mystery of why God would allow His Son, who is also God incarnate, second person of the Trinity, to die for humanity's sins.

Why would God allow for such a confusing teaching with varying interpretations and theories? Why would God's religion include such an absurd idea of God's "son" dying on a cross for the sins of mankind or a selected portion of mankind?

Here are what some early church fathers had said on the topic.

I Clement

I Clement speaks of Christ's blood as "precious" to God, given for salvation and repentance. His death is described as a substitutionary sacrifice for our sins: "He bore our iniquities, wounded for our transgressions... delivered for our sins" (Chap. 16). His sacrifice was for us—His blood for our flesh, His soul for our souls (Chap. 49).

Clement presents a substitutionary view, but remains vague and does not address the theological mechanics of this atonement.

Ignatius of Antioch

Ignatius of Antioch in his Letter to the Smyrnaeans speaks of Christ's suffering for our salvation: "He was nailed to the cross for us in His flesh" (Smyrnaeans 1), and His flesh was "suffered for our sins" (Smyrnaeans 7). In his letter to the Trallians, Ignatius states that by believing in Christ's death, we escape death (Trallians, Ch. 2).

Ignatius clearly has an emphasis on faith over the atonement which creates a theological gap, making it unclear whether Ignatius supports a legal, substitutionary view or something more mystical. Again, why would it be so difficult for God to explain to us what the true atonement belief is?

The Epistle of Barnabas

The Epistle of Barnabas also speaks of Christ's death as a means of sanctification: "He was wounded for our transgressions… He suffered on the tree" (Ch. 5).

Barnabas presents Christ as the suffering servant, but like Clement and Ignatius, his presentation lacks clarity regarding the mechanics of salvation. The substitutionary language is there, but it is not fully explained.

Polycarp's Letter to the Philippians

Polycarp's Letter to the Philippians states that Christ suffered for our sins even unto death (Ch. 1) and calls for acknowledgment of our debt of sin (Ch. 6).

Again, there is no explanation of how Christ's sacrifice actually resolves the sin debt. It does not mention how this is part of God's mercy or justice. Nor does it explain how it doesn't go against His mercy and justice.

Letter to Diognetus

In the Letter to Diognetus, Jesus takes on the burden of our iniquities, offering Himself as a "ransom" for us: "The holy One for transgressors… the righteous One for the unrighteous" (Chap. 9).

This passage seems to point toward a ransom theory, but its focus on a "sweet exchange" does little to explain how this transaction between Christ and God operates. Which one is it, is it substitution, ransom, exchange or something else entirely misunderstood from the church fathers?

Justin Martyr

Justin Martyr, in his Dialogue with Trypho, discusses Christ bearing our sins and suffering for the human family: "He was wounded for our transgressions, bruised for our iniquities" (Ch. 13), and that his Father caused him to suffer for us (Ch. 95).

Justin's portrayal is a blend of substitutionary and penal atonement, but his inconsistency complicates matters. While he acknowledges Christ bearing the curse due to sin, his varying focus on suffering and God's plan of salvation leads to an unclear and sometimes contradictory view of the atonement. Why would the Father cause him to suffer? Wasn't there another way?

In summary, the early church fathers offer inconsistent views on Christ's atonement, further complicating any attempt at a reasonable understanding. While some present Christ's death in terms of substitution, others speak of it as a ransom or an exchange. A clear explanation is not provided about how these concepts relate or work together.

Furthermore, one might wonder why such a range of interpretations exists if scripture itself is clear on the matter. Why wouldn't Jesus himself just explain the details of this theory? Why would God leave it to us to figure out?

If the Biblical foundation for the atonement were as straightforward as some argue, the early Church should have arrived at a more uniform understanding, yet the presence of differing views suggests confusion in the interpretation of Christ's sacrificial death.

6.4 Contradictions of Events

The crucifixion and resurrection of Jesus are pivotal moments in Christianity, yet the four Gospels—Matthew, Mark, Luke, and John—present contradicting details about these events. From Jesus' trial before Pilate to his final words to his disciples, each Gospel offers something different.

I encourage the reader to read the final parts of each Gospel horizontally and compare them. Mark 14, Matthew 26, Luke 22, and John 18 cover the betrayal and arrest of Jesus.

Mark 15, Matthew 27, Luke 23, and John 18-19 cover the trial of Jesus and his crucifixion.

Mark 16, Matthew 28, Luke 24, and John 20 cover the resurrection of Jesus.

This horizontal reading of the Bible, exposes several inconsistencies. These discrepancies raise doubts about the trustworthiness of the Bible as we have it today and the accuracy of its contents.

Much like a detective who hears conflicting testimonies from supposed eyewitnesses, he begins to question the validity of their story. So too are religious scholars and readers forced to reconsider the reliability of the Biblical accounts when faced with differing versions of the same events.

Here are some contradictions and differences between the Gospel accounts of the crucifixion.

What was the Method of the Betrayal?
   Judas betrays Jesus with a kiss. (Matthew 26:48-50, Mark 14:44-46, Luke 22:47-48)
   Judas leads a group of soldiers, but there is no mention of a kiss. (John 18:3-9)

The cross is one of the main symbols of Christianity, representing Jesus' crucifixion. But when we look at the Gospel accounts, one question stands out: **Who actually carried the cross?**
   Mark, Luke and Matthew all say it was Simon of Cyrene. (Mark 15:21, Luke 23:26 & Matthew 27:32)

   But John say it was Jesus. (John 19:16-17)

Before being crucified, **Jesus was offered a drink, but the details differ between the Gospels.**
   "And they offered him wine mixed with myrrh, but he did not take it." (Mark 15:23, ESV)

   "They offered him wine to drink, mixed with gall, but when he tasted it, he would not drink it." (Matthew 27:34, ESV)

Luke and John don't mention this drink at all.

Crucifixion and Resurrection

The time of Jesus' crucifixion also varies between the Gospels, which is an important detail when trying to understand the timeline of events.

"And it was the third hour, and they crucified him." (Mark 15:25, ESV)

"And it was the preparation of the Passover, and about the sixth hour: and he saith unto the Jews, Behold your King!" (John 19:14, ESV)

As Jesus was crucified, a sign was placed above his head, but **the wording of the sign** is different in each Gospel.

"And the inscription of the charge against him read, **"The King of the Jews.""** (Mark 15:26, ESV)

"And over his head they put the charge against him, which read, **"This is Jesus, the King of the Jews.""** (Matthew 27:37, ESV)

"There was also an inscription over him,[a] **"This is the King of the Jews.""** (Luke 23:38, ESV)

"Pilate also wrote an inscription and put it on the cross. It read, **"Jesus of Nazareth, the King of the Jews.""** (John 19:19, ESV)

Each Gospel has a different version of what was written. With these differences, we're left to question how accurate these details really are.

The Gospels tell us that two thieves were crucified alongside Jesus, but **did one or both mock him**?

"And the robbers who were crucified with him also reviled him in the same way." (Matthew 27:44, ESV)

"Those who were crucified with him also reviled him." (Mark 15:32, ESV)

"One of the criminals who were hanged railed at him, saying, "Are you not the Christ? Save yourself and us!"" (Luke 23:39, ESV)

Luke's version differs from Matthew and Mark, while John doesn't mention the conversation at all.

Did darkness cover the land?

Darkness covers the land from noon until 3 PM. (Matthew 27:45, Mark 15:33, Luke 23:44)

John: There is no mention of darkness during the crucifixion. (John 19:17-30)

What were Jesus' Last Words?

Jesus cries out, "My God, my God, why have you forsaken me?" (Matthew 27:46, Mark 15:34, ESV)

Jesus says, "Father, into your hands I commit my spirit." (Luke 23:46, ESV)

Jesus says, "It is finished." (John 19:30, ESV)

What was the Centurion's declaration?
The Roman centurion at the cross declares, "Truly this was the Son of God." (Matthew 27:54, Mark 15:39, ESV)

The centurion says, "Certainly this man was innocent!" (or "the Son of God" in some translations), but it's less specific. (Luke 23:47, ESV)

The centurion's declaration is not recorded. (John 19:31-37)

Who exactly was Joseph of Arimathea? Was he a disciple or just a counselor?
"When it was evening, there came a rich man from Arimathea, named Joseph, who also was a disciple of Jesus." (Matthew 27:57, ESV)

"Joseph of Arimathea, a respected member of the council, who was also himself looking for the kingdom of God, took courage and went to Pilate and asked for the body of Jesus." (Mark 15:43, ESV)

"Now there was a man named Joseph, from the Jewish town of Arimathea. He was a member of the council, a good and righteous man" (Luke 23:50, ESV)

The Events Around Jesus' Death:

There is an earthquake, the veil of the temple tears, and many dead saints are resurrected. (Matthew 27:51-53)

No mention of saints being resurrected, though the temple veil tears and there's an earthquake. (Mark 15:38, Luke 23:45)

There's no mention of an earthquake or the resurrection of saints. (John 19:30-37)

Who buried Jesus?

Jesus is buried by Joseph of Arimathea alone. (Matthew 27:57-61, Mark 15:40-47, Luke 23:50-56)

Jesus' body is buried by both Joseph of Arimathea and Nicodemus. (John 19:38-42)

While these contradictions may appear superficial or of little importance, the contradictions surrounding the resurrection are anything but.

Resurrection Discrepancies

The resurrection of Jesus is central to Christian faith, often held as the ultimate proof of Jesus' divine nature. However, the gospel accounts of the resurrection present notable variations that have long been a point of discussion among scholars. The below are some of many inconsistencies and discrepancies found within the resurrection story.

Crucifixion and Resurrection

1. Who Found the Empty Tomb?

When it comes to **who found Jesus' empty tomb and when**, the Gospels don't agree on the details.

> "When the Sabbath was past, Mary Magdalene, Mary the mother of James, and Salome bought spices, so that they might go and anoint him. And very early on the first day of the week, when the sun had risen, they went to the tomb." (Mark 16:1-2, ESV)

> "Now after the Sabbath, toward the dawn of the first day of the week, Mary Magdalene and the other Mary went to see the tomb." (Matthew 28:1, ESV)

> "Now upon the first day of the week, very early in the morning, they came unto the sepulchre, bringing the spices which they had prepared, and certain others with them." (Luke 24:1, KJV)

> "Now on the first day of the week Mary Magdalene came to the tomb early, while it was still dark, and saw that the stone had been taken away from the tomb." (John 20:1, ESV)

Mark says they came at sunrise, while John says it was still dark when Mary arrived. The timing and the people involved don't match up. These differences in the Gospel accounts force us to pause and consider the reliability of these stories, especially when they contradict each other so clearly on key details.

If the discovery of the empty tomb is foundational to the resurrection claim, why do the witnesses vary so widely? These discrepancies challenge the idea of a unified, eyewitness account.

297

2. What Did They See at the Tomb?

A young man in a white robe sitting inside the tomb. (Mark 16:5)

An angel of the Lord descends, rolls back the stone, and sits on it. (Matthew 28:2-5)

Two men in dazzling clothes appear inside the tomb. (Luke 24:4)

Mary Magdalene sees two angels in white sitting where Jesus' body had been. (John 20:12)

Were there one or two angels? Were they outside or inside?

3. What Did the Women Do After Finding the Tomb?

The women flee in terror and say nothing to anyone. (Mark 16:8)

The women run to tell the disciples but are met by Jesus on the way. (Matthew 28:8-10)

The women report the news to the disciples, who are skeptical. (Luke 24:9-11)

Mary Magdalene runs to Peter and the "other disciple" to report that the body has been taken. (John 20:2, ESV)

Mark's abrupt ending may underscore the mystery and awe of the resurrection, while Matthew and Luke stress the women's role as the first proclaimers of the good news.

Crucifixion and Resurrection

4. Who Did Jesus Appear To?

(Later addition) Jesus appears first to Mary Magdalene, then to two disciples, and finally to the eleven. (Mark 16:9-20)

Jesus appears to the women, then to the eleven in Galilee. (Matthew 28:9-10, 16-20)

Jesus appears to two disciples on the road to Emmaus and later to the eleven in Jerusalem. (Luke 24:13-49)

Jesus appears to Mary Magdalene, then to the disciples twice (once without Thomas and once with him). (John 20:11-29)

5. Where Did the Disciples See Jesus?

(Later addition) Implies appearances in Jerusalem and elsewhere. (Mark 16)

The eleven see Jesus on a mountain in Galilee.
(Matthew 28:16-20)

Jesus appears in Jerusalem and ascends to heaven from Bethany. (Luke 24:50-51)

The disciples meet Jesus in Jerusalem. (John 20:19-29)
The geographic inconsistencies between Jerusalem and Galilee could reflect early Christian attempts to anchor the resurrection story in different communities. For example, Matthew's emphasis on Galilee aligns with its theme of Jesus' ministry to the Gentiles.

6. The Timing of Events

"Very early on the first day of the week, when the sun had risen." (Mark 16:2, ESV)

"Dawn of the first day of the week." (Matthew 28:1, ESV)

"At early dawn." (Luke 24:1, ESV)

"While it was still dark." (John 20:1, ESV)

These subtle variations may not seem significant, but they provide further inconsistences between supposedly strict historical accounts.

7. Who Moved the Stone?

The women find the stone "rolled away" when they arrive. (Mark 16:4)

An angel of the Lord descends, rolls back the stone, and sits on it. (Matthew 28:2)

The women find the stone already rolled away, but no explanation is given. (Luke 24:2)

Mary Magdalene sees that the stone has been moved. (John 20:1)

Matthew emphasizes a dramatic angelic action, while the other gospels simply note the stone's removal without elaboration.

8. Did Anyone See Jesus Leave the Tomb?

None of the gospels explicitly describe Jesus leaving the tomb, but their narratives differ in what happens afterward:

(Later addition) Jesus does not appear until later (Mark 16:15-20).

Jesus meets the women as they leave the tomb. (Matthew 28:9)

Jesus first appears to two disciples on the road to Emmaus. (Luke 24:13-35)

Jesus appears to Mary Magdalene outside the tomb. (John 20:14-17)

The gospels differ on who first sees Jesus, reflecting distinct theological priorities—John, for instance, emphasizes Mary Magdalene's personal encounter.

9. How Did the Disciples React?

There is no mention of the disciples' reaction (in the original ending). (Mark 16:8)

The disciples go to Galilee as instructed and worship Jesus, though some doubt. (Matthew 28:16-17)

The disciples dismiss the women's story as nonsense. (Luke 24:11)

Peter and the "other disciple" run to the tomb to investigate. (John 20:3-10, ESV)

These reactions range from skepticism to immediate faith, illustrating different emphases. Luke's account underscores the disciples' initial disbelief, while John highlights the role of individual encounters in confirming the resurrection. Which one is it?

10. When and How Did Jesus Ascend?

(Later addition) Jesus ascends to heaven after appearing to the disciples. (Mark 16:19)

Matthew makes no mention of the ascension.

Jesus ascends to heaven on the same day as his resurrection. (Luke 24:50-51)

Luke (author of Acts) places the ascension 40 days after the resurrection. (Acts 1:9-11)

11. Did the Guards Report the Resurrection?

Guards are placed at the tomb. (Matthew 27:62-66)

The guards report the resurrection to the chief priests, who bribe them to spread the story that the disciples stole Jesus' body. (Matthew 28:11-15)

No other gospel mentions these guards

Crucifixion and Resurrection

Why would Matthew mention these guards when no other gospel has? Is Matthew trying to reinforce the idea that Jesus' body was carefully guarded, in an attempt to prove there was no way it could have been stolen by the disciples? Shouldn't we be suspicious of this addition to the story?

12. What Was Jesus' Final Commission?

(Later addition) Jesus tells the disciples to preach the gospel to all creation and promises miraculous signs for believers. (Mark 16:15-18)

Jesus delivers the "Great Commission," instructing the disciples to make disciples of all nations, baptizing them and teaching obedience. (Matthew 28:19-20)

Jesus commands the disciples to preach repentance and forgiveness, starting in Jerusalem, and promises the Holy Spirit. (Luke 24:47-49)

Jesus sends the disciples as the Father sent him and grants them the authority to forgive sins. (John 20:21-23)

The discrepancies found in the Gospel accounts of the resurrection raise important questions about the consistency and reliability of the narratives. The wide variations in details—such as who discovered the empty tomb, what they saw, and how the disciples reacted—suggest that the resurrection story within the New Testament is not as reliable and trustworthy as Christians claim it to be.

While these differences challenge the idea of a unified, eyewitness account, they also highlight theological priorities of each Gospel writer.

Chapter 6 Crucifixion and Resurrection

References:

Anselm of Canterbury (1033–1100AD) Cur Deus Homo? [Why did God become Man?] (1098)

Bounds, C.T., 2012. The scope of the atonement in the Early Church Fathers.

Demarest, B., 2006. The Cross and Salvation (Hardcover): The Doctrine of Salvation. Crossway.

Finlan, S. (2005). Problems with atonement. Collegeville, Minn.: Liturgical Press.

Haag, H., 1969. Is original sin in Scripture?. Sheed and Ward.

Henry Corbin, Swedenborg and Esoteric Islam, (Westchester, Pennsylvania: Swedenborg

Henry, M., 1991. Commentary on the whole Bible (Vol. 4). FH Revell.

Irenaeus, 2004. Irenaeus Against Heresies (Vol. 4). Kessinger Publishing.

Martyr, J., 1948. The first apology. Ante-Nicene Fathers, 1.

Translated by Charles Gordon Browne and James Edward Swallow. From Nicene and Post-Nicene Fathers, Second Series, Vol. 7. Edited by Philip Schaff and Henry Wace. (Buffalo, NY: Christian Literature Publishing Co., 1894.)

Smith, D.A., 2007. The post-mortem vindication of Jesus in the sayings Gospel Q. Bloomsbury Publishing.

Todd Lawson, The Crucifixion and the Qur'an: A Study in the History of Muslim Thought, (Oxford: Oneworld Publications, 2009).

Wetzel, J., 2000. Augustine on Free Will and Predestination. Dodaro and Lawless (eds.).

7

"If anyone adds anything to them, God will add to that person the plagues described in this scroll. And if anyone takes words away from this scroll of prophecy, God will take away from that person any share in the tree of life and in the Holy City, which are described in this scroll." (Revelation 22:18–19, NIV)

Canon

"There is a group of them who alter their voice while reading out a text [that they have themselves authored], so that you may suppose it to be from the Book, though it is not from the Book, and they say, 'It is from Allah,' though it is not from Allah, and they attribute lies to Allah, and they know [it]." (Qur'an 3:78)

7.1 Gnostic and Apocryphal Writings

Many Christians believe that the Bible is not only a collection of books of guidance, but also the infallible Word of God. This begs the question, if God inspired sixty-six or seventy-three books (Protestant or Catholic), how do we know there weren't other books that were not part of God's Word?

If we engage in a historical study of the early Christian movement, we realize that plenty of Christians from different parts of the world believed and accepted other books as the 'Word of God'. Interestingly, church leaders later removed some books that had originally made it into the canon (McDowell 1999).

For example, the Apocalypse of John and the book of Revelation were denounced as false teachings. The Apocalypse of Peter was eventually accepted, but initially, it was not—which is also the case for 1 and 2 Timothy and Titus.

Some Christians accepted the Gospel of Peter but rejected the Gospel of John. And some accepted portions of the Gospel of Luke as well as the Gospel of Thomas, which is not even part of the canon we have today. The Epistle of Barnabas, Third Corinthians, the Gospel of the Ebionites, and the Coptic apocalypse of Peter are other examples of writings that were once accepted by at least some Christians, but never made it into the modern Bible (Ehrman 2000).

Who decided what went into the Bible? Why are there only 66 books in some versions of the Bible when others have more? This is because some branches of Christianity accept more books as being worthy of inclusion in the Bible than other branches.

Gnosticism

Gnosticism had a significant impact on early Christianity, pulling it away from its Hebrew roots and introducing ideas that often clashed with the Bible.

Gnostics and their related philosophy, Neoplatonism, promoted the belief in a distant, unknowable God who could have multiple personalities. They also viewed the material world as inherently evil, believing it was created by a lesser, malevolent deity.

These views ran counter to biblical teachings, which affirm that creation reflects the work of a good and personal God. This influence shaped doctrines like the Trinity, which was framed as a mystery beyond human understanding. Many Christians today accept it without question, leaving the details to theologians.

The Gnostic belief that physicality was corrupt also led some early scribes to adjust scripture to emphasize Jesus' humanity. For example, Luke 22:44's mention of Jesus sweating blood has been argued by scholars like Bart Ehrman to be a later addition, intended to counter Gnostic claims that Jesus wasn't truly human.

Gnostic ideas persist in modern Christianity. Practices like rejecting dancing in worship reflect the Gnostic disdain for physical expression. Some Gnostic writings were rediscovered in the Nag Hammadi Library in Egypt in 1945, shedding light on their beliefs and their alternative take on Christianity.

Apocryphal writings

Apocryphal writings are books that didn't make it into the official Bible, or Canon. They might have been popular in some early Christian communities but were excluded from the Bible for various reasons — maybe they didn't fit the theology, seemed historically shaky, or just weren't widely accepted.

The word "Apocrypha" itself comes from Greek and means "hidden" or "obscure." These books are not part of the Hebrew Bible's canonical texts recognized by Jews and Protestant Christians. However, they are accepted as canonical by Eastern Orthodox, Oriental Orthodox, and Catholic Christians, and are included in their versions of the Old Testament. Dispute over the canonicity of these books involves the Latin translation of the Bible (*Vulgate*) by Saint Jerome.

Sometimes called "Deuterocanonical" books, they include stories like Tobit and Judith. New Testament Apocryphal writings are books about Jesus and the apostles that didn't make the cut, often because they contradicted orthodox teachings. Below is a list of some Gnostic texts, mostly from the Nag Hammadi Library.

The Gospel of Thomas: A collection of Jesus' sayings, with no miracles or resurrection stories.

The Gospel of Mary: Puts Mary Magdalene front and center, showing her as one of Jesus' closest followers.

The Gospel of Philip: Talks about sacraments and suggests a special relationship between Jesus and Mary Magdalene.

The Apocryphon of John: Explains how the flawed material world was created by a lesser divine being.

The Pistis Sophia: Details spiritual journeys and the battle for enlightenment.

The Gospel of Judas: Paints Judas as a hero who helped Jesus fulfill his mission.

The Apocalypse of Peter: Gives a Gnostic twist to ideas about the afterlife.

The Treatise on the Resurrection: Says resurrection is spiritual, not physical.

The Thunder, Perfect Mind: A mysterious poem exploring divine wisdom.

The Second Treatise of the Great Seth: Claims Jesus' crucifixion was an illusion.

In contrast, some of these gospels are entirely lost, known only through references in other writings, while others survive in fragments, quotations, or translations, providing limited insight into their content.

They could reflect the beliefs, practices, and theological perspectives of the diverse communities that valued them, shedding light on the complexity of early Christian thought. These books include:

The Gospel of the **Ebionites**, The Gospel of the **Nazarenes**, The Gospel of **Matthias**, The Gospel of the **Twelve Apostles**, The Gospel of **Basilides**, The Gospel of **Mani**, The Gospel of **Perfection**, and The Gospel of **Bartholomew**.

The Old Testament Apocrypha are books that are part of the Catholic and Orthodox Bible but not the Protestant one. They include:

Tobit: A story about faith, marriage, and an angelic rescue mission.

Judith: A heroic tale about a widow who saves her people.

Canon

Wisdom of Solomon: Philosophical reflections on wisdom and justice.

Sirach (Ecclesiasticus): A collection of proverbs and teachings about life.

Baruch: Encouragement and prayers during exile.

1 Maccabees: A history of the Jewish revolt against Greek rulers.

2 Maccabees: Focuses on martyrs and God's intervention in Jewish history.

Additions to Esther: Extra parts of the Book of Esther, with more prayers and divine action.

Additions to Daniel: Includes stories like "Bel and the Dragon" and "The Song of the Three Holy Children."

The existence of numerous gospels, many of which were excluded from the Bible, raises significant questions about the preservation and consistency of the Christian message.

The sheer number of lost, rejected, or partially preserved gospels—like the Gospel of Thomas, the Gospel of Peter, and the Gospel of Mary Magdalene—highlights how early Christian communities held diverse views of Jesus and his teachings.

These texts, often labeled "apocryphal," were excluded from the canon not because they were false, but because they conflicted with the doctrines later deemed "orthodox."

According to Ehrman in his book 'Lost Christianities' he writes on page 149:

"Hermas, whose written account, the Shephard, was accepted as an authoritative book by many Christians of the early centuries. Quoted by several church fathers as scripture, the book, like the

Epistle of Barnabas, was included as one of the books of the New Testament in the fourth-century Codex Sinaiticus. It was eventually excluded..."

He also states on page 9:
"The same holds true for nearly all of the Gospels, Acts, Epistles, and Apocalypses that came to be excluded from the canon: forgeries in the names of famous apostles and their companions. That Christians in the early centuries would forge such books should come as no surprise. Scholars have long recognized that even some of the books accepted into the canon are probably forgeries. Christian scholars, of course, have been loathe to call them that and so more commonly refer to them as "pseudonymous" writings. ...it does little to solve the problem of a potential deceit..."

Additionally, the Bible itself exists in a multitude of translations and versions, with differences in wording and interpretation that can alter theological understanding.

This process of selection, exclusion, and reinterpretation undermines claims of divine preservation.

If the Bible is truly God's word, why were certain texts lost, and why does its message vary across communities and translations? How do we know which books, whether canonical or apocryphal, are truly "God-breathed"? Were the authors of these excluded texts not inspired by the Holy Spirit? What criteria can we trust to determine whether a book reflects divine truth, especially given the debates and disagreements that shaped the canon?

Canon

These questions highlight the challenge of discerning the voice of God amidst the diverse and often conflicting voices of early Christianity.

7.2 Differing Views in Early Christianity

In order to put things in their proper context, understanding the diversity of early Christian movements is vital.

Many are under the impression that the beginning of Christianity was a monolithic dogma preached by Jesus, interpreted by Paul many years later, starting from churches of the Middle Ages to present times. In reality, this is inaccurate.

As early as 150 years after the death of Jesus, we find various Christian groups claiming to represent different ideas of Jesus and his disciples, some of which completely opposed each other. Below are some examples of debates throughout the history of Christian councils (Metzger 1988).

325AD	Council of Nicaea: Is the Son eternal? Arianism condemned; Nicene Creed created. Arian and semi–Arian Christians rejected this council.
381AD	Council of Constantinople: Is the Holy Spirit the third person in the Trinity? The council defined the Holy Spirit as divine. Macedonians (*Pneumatomachian*) and Monarchians rejected the Spirit as divine.

431AD	Council of Ephesus: Was Mary the bearer of Christ's divine nature? Affirmed Mary as Theotokos ("God-bearer"). The Assyrian Church of the East reject this till this day and do not worship/venerate Mary as mother of God instead believe in her as "Mother of Christ".
451AD	Council of Chalcedon: Did Jesus have two natures? If so, how is that possible? Council declares Jesus having two natures. Coptic Orthodox, Ethiopian Orthodox, Syriac Orthodox, Armenian Apostolic (all Oriental Orthodox Churches) affirm one united nature instead of two. This Miaphysitism vs Dyophysitism split remains till today.
553AD	Second Council of Constantinople: How can we interpret the dual natures without dividing Jesus into two beings? Council condemned "Three Chapters" (Nestorian writings on Christ being two distinct persons). Miaphysite churches (e.g., Coptic, Syriac) remained unconvinced; Western bishops rejected the council.

681AD	Third Council of Constantinople: Did Jesus have one or two wills? Affirmed Christ has two wills (Dyothelitism) and rejected (Monothelitism) one will. Some Maronite Christians rejected this council until the 9th century.
787AD	Second Council of Nicaea: Can we worship icons of Jesus? If so, how? Allowed venerating but not worshipping icons. Protestants (e.g., Evangelicals, Baptists, Puritans) reject icon veneration as idolatrous till this day.

Bear in mind that non-Trinitarians (such as Oneness Pentecostals, Unitarians, Mormons, and Jehovah's Witnesses) reject the teachings from all of these councils.

The table above reflects a constant struggle within Christianity to define its own truths. Over centuries, theologians, emperors, and bishops have debated essential questions about who Jesus is, what the Trinity means, and how Christians should live and worship. These are ongoing theological developments and sometimes forced through political pressures.

For example, Coptic Christians, numbering in the millions today reject the Chalcedonian definition of Christ having two natures. They believe in one composite nature of Christ, fully divine and fully human, united. From their perspective, this affirms the unity of Christ; from a Chalcedonian view, it is heresy. Which Christians are truly saved and which are deemed lost and heretic destined for punishment? (Kitchen 2012)

The Ebionites are a clear example of an early group that denied the divinity of Christ. They were a group of converted Christians who insisted on practicing Jewish aspects of the faith, following the laws of Moses based on the Hebrew Bible.

The scholarly consensus about the name *Ebionites* derives from the Hebrew word *ebyon* meaning 'the poor' (Ehrman 2000). Scholars suggest the Ebionites most likely held views very similar to those of the first followers of Jesus (e.g., James and Peter).

According to Klijn and Reinink, 1973 the Ebionites are Christians who observe Jewish customs. Although it is extremely difficult to provide a clear and historically trustworthy examination of all the beliefs of the Ebionites, some distinctive features of the movement can be identified, especially through the works of church fathers who almost always wrote about them in a hostile manner.

On page 20 they state:

"Irenaeus makes other observations about the Ebionites without any commentary. He writes that they use only the Gospel of Matthew and that they repudiate Paul (cf. In 15 1) because he abandoned the Law. They explain the prophets curiosius, which means "carefully" or "diligently" not "in a remarkable way". They have themselves circumcised and follow a Jewish way of life. Finally, it is said that they honour Jerusalem as the house of God and face towards Jerusalem when they pray…".

Eventually the apostle Paul is introduced, preaching ideas contrary to what the early disciples taught and to Ebionite and other Jewish Christian foundations. Paul taught that the Gentiles did not need to become Jewish to follow Jesus. In contrast, the Ebionites denied claims of Jesus' divinity. To them, Jesus was a prophet delivering the truth and Word of God—not God himself delivering his divine son (Cook, 2013).

William Cook in his article: "The Ebionites: *Eccentricor Essential Early Christians?*" states:

> "An intriguing example of one form of "early Christianity" which challenges one's expectations is a group known as the Ebionites, Jewish Christians who did not accept the divinity of Christ, believed that Jesus actually increased an emphasis on the "law" and saw Paul of Tarsus as an enemy."

As mentioned above the memory of the Ebionites remains alive only through descriptions of them in the works of their opponents.

According to Luomanen (2007):

> "the Ebionites and the Nazarenes are known only from the writings of the Church Fathers who present short summaries of their teachings and quotations from their writing, usually in order to confute what they consider to be heresy."

The earliest mention of them is dated around 180AD through the works of Irenaeus' Adversus Haereses.

The Marcionites on the other hand were followers of Marcion, a famous theologian of the second century, from what is now Turkey. The Marcionites regarded Paul as the only apostle who truly understood Jesus, and they denied the humanity of Jesus.

They believed that the God of the Old Testament was a wrathful and vengeful God of judgment, while the God of Jesus (in the New Testament) was a loving and merciful God of salvation. Marcion concluded that the distinguished characters of God in both scriptures were ultimately two distinct Gods (Ehrman 2000).

Another group that emerged early in the Christian movement were the Gnostics, who we touched on earlier. The Gnostics believed in an esoteric creation consisting of many divine beings in the heavenly spheres, and that this world is the creation of lesser, unfortunate divine beings.

Very popular in different parts of the early church, the Gnostics believed that one was granted salvation by understanding the secret teachings, as opposed to faith in Christ and his resurrection (Telford 2002).

As Christians developed a Christology centered on incarnation, as opposed to exaltation, serious debates arose around the following questions: Was Jesus a divine being? Was he a human being? Were there two divine beings? Are these two conflicting?

A view called Docetism emerged in the second century under the position that Christ was in fact God but only seemed to be human. Docetism was eventually proclaimed heretic, as theologians insisted that Jesus must have been both divine and human in order to really be a sacrifice for our sins—real blood needed to have been shed.

There were also early Christian groups that believed in the standard view of modalism. An example of modalism is to say, 'I myself am one, yet at the same time a brother, cousin, and son.' I am a brother to my sister, son to my father and cousin to my cousin. I am all three at the same time. This formula was applied to the Father, Son, and Holy Spirit, with God existing in three modes.

Although it was very popular in Rome, modalism eventually faded away, though not entirely, as some Christians still subscribe to the idea today. Many different early Christian views existed and gradually evolved, some more dramatically than others (Ehrman 2000).

The Proto-Orthodox Christians were actually successful in the struggle to convert non-Christians. At the start of the fourth century, The Roman Emperor Constantine converted to this popular form of Christianity and it subsequently became the official religion of the empire though there remained some variation within it. Eventually, Proto-Orthodox Christianity was declared the correct form of Christianity, hence the term orthodoxy. In Greek, the word *orthos* means 'right' and *doxa* means 'opinion' (Ehrman 2000).

We know the most about this group of Christianity, as their writings were better preserved than other Christian groups'.
Their writers are responsible for carving out their views, which became widely accepted. Some of their influential and historical figures whom the writers mentioned were:

- Justin Martyr (AD 100)
- Irenaeus (AD 130)
- Tertullian (AD 160)
- Clement of Alexandria (AD 150)

7.3 Canon in a Nutshell

Today, the vast majority of Christians assume that the New Testament accurately reflects the authentic words and teachings of Jesus, but most are unaware of the historical process of its formation. Many do not realize that there was a time when the New Testament canon did not exist (Kruger 2012).

Jesus did not write it himself, nor did he instruct his followers to write it. In fact, there is not one person, church council, or Christian community that can claim to have produced the New Testament canon as we know it today.

The order of the New Testament books was still being vigorously debated hundreds of years after the death of Jesus and even till today. Missionaries and apologists are ill inclined to discuss is that there were numerous other canons of the Bible.

This subject requires countless volumes in order to fully grasp the intricacies attached to it. In order to simplify it, here is a list of the canons that were selected by various Church authorities showing what they thought constituted the New Testament (Metzger 1988).

The Muratorian Canon (170AD)
The Canon of Origen (c. 185–254AD)
The Canon of Eusebius of Caesarea (265–340AD)
The Canon of Cyril of Jerusalem (c. 350AD)
The Cheltenham Canon (c. 360AD)
The Canon approved by the Synod of Laodicea (c. 363AD)
The Canon of Athanasius (367AD)
The Canon Approved by the 'Apostolic Canons' (c. 380AD)
The Canon of Gregory of Nazianzus (329–389AD)

Canon

The Canon of Amphilochius of Iconium (394AD)
The Canon approved by the Third Synod of Carthage (397AD)
Rufinus of Aquileia (400AD)
Codex Charomontanus (400AD)
Decree of Gelasius (550AD)
John of Damascus (730AD)

Many people assume that the biblical canon was decided by a formal vote during a major church council, such as the Council of Nicaea in 325AD. However, this is not accurate. The question of the canon was not discussed at Nicaea or any other major council. Nor was the canon established by a singular authority, such as a Pope or Emperor (not even Constantine, who seemingly paid it no attention).

In reality, the canon was never officially decided in an early, formal sense. Apart from a few minor church synods, no definitive rulings on the canon were made until the Council of Trent (AD 1545-63) during the Counter-Reformation (F.F. Bruce, 1988).

For centuries, the church operated without a formally established canon. Instead, there was a gradual, informal consensus among Christian communities. By the fifth century, a general agreement had formed in orthodox circles, rendering the issue relatively settled.

Certain writings gained authority for doctrinal, spiritual, and practical purposes, while others were regarded as useful but not divinely inspired. For example, the Gospel of James, which narrates the early life of Mary, and the Apocalypse of Paul, which explores heaven and hell, were considered insightful but never part of the sacred canon (Ehrman, 2005).

The books included in the canon were not without internal differences. Ironically, rather than celebrating this diversity, the canonization process sought to eliminate it. All the texts were read as part of a single, internally consistent collection.

Yet, the reality is that early orthodox Christianity was never a unified entity. It encompassed a variety of theological, ethical, and practical perspectives. The four Gospels, for instance, present differing portrayals of Jesus. Similarly, the letters attributed to Paul, including those later written in his name, sometimes conflict with one another. The writings of James, Peter, John, and Jude also convey distinct and occasionally contradictory messages.

By 160AD, several books now considered part of the New Testament were not widely acknowledged as canonical. These included Acts, Hebrews, James, 1 and 2 Peter, 1, 2, and 3 John, Jude, and Revelation—10 out of the 27 books.

Justin Martyr (d. c. 165) didn't recognize Philippians or 1 Timothy, and his collection of Gospels included material from apocryphal texts. Clement of Alexandria and Origen, writing before the mid-3rd century, regarded the Epistle of Barnabas as inspired Scripture.

For example, in his work Stromata, Clement refers to the Epistle of Barnabas as an important Christian text. Specifically, in Stromata book 2, Clement mentions sayings of Barnabas along with other Hebrew scriptures.

Canon

Ehrman (2005) further highlights that early Christian texts were not universally agreed upon, and some teachings deviated from orthodox Christianity. He states on page 156:

> "Both Barnabas and 1 Clement were considered by some orthodox Christians of later times to be canonical authorities and so were included in some manuscripts of the New Testament. Yet other non-canonical letters embody "heretical" concerns, including several that are clearly gnostic creations— which try, in fact, to convince proto-orthodox readers that a gnostic point of view is correct (e.g., Ptolemy's Letter to Flora and the Letter to Rheginus)."

They also held the same view of the Didache and The Shepherd of Hermas—a view shared by Irenaeus and Tertullian in the case of Hermas. Clement of Alexandria (d. c. 215) even considered The Apocalypse of Peter and the Gospel of the Hebrews as Scripture, while Origen included the Acts of Paul in his list. Ehrman (2005):

> "One other apocalypse was widely considered canonical by orthodox Christians—the Apocalypse of Peter (one of three surviving texts that go by that name)—and another is included as Scripture in one of our oldest manuscripts of the New Testament (the Shepherd of Hermas)."

No early Church Father accurately identified all the books that would eventually be deemed canonical while excluding those later determined to be non-canonical until St. Athanasius did so in 367AD, more than three centuries after the death of Christ. The well-known Muratorian Canon (c. 190AD) excluded Hebrews, James, and 1 and 2

Peter while including The Apocalypse of Peter and Wisdom of Solomon.

Ehrman (2005) states on page 331:

"Twenty-two of the twenty-seven books of the New Testament canon are included here—all except Hebrews, James, 1 and 2 Peter, and 3 John. But the author **also accepts as canonical** the Wisdom of Solomon and the Apocalypse of Peter".

At the Council of Nicaea in 325, questions were raised about the canonicity of James, 2 Peter, 2 and 3 John, and Jude. James, in particular, wasn't even cited in Western writings until around 350AD Meanwhile, Revelation was rejected by notable figures such as Cyril of Jerusalem, John Chrysostom, and Gregory Nazianzen.

Even into the late 4th century, texts like the Epistle of Barnabas and The Shepherd of Hermas were included in major manuscripts, such as the Codex Sinaiticus (Ehrman, 2005).

This inconsistent approach to canonization, coupled with the inclusion and exclusion of books based on shifting theological and political priorities, undermines the claim that the process was divinely guided or preserved. The lack of clarity and widespread disagreement over centuries suggests that the formation of the New Testament canon was more a product of human decisions and disputes than of divine revelation or consistent preservation.

7.4 Church Fathers on the Canon

If God intended to deliver a clear and unified message through Scripture, why would he allow centuries of debates, contradictions, and confusion over its contents, leaving believers to wrestle with uncertainty about what truly constitutes his Word?

Below are some of the conflicting views church fathers had on the topic of the canon.

Melito of Sardis: "I have accurately learned the books of the Old Testament. Their names are as follows: Five books of Moses: Genesis, Exodus, Leviticus, Numbers, and Deuteronomy. Joshua, Judges, Ruth. Four books of Kings [two of Samuel and two of Kings], two of Paralipomenon [Chronicles]. The Psalms of David, the Proverbs of Solomon (which is also Wisdom), Ecclesiastes, the Song of Songs, Job. Of the prophets, Isaiah, Jeremiah; and of the twelve prophets, one book; Daniel, Ezekiel, Esdras." Esther is notably missing. (As cited by Eusebius, Ecclesiastical History, Book 4, Section 26).

Origen: "The collective books, as handed down by the Hebrews, are twenty-two, according to the number of letters in their alphabet." Excludes deuterocanonical texts such as Tobit and Judith. (As cited by Eusebius, Ecclesiastical History, Book 6, Section 25).

Victorinus of Pettau: "The books of the Old Testament that are received are twenty-four." Adds two more books compared to Origen by counting Tobit and Judith. (Commentary on the Apocalypse, Chapter 4, Verses 7-8).

The Council of Laodicea: "The books of the Old Testament which must be read are..." This list goes on to exclude Revelation, a significant omission compared to later canon lists. (Canon 60).

Hilary of Poitiers: "The law of the Old Testament is arranged in twenty-two books, that they may correspond with the number of the Hebrew letters." Also mentions, "Some are pleased to add Tobit and Judith, to make the number twenty-four." Reflects disagreement about whether these two books should be included. (Exposition of the Psalms, Prologue, Section 15).

Athanasius: "The former, my brethren, are included in the Canon, the latter being [merely] read." Includes 22 books but allows non-canonical texts like Judith, Tobit, and the Shepherd of Hermas for reading. (39th Festal Letter, Section 7).

Cyril of Jerusalem: "Of the Old Testament, as we have said, study the two and twenty books." Excludes apocryphal writings and adheres strictly to the Hebrew tradition. (Catechetical Lectures, Book 4, Section 35).

Canon

Gregory of Nazianzus: "These twenty-two books of the Old Testament are counted according to the twenty-two letters of the Jews." Rejects "extraneous books" such as Tobit, Judith, and others mentioned by Victorinus and Hilary. (Carmina Dogmatica, Book I, Section I, Carmen XII).

Epiphanius: "These are the twenty-seven books given the Jews by God. They are counted as twenty-two, however, like the letters of their Hebrew alphabet." Mentions disputed status of Sirach and Wisdom of Solomon, which others like Gregory exclude entirely. (The Panarion of Epiphanius of Salamis, Book I, Section I.6,1).

Jerome: "The Church does not recognize the Apocrypha." Excludes deuterocanonical books but permits them for edification. (Against Rufinus, Book 2, Section 27).

Rufinus: "There are also other books which our fathers call not 'Canonical' but 'Ecclesiastical.'" Excludes Tobit, Judith, and Maccabees from the canon but allows them to be read. (Commentary on the Apostles' Creed, Section 38).

Amphilochius of Iconium: "Four prophets, Isaiah the great free-speaker, Jeremiah the sympathetic and mystic, Ezekiel, and Daniel the last." Lists 22 books but acknowledges that some include Esther, reflecting ongoing debates. (As cited by C. E. Stowe, The Apocryphal Books of the Old Testament, p. 302).

Primasius: "The books of the Old Testament, which we take up on canonical authority, are twenty-four." Aligns with Victorinus and Hilary in counting 24 books. (Commentary on the Apocalypse of John, Book I, Chapter IV).

John of Damascus: "There are two and twenty books of the Old Testament, one for each letter of the Hebrew tongue." Excludes Sirach and Wisdom, in line with Cyril and Gregory. (Exposition of the Orthodox Faith, Book 4, Chapter 17).

Pope Gregory the Great: "With reference to which particular we are not acting irregularly, if from the books, though not Canonical, yet brought out for the edification of the Church, we bring forward testimony." Acknowledges non-canonical texts like 1 Maccabees. (Morals on the Book of Job, Volume 2, Part 4, Book 19, Section 34).

The Venerable Bede: "Six wings of four animals, which makes twenty-four, suggest the books of the entire Old Testament." Agrees with Victorinus, Hilary, and Primasius in counting 24 books. (Commentary on Revelation, [PL 93.144]).

Cardinal Cajetan: "For the rest (that is, Judith, Tobit, and the books of Maccabees) are counted by St. Jerome out of the canonical books." Distinguishes between books for edification and those for doctrine. (Commentary on all the Authentic Historical Books of the Old Testament, as cited by William Whitaker, A Disputation on Holy Scripture, p. 48).

The vastly differing views among Church Fathers on the number of books or letters considered canonical—ranging from 22 to 27 in the Old Testament alone—only add confusion as to the reliability of the Bible. How can the Bible be the Word of God if no one can even agree on what the Bible is?

7.5 Scholarly Treatment of Canon

The centuries-long debates and disagreements over the biblical canon reveal a striking lack of certainty in what should be regarded as the Word of God. Instead of an immediately evident and divinely established collection, the canon developed amid differing traditions, interpretations, and theological emphases.

The varying lists of books among Church Fathers and councils, coupled with the absence of consensus even within early Christianity, raise the question of why God would allow such confusion if the Bible was meant to be His clear and definitive revelation? Scholars further underscore these issues, noting how the ongoing debates and unresolved tensions around the canon contribute to doubts about its claimed divine authority.

Below are some examples of these debates and tensions.

1. In the four centuries previous to Christ, **"it cannot be proved** that there was already a complete Canon" (New Bible Dictionary 1975). See also, F. F. Bruce, The Canon of Scripture.

2. There was no Jewish "synod of Jamnia" per se, but rather a series of scholarly discussions, from the period of 70-100AD, and **even these did not finally settle the issue of the OT canon** (The New Bible Dictionary; Norman Geisler, From God to Us: How we

Got our Bible; Oxford Dictionary of the Christian Church; F. F. Bruce, The Canon of Scripture).

3. These discussions were still dealing with the disputed canonicity of books like Esther, Proverbs, Ecclesiastes, Canticles, and even Ezekiel after the death of Jesus and after most or all of the New Testament was completed (New Bible Dictionary 1975). So Paul (or any New Testament writer) could hardly have assumed a commonly accepted Old Testament canon before this time.

4. The Jewish historian Josephus "also uses books which we count among the Apocrypha, e.g. **1 Esdras and the additions to Esther.**" (New Bible Dictionary 1975)

5. The Jews of the Dispersion (particularly the Alexandrian, Greek-speaking Jews) regarded several additional Greek books as equally inspired, — i.e., the so-called Apocrypha. (Oxford Dictionary of the Christian Church)

6. "During the first three centuries these were regularly used also in the Church... St. Ambrose, St. Augustine, and others placed them on the same footing as the other OT books." (Oxford Dictionary of the Christian Church)

7. The Septuagint (LXX), incorporated all of the so-called "Apocryphal" books except 2 Esdras, and they **were in no way differentiated from the other Books of the OT**. (Oxford Dictionary of the Christian Church)

Canon

8. "Christians... at first received all the Books of the Septuagint equally as Scripture... Down to the 4th cent. the Church generally accepted all the Books of the Septuagint as canonical. Gk. and Lat. Fathers alike (e.g., Irenaeus, Tertullian, Cyprian) cite both classes of Books without distinction... **[the "Apocrypha" was] read as Scripture by the pre-Nicene Church and many post-Nicene Fathers**..." (Oxford Dictionary of the Christian Church)

9. "In the 4th cent., however, many Fathers... came to recognize a distinction between those canonical in Heb. and the rest, though the latter were **still customarily cited as Scripture**." (Oxford Dictionary of the Christian Church)

10. "Luther, however, included the Apocrypha (except 1 and 2 Esd.) as an appendix to his translation of the Bible (1534), and in his preface allowed them to be 'useful and good to be read'" (Oxford Dictionary of the Christian Church)

11. According to F.F Bruce in his work 'The canon of Scripture', There are quotations in the New Testament introduced as though they were taken from holy scripture, but their source can no longer be identified.

For instance, the words "He would be called a Nazarene," quoted in Matthew 2:23 as "what was spoken by the prophets," (ESV) have no clear source in the Old Testament. Similarly, in John 7:38, the phrase "as the scripture has said" (ESV) is used, but it's unclear which scripture is being referred to. Additionally, 1

Corinthians 2:9 and James 4:5 are introduced as being based on scripture, but the exact sources for these quotations are uncertain

12. The Dead Sea Scrolls from the Qumran community revealed that **they did not have Esther included in their canon** (Bruce 1998). And yet we currently have this book in the Bible today.

13. "As Athanasius includes Baruch and the 'Letter of Jeremiah'... **so he probably includes the Greek additions to Daniel** in the canonical book of that name... " (Bruce 1998)

14. St. Athanasius **excludes Esther from the canon.** (Bruce 1998)

15. Yet Hippo and Carthage, along with "The Sixth Council of Carthage (419)" **included "the apocryphal books."** (Bruce 1998)

16. "Throughout the following centuries most users of the Bible made no distinction between the apocryphal books and the others: **all alike were handed down as part of the Vulgate**..." (Bruce 1998)

Chapter 7 Canon

References:
Bruce, F.F., The Canon Of The Scripture, 1988, Chapter House Ltd.: Glasgow.

Chapman, S.B., 2010. The Canon Debate: What It Is and Why It Matters. Journal of Theological Interpretation, 4(2).

Clement, O.A., 1885. The Stromata, or Miscellanies. Ante-Nicene Fathers, 2.

Cook Jr, W.J., 2013. The Ebionites: Eccentric or Essential Early Christians?. Journal of Arts and Humanities, 2(7).

Davidson, S., 2020. The Canon of the Bible. BoD–Books on Demand.

Ehrman, B.D., 2000. The New Testament: A historical introduction to the early Christian writings. Oxford University Press, USA.

Ehrman, B.D., 2005. Lost Scriptures: Books that did not make it into the New Testament. Oxford University Press.

Ehrman, B.D., 2005. Lost Christianities: The battles for scripture and the faiths we never knew. Oxford University Press, USA.

From Nicene and Post-Nicene Fathers, Second Series, Vol. 7. Edited by Philip Schaff and Henry Wace. Translated by C.G. Browne and J.E. Swallow. (Christian Literature Publishing Co., 1894.)

Kitchen, R.A., 2012. The Assyrian Church of the East. In The Orthodox Christian World (pp. 78-88). Routledge.

Klijn, A.F.J. and Reinink, G.J., 1973. Ebionites. In Patristic evidence for Jewish-Christian sects. Brill.

Kruger, M.J., 2012. Canon revisited: establishing the origins and authority of the New Testament books. Crossway.

Luomanen, P., 2007. Ebionites and Nazarenes. Jewish Christianity Reconsidered.

McDonald, L.M. and Sanders, J.A. eds., 2001. The canon debate. Baker Academic.

New Bible Dictionary, (Wm. B. Eerdmans Pub., Grand Rapids, MI, 1975).

Metzger, B. M., The Canon Of The New Testament: Its Origin, Significance and Development, 1997, op cit.

McDowell, J., The New Evidence That Demands A Verdict: Evidence I and II Fully Updated In One Volume To Answer Questions Challenging Christians In The 21st Century, 1999, Thomas Nelson Publishers: Nashville.

Telford, W. (2002). The New Testament. Oxford, England: Oneworld.

8

"Surely the Sovereign Lord does nothing without revealing his plan to his servants the prophets." (Amos 3:7, NIV)

Pagan Influences

"Whoever obeys Allah and the Apostle—they are with those whom Allah has blessed, including the prophets and the truthful, the martyrs and the righteous, and excellent companions are they!"

(Qur'an 4:69)

8.1 Incarnation

The idea of the 'Incarnation,' as most Christians understand it, is that Jesus wasn't a created being but actually God himself in human form.

The historical development of the doctrine of the "Incarnation," now a cornerstone of Christian faith, did not arise directly from Scripture. Instead, it was influenced by prevailing beliefs and attitudes surrounding the Christian church after the first century, including pagan mythology, Gnostic concepts of redemption and pre-existence, and misinterpretations of Johannine language.

Together, these factors contributed to the teaching that God himself became a man, forming the essence of "Incarnational theology."

Although widely assumed to be a foundational tenet of Christianity, the term "Incarnation" does not appear in Scripture. Trinitarian scholars concede this, noting that "Incarnation, in its full and proper sense, is not something directly presented in Scripture" (Wiles, 1982).

The doctrine was formally developed over several centuries, as confirmed by the Oxford Dictionary of the Christian Church:

> "The doctrine, which took classical shape under the influence of the controversies of the 4th-5th centuries, was formally defined at the Council of Chalcedon of 451. It was largely molded by the diversity of tradition in the schools of Antioch and Alexandria... further refinements were added in the later Patristic and Medieval periods". (Cross 1983).

This prolonged development reflects its lack of explicit biblical foundation. The councils took centuries to refine the doctrine, which

Pagan Influences

remains reliant on interpretations of Scripture that can be understood without invoking the Incarnation.

Teaching the Jews of Jesus' time that God became a man would have deeply offended their monotheistic beliefs and contradicted their understanding of the Messianic Scriptures. The Gospel of John, particularly John 1:14 ("The Word became flesh", ESV), is often cited as a basis for this doctrine.

However, Jewish audiences would have understood "the Word" as referring to God's plan or purpose rather than a pre-existent divine being. This interpretation aligns with Genesis 3:15, where the promised "seed" of a woman signifies God's plan for humanity.

John 1:14 emphasizes God's plan being realized in Jesus rather than establishing a doctrine of pre-existence or Incarnation. The traditional understanding of the Incarnation is that God, without ceasing to be God, became man (New Bible Dictionary 1975).

However, one would argue that by God becoming man or being man is actually against the essence of a creator "God is not human." (Numbers 23:19)

Trinitarian sources define it as follows:

> "It appears to mean that the divine Maker became one of his own creatures, which is a prima facie contradiction in theological terms." (New Bible Dictionary 1975)

When the Word "became flesh," it is argued, God's deity was neither abandoned nor diminished but was accompanied by human nature. However, this raises logical and theological problems for Christians who believe this.

How can a pre-existent "God the Son" live a "fully human" life while continuing to exercise divine functions? This alleged paradox is often described as part of the 'mystery' of the Incarnation.

The New Bible Dictionary admits that the concept is not developed or discussed in the New Testament:

> "The only sense in which the New Testament writers ever attempt to explain the incarnation is by showing how it fits into God's overall plan for redeeming mankind…This evangelical interest throws light on the otherwise puzzling fact that the New Testament nowhere reflects on the virgin birth of Jesus as witnessing to the conjunction of deity and manhood in his person—a line of thought much canvassed by later theology." (New Bible Dictionary 1975)

Paul's warnings about turning from truth to fables (2 Timothy 4:3-4) align with this phenomenon, as the early Church increasingly adopted ideas influenced by pagan culture. The thought of God or any spirit being becoming a baby doesn't match up with biblical evidence.

While the Incarnation wasn't directly invented from pagan myths, the evidence suggests that early church leaders in the third and fourth centuries misinterpreted Scripture and let outside influences shape the doctrine.

This concept very much resembles myths about gods coming to earth in human form. For example, Acts 14:11-15 shows Paul and Barnabas actively rejecting the idea of gods appearing as humans, pointing instead to the one true God who made the heavens and the Earth.

> "And when the crowds saw what Paul had done, they lifted up their voices, saying in Lycaonian, "The gods have come down to us in

Pagan Influences

the likeness of men!" Barnabas they called Zeus, and Paul, Hermes, because he was the chief speaker. And the priest of Zeus, whose temple was at the entrance to the city, brought oxen and garlands to the gates and wanted to offer sacrifice with the crowds. But when the apostles Barnabas and Paul heard of it, they tore their garments and rushed out into the crowd, crying out, "Men, why are you doing these things? We also are men, of like nature with you, and we bring you good news, that you should turn from these vain things to a living God, who made the heaven and the earth and the sea and all that is in them." (Acts 14:11-15, ESV)

This passage makes it clear that pagan beliefs risked infiltrating the original Christian message as early as the time of Paul. Christians were not immune to being influenced by the mythological backdrop of the first-century world.

Pagan cultures, like the Romans and Greeks, had plenty of stories about gods becoming human, such as Hercules, Dionysus, or Romulus. These stories often involved divine beings being born to mortal women, which sounds a lot like what later became the idea of the Incarnation.

Critics of Christianity, like A.N. Wilson, argue that the concept of "God becoming man" feels borrowed from these mythological ideas.

In the Bible, though, the focus is always on God's distinct nature. The prophecies about the Messiah describe a human being empowered by God, not God himself in disguise.

For example, Isaiah 11:2 speaks of the Spirit of the Lord resting on the Messiah—not that the Messiah is God.

Nowhere in the Old Testament does it say God planned to become a man. Instead, the Messiah was expected to be fully human, representing God perfectly on earth.

The Incarnation also creates some major theological problems. If Jesus were God, then his temptations and struggles wouldn't be real—because God can't sin or even be tempted (James 1:13).

Philippians 2:8-11 highlights that Jesus' humility and obedience led to his exaltation, not some divine pre-existence. And if Jesus was both fully human and fully God at the same time, how could he truly experience the limitations of humanity?

The Bible consistently presents Jesus as a man chosen and empowered by God, not a divine being who somehow became human (Robinson, 2002). The prophecies and accounts of Jesus' life make much more sense when we see him as a human Messiah who overcame challenges through faith and obedience. The idea that God would come down and "become a baby" just doesn't align with the story Scripture tells.

The Bible clearly states, "God is not a man…" (Numbers 23:19, ESV), establishing a firm distinction between the divine and human.

Additionally, the notion that Jesus is "God in human flesh" creates contradictions. For instance, in Gethsemane, Jesus prayed, "…not my will, but yours, be done." (Luke 22:42, ESV). If Jesus is God, this prayer becomes perplexing, suggesting a conflict between his human and divine wills. Hebrews 4:15 states that Jesus was "in every respect has been tempted as we are," (ESV) but God cannot be tempted.

The idea of Christ's pre-existence largely stems from a literal interpretation of passages in John's Gospel. James D.G. Dunn observes that the concept of "pre-existent divine sonship" emerged only by the end of the first century and became dominant in later centuries:

> "Only in the Fourth Gospel does the understanding of a personal pre-existence fully emerge, of Jesus as the divine Son of God before the world began sent into the world by the Father… at the end of the first century a clear concept of pre-existent divine sonship has emerged, to become the dominant (and often the only) emphasis in subsequent centuries." (Dunn, 1996)

There is also the issue that if Jesus did preexist, his birth narratives in Matthew and Luke would contradict this idea. Matthew 1:18 explicitly describes Jesus' beginning using the Greek word "genesis," meaning "origin."

The doctrine of the Incarnation is unsupported by Scripture. The Bible consistently portrays Jesus as God's creation, not his incarnation. The central message of the Gospel is not "God became a man," but that a man, Jesus, through his obedience, was the Christ. Acts 2:22 declares:

> "Men of Israel, hear these words: Jesus of Nazareth, a man attested to you by God with mighty works and wonders and signs that God did through him in your midst, as you yourselves know." (ESV)

8.2 Pagan Roots of Christian Holidays

Many Christian holidays are celebrated as sacred events commemorating pivotal moments in the religion, but a closer look reveals they are not entirely rooted in Scripture. Over time, these holidays absorbed elements from pre-Christian traditions, blending biblical narratives with pagan customs to create the celebrations we know today.

For example, Christmas, celebrated on December 25, is one of the most beloved Christian holidays. Yet, there is no biblical basis for this date as Jesus' birth date is never explicitly mentioned in Scripture. In fact, Luke 2:1-20 mentions shepherds in fields, suggesting a non-winter timeframe.

Early Christians adopted this date to coincide with pagan celebrations such as the Roman Saturnalia and Sol Invictus, which marked the winter solstice (Davis, 2009). These festivals involved feasting, gift-giving, and honoring the rebirth of the sun. Christian leaders likely chose this date to present Jesus as the "light of the world" (John 8:12, ESV), symbolically aligning his birth with the return of longer daylight (Schaff 1866).

Even traditional customs, like decorating trees and lighting logs, reflect older solstice practices that celebrated life during the darkest time of the year.

Another example is Easter. Easter is believed to commemorate the resurrection of Christ (Matthew 28:1-10), but its timing and many of its symbols stem from pagan spring festivals. According to Professor Carole Cusack from the University of Sydney, these ancient celebrations honoured fertility and renewal (Cusack, 2007).

In 325AD, the Council of Nicaea, the first significant church council, decided that Easter should be celebrated on the Sunday following the first full moon after the Spring equinox (or the Autumn equinox in the Southern Hemisphere).

As a result, Easter Sunday for Catholic and Protestant Christians falls on a date between March 22 and April 25 (Cusack, 2007). On the

Pagan Influences

other hand, Orthodox Churches continue to follow the Julian Calendar, introduced by Julius Caesar. This calendar was replaced in Western Europe in 1582 when Pope Gregory XIII introduced the Gregorian Calendar, named after himself.

The word "Easter" originates from Eostre, an Anglo-Saxon goddess of dawn and spring, while in German, "Ostern" comes from the related goddess Ostara. Many other languages use names for Easter derived from the Hebrew "Pesach" (Passover), such as "Paskha" (Greek), "Pasqua" (Italian), and "Pâques" (French).

Easter eggs symbolize new life and resurrection, with decorated eggs being enjoyed after Lent as early as the Middle Ages. Chocolate eggs became popular in the 19th century. The Easter bunny, linked to fertility and folklore about hares hiding eggs, also gained prominence in 19th-century Germany, especially with the rise of greeting cards.

One would naturally question these traditions. What do eggs, bunnies, and references to spring goddesses have to do with Jesus and Christianity? Such elements seem far removed from the biblical narrative of Christ sent to the children of Israel with teachings of oneness of God and worshipping God alone without any idols, stones or pagan rituals.

A final example we can look to is Halloween. Dr Dominique Wilson from the University of Sydney's Department of Studies in Religion explains that Halloween has roots in Celtic and Catholic traditions gaining popularity globally (Wilson 2016).

Originating from the ancient Celtic festival of Samhain, celebrated on October 31, it marked a time when the barrier between the natural and supernatural worlds was believed to thin, allowing spirits to roam. In the 8th and 9th centuries, the Catholic Church established All

Saints' Day (November 1) and All Souls' Day (November 2), with All Hallow's Eve (Halloween) preceding them, aligning with Samhain's timing.

One must question why the church would adopt such holidays. Would they have ever been accepted by Christ or his followers? Given their commitment to upholding the teachings of the Torah and distancing themselves from idolatrous practices, it's hard to believe they would.

The early Christian movement emphasized worshiping God in spirit and truth (John 4:24) and often rejected pagan customs, which were seen as contradictory to the monotheistic worship of God.

So are these Christian Holidays really Godly?

8.3 Conclusion

Our journey through the Bible has uncovered many important issues that challenge its reliability as the word of God. We have explored textual criticism, highlighting contradictions, discrepancies, and instances where the text was altered intentionally due to theological agendas.

These changes raise questions about the authenticity of its message and its transmission over time.

The gospels, with their varying accounts and the influence of the synoptic writers, raise serious doubts about their accuracy through the *'Snowball effect'*. Furthermore, some of the more disturbing passages, especially those that are violent or unnecessarily sexual and graphic, make it difficult to accept that this is the word of a good God.

Pagan Influences

We've found that the Bible doesn't offer a clear and consistent message supporting key Christian beliefs such as the divinity of Jesus. In fact, it consistently denies them.

The concept of the Trinity, which became central to Christian doctrine, doesn't have a solid biblical backing. Rather it is shaped by enigmatic verses and later theological debates as seen through the writings of early church fathers and the outcomes of various councils.

Another problem within the New Testament, is the issue of *"Paulitics"*, Paul's heavy influence on Christianity. This raises important questions about whether we're seeing the original message of Christ or rather Paul's perspective on it. Unfortunately, we do not have the writings of the opponents of Paul, so we are left with mostly one side of the story.

The concept of Jesus as the sacrifice for sin, central to the faith, is riddled with challenges, as shown by the many different atonement theories that have emerged since the early days of Christianity, and which continue to emerge till this day.

Looking at the history of the Bible's canon, it becomes clear that what we have today was shaped by political aspects and not *'God-breathed'* or inspired revelation. Despite the writings that were once added and later excluded, there remains uncertainty about what should or shouldn't be considered canonical, as different historical contexts and shifting views have influenced these decisions over time.

The influence of pagan traditions, especially in the development of Christian holidays and beliefs, further challenges the idea that Christianity is a purely incorruptible faith.

All in all, the Bible is far from flawless, and the Christianity we see today seems to be a product of human history, opinion, and interpretation rather than direct divine guidance.

While the Bible does contain many reliable elements and truths, overall, it is clearly not an infallible source of truth. Its inconsistencies, contradictions, and historical influences make it challenging to view as a definitive guide for all humanity.

I hope that through this exploration, readers have gained a deeper understanding of the complexities surrounding the Bible and the foundations of Christianity.

While this book presents challenges to the traditional view of the Bible, it's crucial for everyone to engage in their own research and ask critical questions. By doing so, we can all move closer to a more informed, thoughtful understanding of faith, scripture, and history.

Let us keep questioning, exploring, but most importantly "let us reason together" (Isaiah 1:18, KJV). There is always more to discover.

Chapter 8 Pagan Influence

References:

Anderson, B.W., 1986. Understanding the old testament.

Appleton, R. and Knight, K., 1908. The Catholic Encyclopedia.

Aramaic Lexicon and Concordance, Atour.

Atour.com (n.d.) *God and*. Available at: http://www.atour.com/cgibin/dictionary.cgi?string=godandSearch_Field=Meaning [Accessed 14 February 2025].

Berlin, A., Brettler, M.Z. and Fishbane, M.A., 2004. *The Jewish Study Bible: Jewish Publication Society Tanakh Translation*. Oxford University Press, USA.

Codex Sinaiticus. (n.d.). The Gospel of John, Chapter 14, Verse 26. Retrieved from: http://codexsinaiticus.org/en/manuscript.aspx?book=36&chapter=14&lid=en&side=r&verse=26&zoomSlider=0

Brown, F., Driver, S.R., Briggs, C.A., Gesenius, W., Robinson, E. and Strong, J., 1996. *The Brown-Driver-Briggs Hebrew and English Lexicon: With an Appendix Containing the Biblical Aramaic: Coded with the Numbering System from Strong's Exhaustive Concordance of the Bible*. Hendrickson Pub.

Bultmann, R., 2014. *The Gospel of John: a commentary*. Wipf and Stock Publishers.

Charlesworth, J.H. ed., 1992. *Jesus and the Dead Sea Scrolls*. Anchor Books.

Childers, C.L., 1964. Beacon Bible commentary.

Cross, F. L., ed. The Oxford Dictionary of the Christian Church (Oxford University Press, N.Y., 1983).

Cusack, C., 2007. The Goddess Eostre: Bede's Text and Contemporary Pagan Tradition (s). Pomegranate, 9(1).

Davis, K.C., 2009. *Don't know much about mythology: everything you need to know about the greatest stories in human history but never learned*. Harper Collins.

Dunn, J.D., 1996. *Christology in the Making: A New Testament Inquiry into the Origins of the Doctrine of the Incarnation*. Wm. B. Eerdmans Publishing.

Dow, J.L., 1974. *Collins Gem Dictionary of the Bible*. Collins.

Gill, J., 2009. John Gill's exposition of the entire Bible. *Found in his comments on Matthew, 27*.

Haag, H., 1969. *Is original sin in Scripture?*. Sheed and Ward.

Hayes, J.H., 1971. *Introduction to the Bible*. Westminster John Knox Press.

Henry, M., 1991. *Commentary on the whole Bible* (Vol. 4). FH Revell.

Kent, C.F., 1911. *Biblical Geography and History*. Scribner.

Lapidus, I.M., 2002. *A history of Islamic societies*. Cambridge University Press.

Metzger, B.M., 1957. *An introduction to the Apocrypha*. Oxford University Press.

Myers, A.C., 1987. *The Eerdmans Bible Dictionary*. Eerdmans Pub Co.

Newby, G., 2013. *A concise encyclopedia of Islam*. Oneworld Publications.

New Bible Dictionary, (Wm. B. Eerdmans Pub., Grand Rapids, MI, 1975).

Nicoll, W.R., 1983. Expositor's Greek New Testament 5 vols. *Grand Rapids, Eerdmans*.

Parrinder, G. and Parrinder, E.G., 1998. *A concise encyclopedia of Christianity*. Oneworld Publications Limited.

Chabad.org (2019) *Rashi's Commentary on the Torah: Deuteronomy 18*. Available at: http://www.chabad.org/library/bible_cdo/aid/9982#showrashi=trueandlt=primary [Accessed 14 February 2025].

Reston Jr, J., 2006. *Dogs of God: Columbus, the Inquisition, and the Defeat of the Moors*. Anchor.

Sanders, E., 1993. *The historical figure of Jesus*. Penguin UK.

Sheridan, R., 2007. The Paraclete and Jesus in the Johannine Farewell Discourse. *Pacifica: Australasian Theological Studies*, 20(2).

Smith, D.E. and Tyson, J.B. eds., 2013. *Acts and Christian Beginnings: The Acts Seminar Report.*

Smith, W., Peloubet, F.N. and Peloubet, M.A.T., 1967. *Smith's Bible Dictionary*. Pyramid Books.

Stanton, G., 2002. *The gospels and Jesus*. Oxford University Press.

Wiles, M., 1982. Reflections on James Dunn's Christology in the Making. Theology, 85(704).

Wilson, D. (2016) The origins of Halloween. The University of Sydney. Available at: [https://www.sydney.edu.au/news-opinion/news/2016/10/27/the-origins-of-halloween.html] [Accessed 21 November 2024].

Tim LaHaye, Jesus: Who Is He? (Multnomah Books, Sisters, OR, 1996).

Robinson, J.A.T., 2002. Honest to god. Westminster John Knox Press.

Philip Schaff, 1866, History of the Christian Church, Volume III: Nicene and Post-Nicene Christianity. AD 311-600

Wilson, D.B. and Cusack, C.M., 2017. Australian Pagans: Fashion, music, and festivals. Walking the Old Ways in a New World. Edited by Adam Anczyk and Joanna Malita-Król. Katowice: Sacrum Publishing.

www.ingramcontent.com/pod-product-compliance
Lightning Source LLC
Chambersburg PA
CBHW052010070526
44584CB00016B/1692